Ever since the age of enlightenment there has been a cultural chasm between science and Christianity, a divide that is seen at its widest in the different opinions regarding the nature of Jesus Christ.

To some he is the incarnate god, born of a virgin, who was crucified and resurrected. To others he was a charismatic preacher but still a mere man.

The one opinion is not scientifically credible, the other is spiritually unsatisfying.

Yet Christianity was born in an age of extraordinary scientific achievements with great intellectual thinkers.

It is time surely to bridge that cultural divide. It is time to abandon the quest for the historical Christ and rediscover the logos.

For Karen

Thanks for your patience.

First Edition

Copyright © 2012, Dominick Garden

All rights reserved. No part of this book may be reproduced, stored, or transmitted by any means—whether auditory, graphic, mechanical, or electronic—without written permission of both publisher and author, except in the case of brief excerpts used in critical articles and reviews. Unauthorized reproduction of any part of this work is illegal and is punishable by law.

ISBN 978-1478344308

Contents

CONTENTS 1

PROLOGUE 8

   Faith 8

   Reason 9

   Spirit 10

PART I 16

   12th year of Nero's reign (66 CE) - 3 18

   Alexandria and Judaea 21

      15TH YEAR OF TIBERIUS' REIGN (28 CE) 21

      16TH YEAR OF TIBERIUS' REIGN (29 CE) 24

   The tripartite soul 26

      21ST YEAR OF TIBERIUS' REIGN (34 CE) 26

      7TH YEAR OF NERO'S REIGN (61 CE) 28

      22ND YEAR OF TIBERIUS' REIGN (35 CE) - 1 32

      22ND YEAR OF TIBERIUS' REIGN (35 CE) - 2 34

   Healing 36

      3RD YEAR OF TIBERIUS' REIGN (36 CE) - 1 36

      23RD YEAR OF TIBERIUS' REIGN (36 CE) - 2 38

CONTENTS

Conflict 39
- 4TH YEAR OF CALIGULA'S REIGN (40 CE) 39
- 1ST YEAR OF CALIGULA'S REIGN (37 CE) 41
- 2ND YEAR OF CALIGULA'S REIGN (38 CE) - 1 43

Judas 46
- 2ND YEAR OF CALIGULA'S REIGN (38 CE) - 2 46
- 2ND YEAR OF CALIGULA'S REIGN (38 CE) – 3 47
- 4TH YEAR OF VESPASIAN'S REIGN (73 CE) - 1 48

James 49
- 6TH YEAR OF CLAUDIUS' REIGN (46 CE) 49
- 1ST YEAR OF NERO'S REIGN (55 CE) 51
- 6TH YEAR OF NERO'S REIGN (60 CE) 52

Joseph 53
- 15TH YEAR OF NERO'S REIGN (69 CE) - 2 53
- 8TH YEAR OF CLAUDIUS' REIGN (48 CE) 54
- 9TH YEAR OF CLAUDIUS' REIGN (49 CE) 57
- 10TH YEAR OF CLAUDIUS' REIGN (50 CE) 58

Simon 59
- 3RD YEAR OF NERO'S REIGN (57 CE) 59
- 13TH YEAR OF NERO'S REIGN (67 CE) 60

War 62

- 8TH YEAR OF NERO'S REIGN (62 CE) 62
- 10TH YEAR OF NERO'S REIGN (64 CE) 63
- 12TH YEAR OF NERO'S REIGN (66 CE) – 1 63
- 12TH YEAR OF NERO'S REIGN (66 CE) – 2 65
- 15TH YEAR OF NERO'S REIGN (69 CE) - 3 66
- 15TH YEAR OF NERO'S REIGN (69 CE) - 1 67

The everlasting name 68

- 12TH YEAR OF NERO'S REIGN (66 CE) – 4 68
- 1ST YEAR OF VESPASIAN'S REIGN (70 CE) - 1 69

Sin 72

PART II 80

Christianity 80

- ALEXANDRIA 82
- JUDAEA 97

The tripartite soul 104

- PLATO AND THE TRIPARTITE PSYCHE 104
- THE UNIVERSAL PSYCHE 109
- WOMEN 116
- NUMBERS 123

Healing 130

- THE GALILEAN HEALING MIRACLES 130

CONTENTS

Conflict 133
The messianic secret 133
Flaccus 135

Judas 140
Judas the Galilean 140
Society and spirit without faith in the divine 144
The fourth philosophy 147
Judas Iscariot 149

James 153
The decline of an ideology 153
James 159
Jesus 164

Joseph 170
Qumran 170
Rebuilding David's fallen tent 174
The Teacher of Righteousness 178
The Jerusalem Council 181
Joseph of Arimathea 185

Simon 190
Paul 190
Paul and James 195

INTERPRETING MARK

- Simon 198
- Mary the mother of Jesus 201

War 203
- The coming rebellion 203
- Stephen 205
- Prophecy 207
- Conflict 210
- Josephus 214
- The Capernaum demoniac 220
- The Gerasene demoniac 222

The everlasting name 231
- Abraham, Isaac and Jacob 231
- The God of Abraham 233
- The God of Jacob 236
- The God of Isaac 240

Sin 243
- Harmony and discord 243
- Sins of the Passion 245

Divine reason 252
- Salome, Mary Magdalene and Mary the mother of James and Joseph 252

Contents

Worship 254

Part III 255

The Catholic Church 255

Introductory rites 258

Greeting 258

Penitential Rite and Kyrie 261

Gloria 264

Liturgy of the word 269

First Reading 269

Second Reading 273

Gospel 276

Credo 280

Intercessions 284

Liturgy of the Eucharist 289

Sanctus 289

Agnus Dei 293

Interlude 295

Communion 297

Concluding rite 299

Dismissal 299

Epilogue 302

Spirit 304

Reason 307

Faith 313

Appendix – Psychological and social fractures 317

References 318

Prologue

Definitions:

Chaos (noun):

1. *a state of utter confusion or disorder; a total lack of organization or order.*

2. *The infinity of space or formless matter supposed to have preceded the existence of the ordered universe.*

Cosmos (noun):

1. *The universe regarded as an orderly, harmonious whole.*

Faith

The Church has always venerated the divine Scriptures just as she venerates the body of the Lord.... All the preaching of the Church should be nourished and governed by Sacred Scripture. For in the sacred books, the Father who is in heaven meets his children with great love and speaks to them; and the power and goodness in the word of God is so great that it stands as the support and energy of the Church, the strength of faith for her sons and daughters, the food of the soul, a pure and perennial fountain of spiritual life.

[Second Vatican Council, Dei Verbum 21]

Reason

In 1980, a thirteen part series on science entitled *"Cosmos, a personal voyage"* was first aired on American television. Fronted and co-created by the charismatic astronomer Carl Sagan, the series was hugely popular. It benefits from Sagan's easy charm and poetic language and the special effects that for the time it was made were truly ground breaking. Episode One is titled *"The Shores of the Cosmic Ocean"* and introduces the viewer to the ancient library of Alexandria. As Professor Sagan appears to walk around the library with a mural of Alexander in the great hall, he talks about the geniuses that Alexandria nurtured; the geographer Eratosthenes, the astronomers Hipparchus and Ptolemy, the mathematician Euclid and the great polymath Archimedes. The clip still has the capacity to stimulate the imagination as Professor Sagan appears genuinely awestruck by the achievements of these ancient scientists. In the final episode to the series, titled *"Who speaks for the earth?"*, the professor revisits the virtual library of Alexandria and the accompanying narrative truly captures the spirit of that ancient city:

> *Alexandria was the greatest city the Western world had ever seen. People of all nations came there to live, to trade, to learn. On any given day, its harbors were thronged with merchants, scholars and tourists. This was a city where Greeks, Egyptians, Arabs, Syrians, Hebrews, Persians, Nubians, Phoenicians, Italians, Gauls and Iberians exchanged merchandise and ideas. It is probably here that the word cosmopolitan realized its true meaning -- citizen, not just of a nation, but of the Cosmos. To be a citizen of the Cosmos...*
>
> [Carl Sagan: from Cosmos]

PROLOGUE

Spirit

"Well said, teacher," the man replied. "You are right in saying that God is one and there is no other but him. To love him with all your heart, with all your understanding and with all your strength, and to love your neighbor as yourself is more important than all burnt offerings and sacrifices."

[Mark 12: 32-33]

From the babe in the manger to the ubiquitous crucifix, images of Christ are common-place. The slumped and suffering loin cloth clad figure, crowned with thorns and nailed to the cross is emblazoned in the mind of most Christians.

Between Paul's earliest letters and his latest we can see the development of a Christology that culminates in this statement in his letter to the Romans:

You see, at just the right time, when we were still powerless, Christ died for the ungodly.

[Romans 5:6]

With this scriptural backing, the crucifixion imagery feeds into a particular Christian spirituality:

I asked Jesus how much He loved me. He answered "this much". Then He stretched out His arms and died for me.

This is the *"died for our sins"* Christ, the atoning redeemer Christ, the sacrificial *"Lamb of God"* Christ, the *"Alas and did my savior bleed"* Christ. It is a Christianity that is so dominant that it appears to be all pervasive. Yet, it is by no means clear that this spirituality was at all common-place within the early church.

INTERPRETING MARK

Few images of Christ from early Christianity survive. Indeed, before the 4th Century, it seems few images were made. In 1964, however, in a field in Hinton St Mary, Dorset in England, there was an archaeological excavation of part of an approximately 1700 year old Roman villa that uncovered a beautiful floor mosaic comprising two panels. Incorporated into the central roundel of the larger panel is an image that is thought by many to be one of the earliest depictions of Christ,

The image is of the head and shoulders of a clean-shaven, square faced man of solemn appearance with swept back hair and a prominent chin. He wears Roman attire. Behind the head is a monogram, the Chi-Ro, made from the two Greek letters *"chi"* and *"ro"*, the first two letters of the word *"ΧΡΙΣΤΟΣ"* or Christos.

The head is flanked on both sides by a pomegranate, reminiscent of the myth of Persephone who, after eating six pomegranate seeds while captive in the underworld, was condemned to spend six months of each year there. Her mother Demeter, the goddess of the harvest mourns while Persephone is away and the earth loses its fertility. When she is reunited with her daughter the earth is fertile once more.

This is the intertwining of Christian symbolism with pagan resurrection symbolism. The pomegranate represents the earth's seasonal death and rebirth.

Although the *"died for our sins"* spirituality is so dominant within contemporary Christianity, there is another tradition, a mystical tradition, a robust tradition, as old as Christianity itself that sees Christ not as a human sacrifice but as divine reason or logos, part of a divine Trinity. It is spirituality present in the writings of Philo of Alexandria and in the prologue to John's Gospel. It is also strikingly exhibited in that 8th century Irish Celtic prayer known as Saint Patrick's breastplate.

Although there is a reference within this prayer to the crucified Christ comprising two lines out of approximately one hundred, there is no suffering body, no nailed wrists, no nailed feet and no

PROLOGUE

guilt-inducing dying for our sins spirituality. Yet the prayer is no less devout for their absence. The complete work takes the form of an incantation and starts with a call to the Holy Trinity for protection:

> *For my shield this day I call:*
> *A mighty power:*
> *The Holy Trinity!*
> *Affirming threeness,*
> *Confessing oneness*
> *In the making of all*
> *Through love.....*

[From Saint Patrick's Breastplate c. 8th century CE]

The section below comprises a prayerful request for Christ to be with the traveler and all whom he meets.

> *Christ beside me, Christ before me;*
> *Christ behind me, Christ within me;*
> *Christ beneath me, Christ above me;*
> *Christ to right of me, Christ to left of me;*
> *Christ in my lying, my sitting, my rising;*
> *Christ in heart of all who know me,*
> *Christ on tongue of all who meet me,*
> *Christ in eye of all who see me,*
> *Christ in ear of all who hear me.*

[From Saint Patrick's Breastplate c. 8th century CE]

Contemporary Christian spirituality, so tied up with imagery of Christ, is so different from the spirituality exhibited in this prayer that it is surprising that they are born of the same religion. It would surely be beneficial to take heed of the example of Judaism where the use of images of the divine is regarded as idolatrous. For

Christians, the subtle and yet profound doctrine of the Trinity is obscured by both physical and mental images of the historical Christ, the itinerant preacher and miracle worker, born in a Bethlehem stable and later betrayed, condemned, tortured and crucified with arms stretched out, loving you *"this much"*, before on the third day being physically resurrected. The logos is too often lost behind the literal.

Although the figure in the roundel of the St Mary of Hinton Roman floor mosaic is thought by many to represent Christ, the following is one alternative explanation:

Constantine the Great, the first Christian Emperor, was instrumental in establishing the first ecumenical church council that took place in Nicaea in 325 CE. The council formulated a declaration of the Christian faith (or creed) that was used to exclude those who failed to profess it. From this moment the Catholic Church became an institution inextricably linked for many centuries, even after the fall of Rome, with those who wielded political power. When Constantine died in 337 CE, his empire was split between his sons.

From 340 CE, Constans, the youngest son, ruled the western part of the Roman Empire. However, the reputation that Constans gained for cruelty and misrule led to feelings of disenchantment and unrest among many of those who served him.

It was with the support of the Imperial guard units that he commanded that Magnentius, in 350 CE, usurped Constans. His reign was notable for the great tolerance that he demonstrated toward both Christians and pagans. However, his reign was short. The forces of Magnentius were defeated by the forces of Constans' brother, Constantius II. Magnentius died in 353 CE.

Many coins from Magnentius' reign have been found with his image on the obverse. Even in profile, the image is distinctive. It is the image of the head and shoulders of a clean-shaven, square faced man of solemn appearance with swept back hair and a prominent chin. He wears the attire of a Roman Emperor. On the reverse of some coins is the Chi-Ro symbol.

It is perfectly possible, surely, that the image within the Hinton St Mary mosaic is not meant to represent an historical Jesus Christ at all, but Magnentius, in the eyes of some, the embodiment of the logos.

Early Christians were certainly more attuned to the idea of a tripartite soul. On the central roundel of the smaller panel within the St Mary of Hinton Roman floor mosaic, further pagan imagery is depicted. Bellerophon, mounted on his winged horse Pegasus, is spearing the mythical three headed fire-breathing monster, the Chimaera, which has the heads of a goat, a snake and a lion. The monster surely represents an unholy Trinity and although we have no way of knowing what the patron of this mosaic, with its free use of pagan imagery, had in mind when he commissioned this work, he is unlikely to have been a supporter of the newly institutionalized church nor of the sons of the one who created it.

In their genuflection, Catholics give a cursory nod to the Trinity. Yet to most the Trinity is incomprehensible.

It was formed from the philosophical idea of the universal tripartite soul and although this soul may be an abstract ideal, it is not divorced from reality to be debated by philosophers in ivory-towered isolation. Although the Trinity cannot be touched, tasted, smelled, heard or seen, it does, nevertheless, represent something real. It represents that which shapes our relationships.

Indeed, in the very same letter to the Romans where Paul gives backing to the *"died for our sins spirituality"*, he also alludes to *"logos"* spirituality when he writes:

> *For just as each of us has one body with many members, and these members do not all have the same function, so in Christ we, though many, form one body, and each member belongs to all the others.*
>
> [Romans 12:4-5]

The gospel of Mark is one of the great works of literature. The superficial story is gripping enough but woven into this story is an underlying message that resonates through time. The gospel is thought to have been written between 66 and 73 CE during the time of the Jewish war with Rome and the author has long been associated with the ancient city of Alexandria. It is a time and a place that is worthy of study. For when we consider the social and political forces that were at work; when we learn of the historical events that occurred; when we reflect on how the idea of a universal and tripartite soul can help us understand our relationships with others; and above all when we imagine the experiences of the author.

It is then that we sharpen our exegetical tools. It is then that we are prepared for an allegorical excavation of an almost two thousand year old text that can uncover an interpretation that doesn't just fit. It is an interpretation that fits beautifully.

Part I

.. conflicts perpetually arose with the Grecians; and although the governors did every day punish many of them, yet did the sedition grow worse; but at this time especially, when there were tumults in other places also, the disorders among them were put into a greater flame; for when the Alexandrians had once a public assembly, to deliberate about an embassage they were sending to Nero, a great number of Jews came flocking to the theatre; but when their adversaries saw them, they immediately cried out, and called them their enemies, and said they came as spies upon them; upon which they rushed out, and laid violent hands upon them; and as for the rest, they were slain as they ran away; but there were three men whom they caught, and hauled them along, in order to have them burnt alive; but all the Jews came in a body to defend them, who at first threw stones at the Grecians, but after that they took lamps, and rushed with violence into the theatre, and threatened that they would burn the people to a man; and this they had soon done, unless Tiberius Alexander, the governor of the city, had restrained their passions. However, this man did not begin to teach them wisdom by arms, but sent among them privately some of the principal men, and thereby entreated them to be quiet, and not provoke the Roman army against them; but the seditious made a jest of the entreaties of Tiberius, and reproached him

for so doing.

Now when he perceived that those who were for innovations would not be pacified till some great calamity should overtake them, he sent out upon them those two Roman legions that were in the city and together with them five thousand other soldiers, who, by chance, were come together out of Libya, to the ruin of the Jews. They were also permitted not only to kill them, but to plunder them of what they had, and to set fire to their houses. These soldiers rushed violently into that part of the city that was called Delta, where the Jewish people lived together, and did as they were bidden, though not without bloodshed on their own side also; for the Jews got together, and set those that were the best armed among them in the forefront, and made a resistance for a great while; but when once they gave back, they were destroyed unmercifully; and this their destruction was complete, some being caught in the open field, and others forced into their houses, which houses were first plundered of what was in them, and then set on fire by the Romans; wherein no mercy was shown to the infants, and no regard had to the aged; but they went on in the slaughter of persons of every age, till all the place was overflowed with blood, and fifty thousand of them lay dead upon heaps; nor had the remainder been preserved, had they not be-taken themselves to supplication. So Alexander commiserated their condition, and gave orders to the Romans to retire;

PART I

> *accordingly, these being accustomed to obey orders, left off killing at the first intimation; but the populace of Alexandria bare so very great hatred to the Jews, that it was difficult to recall them, and it was a hard thing to make them leave their dead bodies.*
>
> [Josephus: The Jewish War 2:18:7]

12th year of Nero's reign (66 CE) - 3

I worry about my two sons. Rufus is the younger and more impetuous. He takes after his mother. You can still see her in Rufus. He has inherited both the red hair and the temperament, that assertive but sometime aggressive nature that causes him to kick off at the slightest provocation. I didn't spend much time with Rufus when he was young and I regret that now. Rufus looks to others for his sense of self-worth. Alexander is the elder and the more reflective. His sense of self-worth comes from within.

When they were children my sons squabbled frequently but if one minute they were kicking and screaming at each other, the next they were best of friends. It didn't take much for children to be reconciled.

Ruefully, I reflected on how much more difficult it was for adults. Children didn't carry the intellectual baggage that adults carried. Jews after all, regarded themselves as the *"chosen"* people; Greeks regarded themselves as the *"civilized"* ones. There was anger and resentment. Of course, Alexander himself was brutal in his subjugation of nations and Antiochus was barbaric in his treatment of Jews but I hadn't experienced those events. The massacre at Alexandria, however, the night my wife was killed, was seared on my mind.

It was a cold evening and my old bones felt it. When I was first informed, it sounded such a trivial incident that I dismissed it as just another internecine squabble.

There was a gathering of Greeks in the theatre. They were there to discuss a proposal to send an envoy to Nero. Some Jews, pretending to be Greeks, had followed, intending to spy on the proceedings. In truth, Jewish suspicions were largely fuelled by news of the events in Judaea. Their subterfuge did not go undetected. Three of these intruders were captured and the Greek ring leaders, their spirits infused with a heady cocktail of long standing resentment and inflamed passions, threatened to burn them alive.

This was insane talk that was completely out of proportion to the insult and the threat caused the dispute to escalate and the rhetoric to become ever more violent. Some hot headed Jews picked up torches and threatened to burn the theatre itself to the ground with the Greeks inside.

The governor, Tiberius Alexander, summoned the most influential men of both communities to the Imperial Palace and I was included in that number. Tiberius asked us to use our influence to help resolve the dispute. I consider myself a poor rhetorician and I was cold so I was happy to leave the task of talking with the rebels to others. While they went to the theatre, I stayed in the palace courtyard, warming myself at the fire. This was a mistake. I should have gone with the others. I should have tried. The attempts to resolve the conflict came to nothing. The Jewish ringleaders didn't listen. Instead they shouted abuse on Tiberius, who himself was not only a Jew but a nephew of the great philosopher Philo, calling him *"traitor"* and a *"lackey"* of the Emperor. When Tiberius called for the troops, the activists retreated to the Jewish quarter and the soldiers, who up until then were stationed in their barracks, were sent in. There were two Roman legions, XXII Deiotariana and III Cyrenaica. I knew many of the Jews. They were my people. I knew some of the Cyrenaica legion. They were my people too.

It is painful for me to describe the events that followed. The Jews fought valiantly and the soldiers suffered many casualties but after the initial defenses were breached, the soldiers were merciless. They slaughtered indiscriminately; young and old; men and women; the healthy and infirm. Blood flowed like rivers through the moonlit

PART I

streets and alleyways. I should have done something. I should have spoken out. I should have counseled the ringleaders against such foolhardiness. I should have dissuaded Tiberius from taking such brutal action. I should have protected the vulnerable. But I felt so powerless and so afraid. Instead, I am ashamed to say that I ran and ran; away from the senseless butchery, until I could no longer hear the screams.

The following morning, the soldiers were tasked with removing the dead. Body was piled upon bloody body. All tolled there were 50,000 corpses.

This was wrong. It was unquestionably, unequivocally wrong. But it is wrong to associate all Greeks with this atrocity and it is wrong to associate all Romans with it. We bear our share of blame. It is wrong to separate ourselves from other people.

It is David who we revere; he who demonstrated wanton disregard for the commandments; he who waged war on the flimsiest of pretexts; he who was ruthless in his treatment of his enemies; he who instilled fear into the hearts of his opponents; all with the declared aim of bringing peace. In this David was no different to Alexander.

For the Jewish people it should have been different. We were the people of God.

Why do we celebrate year on year the re-consecration of the Temple after the sins of Antiochus? We nurture the resentment, we cradle the animosity, we foster the hope of a conquering Messiah, a son of David that will come from the House of Judah and we have created a sea of bitterness to divide Jews and gentiles. For the excesses of a group of foolhardy hotheads, a community was decimated.

Something will be born from that bitterness. The movement aimed for something better. I reflected on my own experiences over the years. I reflected on what I had learned from Jewish scripture and in my studies at the Musaeum and I scanned once more those letters that I bought some years ago and knew almost by heart. Then I picked up my pen and started to write.

Alexandria and Judaea

15th Year of Tiberius' reign (28 CE)

I arrived in Alexandria shortly after my eighteenth birthday. It is my first time away from home and I feel apprehensive and excited at the same time.

Alexandria is situated on a spit of land sandwiched between the Mediterranean to the north and Lake Mareotis to the south. The lake is huge, stretching 100 kilometers from east to west and connects to the Nile by a number of canals. It also connects to the canals of Alexandria and from there to the sea. Docks, quays and warehouses are dotted along the northern edge of the lake and its main harbor intrudes into the city just to the west of the Canopic canal.

Compared to my home city, Alexandria is enormous and there is so much to see. From the top of the Paneium, that peculiar man-made fir-cone shaped tower dedicated to the god Pan, you can see the whole of the city below. It was designed in a strict grid pattern with parallel streets running east to west intersecting those running north to south.

To the east of the Paneium is the Canopic canal that brings fresh water from a branch of the Nile that is then diverted into the cavernous subterranean cisterns that lie beneath the city. The canal acts as a boundary to separate the Greek and Jewish populations. The area to the east is the main Jewish district and contains the large roofed, basilica-like structure of the synagogue. Still to the east of the canal, on the seafront, is a promontory called the Lochias. This has a man-made extension, the Diabathra that serves as a breakwater on the eastern side of the harbor. It is on the Lochias that the Imperial Palace is located. The barracks for the Roman

PART I

soldiers are situated at the point where the promontory joins the mainland. Running through the city, from east to west and connecting the different districts, is the major thoroughfare, Canopic Way approximately 30 meters wide that terminates at both ends at gates in the city wall. To the east is the Canopic Gate. To the west is the Sidera.

The Paneium is in the Greek district. This contains the finest public buildings.

To the west, south of Canopic Way, is the Gymnasium, used as a place of public entertainment, where young naked Greek men compete in athletic events and chariot races with the prize of an olive branch crown going to the champions and where after his triumph over the Armenians, Antony, with Cleopatra at his side, bestowed titles upon their royal children. The Gymnasium is most beautiful, with colonnades of more than 200 meters in length.

Opposite the Gymnasium, across Canopic Way is the lavishly constructed Caesareum with its magnificent gateway, decorated porticoes, marble statues, libraries, banqueting halls, groves, spacious courts and open-air rooms founded by Cleopatra in honor of Antony and centrally located overlooking the eastern harbor. The Caesareum is where Cleopatra killed herself after hearing of the news of Antony's suicide. In front of the building are the two red granite obelisks brought from Memphis to the city by the Romans shortly after Cleopatra's death.

To the east of the Caesareum is the theatre where there are regular performances of the works of the great traditional Greek playwrights such as Aeschylus, Aristophanes, Euripides and Sophocles as well as the contemporary Roman ones such as Seneca and Plautus.

Between the Caesareum and the theatre and bounded by a rectangular colonnade, is the open expanse of the agora, the commercial heart of the city.

To the west of the Caesareum is the Musaeum. It is a large three-story building with numerous rooms used as lecture halls and workshops. It has a garden, located inside an inner courtyard, with a wonderful variety of plants and one can often see scholars circumnavigating the courtyard, their minds deep in contemplation. The Musaeum is connected at its northern end to the great library that itself faces out onto the harbor.

The library houses an astonishing collection of works. More than 700,000 scrolls have been collected over the years from all cultures and in all languages. Under the Ptolemys, every ship that entered port was searched for scrolls. Any scroll found would be taken away and copied before being returned to the owner. The best of mankind's intellectual endeavors were classified, catalogued, and stored in that library.

Further west, in the Egyptian district and running at a right angle to Canopic Way and about the same width, is Soma Street. This is terminated by the Gate of the Moon to the north and the Gate of the Sun to the south.

This street leads to the Serapeum in the south of the city. This is a temple to the god Serapis that also acts as an annex for the library.

The Serapeum is magnificent. A series of steps leads up to the building, adorned by a portico supported by a series of columns constructed in the Doric style.

The building has spacious rooms containing wonderfully life-like statues as well as paintings and tapestries and mosaics. It is a place where people can congregate. It is a place where people can study; it is a place where people can pray.

Directly inside the temple doors, one is confronted with the huge statue of the god. He is seated, solidly built and stern-faced. In his left hand he holds a scepter. On his head, worn as a crown, is a modius, a small basket for measuring grain. At his feet sits Cerberus, the three-headed dog of the underworld.

Serapis is said to be a synthesis of the gods Osiris and Apsis, but this god is so unlike the traditional image of the vulnerable Osiris, entombed in a sarcophagus and then torn apart by his brother. This god is a god of authority, sitting in judgment with scepter in hand and at his feet the all so obvious reminder of the afterlife. He won't be measuring grain with the modius he wears; he'll be measuring our sins.

16th Year of Tiberius' reign (29 CE)

Relationships between the communities are civil, if not exactly harmonious. Flaccus, the governor, maintains good order but of course, there are those differences that set us apart and these create the tensions that simmer beneath the surface.

There is the Sabbath, a day that the Greeks treat much like any other. Of course, each Greek has a day of rest but for them it is not the same day for everyone. For us Jews, it is sacrilege to do anything creative on the Sabbath. There is no cooking, no writing, no building and no carrying; nothing except attendance at the synagogue, discourse with others and reading of the scriptures. It is even a compulsory rest day for slaves of Jews. Any Jew caught transgressing this law is guilty of a grievous sin.

The meat of grazing animals is expensive. Beef is unobtainable and goat and lamb have to be imported. Whilst fish and chicken are readily available, many young Jews cannot see the sense in depriving themselves and their children of the cheap, plentiful and tasty pig meat for the sake of tradition.

The Jewish elders do not permit it but there are many young men and boys who want to emulate their Greek friends and take part in the athletics at the Gymnasium. Some disobey the elders but in their nakedness the mark of circumcision is plain to see. Some can cope with the ridicule. Others have come to deeply resent their Jewishness.

Young men and young women are both strongly encouraged to marry within the community. If they are to marry a gentile then their partner must be sympathetic to Judaism and willing to bring up the children in the Jewish faith. Any Jew who chose to marry a gentile who was unsympathetic to the Jewish faith is at risk of being disowned.

There are many Jews, particularly of the older generation, who stay apart from gentiles, as if fraternization risked some sort of contamination.

I always feel uncomfortable with the exuberant celebration of the festivals. We live and work side by side with Egyptians and yet every year at Passover we celebrate the infliction of ten plagues on the Egyptian people and the killing of their first born sons. Similarly, we live and work side by side with Greeks and yet every year at Hanukkah we celebrate the conquest of the Greeks and the overturning of Hellenization.

I am in a large unfamiliar city. I can't identify completely with the Jewish community but I can't identify completely with the Greeks either. I feel somewhat insecure and maybe that is why I feel such empathy with Carabbas. I don't know much about the background of the man but he is evidently without his senses. Night and day, whatever the weather, he will walk up and down Canopic Way and Soma Street completely naked. He is gentle natured and so trusting with everyone irrespective of their nationality or religion. However, there are some who taunt and cruelly mock him.

Carabbas relies on the charity of others for his sustenance and some of the stallholders in the agora give him bread and fruit that they cannot sell. I give him food that I smuggle out from the Musaeum refectory.

Others think me mad for having such concern over a naked beggar but when I see Carabbas, I see my own humanity reflected back at me at its most exposed and vulnerable. Those who torment him don't see that. They just see an object of ridicule and abuse. Unlike Carabbas, they are clothed, of course, in garments that preserve their own vanities.

This is how it is with the Jewish community too. When Jewish people lived apart from Egyptians and Greeks it didn't matter as much but now we live together it matters a great deal. There is an unmistakable air of moral superiority that is deeply unattractive and dangerously divisive.

The tripartite soul

21st Year of Tiberius' reign (34 CE)

I was a diligent student in my youth. In my early years I studied Jewish scripture. I spoke both Hebrew and Aramaic. I learnt Greek and Latin too. It is my good fortune that my parents are wealthy and were willing to fund my education. When I was old enough they sent me to Alexandria to study at the Musaeum which gave me access to both the famed library and the Serapeum.

I remember that extraordinary time measuring device, the clepsydra, a contraption of drums, siphons, wheels, gears, pointers and floats. Built by Ctesibius, the clepsydra stood in the courtyard and was visible from the lecture room windows. Powered by water, it clocked off the hours that passed throughout the day. I couldn't help feeling sorry for the slave boy whose job it was re-calibrate the instrument twice daily and to ensure the upper reservoir of the instrument was constantly topped up with water. It must have been a mind-numbingly boring task.

It was at the Musaeum that I studied rhetoric and philosophy, mostly the works of Aristotle and Plato. I also studied literature, medicine and science and I was fortunate enough to be taught by that great mathematician and experimenter Heron. His lectures were always enjoyable because they were so practical. I particularly liked his demonstration of the aeolipile, that metal sphere partially filled with water and suspended by means of a pivot over a cauldron of water. The sphere had two bent tubes emanating from it that were fitted diametrically opposite to each other. When the fire under the cauldron was heated, the water inside the sphere started to boil. The steam so produced was forced out of the tubes and this caused the sphere to rotate at great speed. Although none of us could conceive of a useful application for this discovery, the demonstration was marvelously entertaining.

My greatest passion, however, was for geometry and astronomy. I studied the geometry of Euclid, of course, and the geometry of Heron himself. I learnt too of the brilliant Archimedes who derived the formula to determine the area of a circle and the volume of a sphere and learnt of his painstaking work deriving the value of pi - that constant whose elusive value is the ratio of the circumference of a circle to its diameter. Archimedes knew how to measure the volume of cylinders, cones, cubes and spheres. These were all regularly shaped objects. Irregularly shaped objects were more of a challenge. My lecturer was fond of relating that unlikely tale propagated by the famous Roman architect, Vitruvius, of how Archimedes, being in his bath and pondering for some time the problem of how to measure the volume of a golden crown, noticed the bath water was overflowing and realized that he could measure the volume of an object by measuring the volume of the water it displaced. At this revelation, or so the story went, he jumped out of the bath and ran, stark naked along the streets of Syracuse shouting *"Eureka"*.

I also learnt of Aristarchus and his bizarre counter-intuitive theory that the earth orbited the sun and the greatest astronomer Hipparchus, his star charts and his use of trigonometry in his measurements of the length of the solar year, the length of the lunar month, the length of the seasons and his calculations of the dates of the equinoxes and solstices.

I learnt how Egyptian astronomers measured the length of the solar year by observation of the stars and measurement of the maximum height of the Nile every year and how they derived a value of the length of this year as being slightly less than 365 ¼. I learnt how Julius Caesar while partaking of the hospitality of Cleopatra, learnt of this value from the astronomer Sosigenes and used this knowledge in his implementation of the Julian calendar.

I spend hours in observation of the stars and contemplation of space and time. It fascinates me.

I have two great heroes. The first is Eratosthenes the Greek.

I am fully aware that this leaves me open to accusations of parochialism. Nevertheless, I feel fully justified. Eratosthenes was brilliant. He was not just a great man of science. He was a radical humanist who condemned those who divided mankind into Greeks and barbarians.

He demonstrated that the world we perceive, the only world that we can perceive is the world we know about — the world that is centered on the Mediterranean. However, this world is just a tiny part of a much, much larger physical body. We know of the local gods, of course, the many and various deities and we know of the strange and alien cultures in the East and there was talk of the primitive cultures of the tribes of the North but there was no doubt, there were people living in as yet, undiscovered societies that had completely different belief systems that worshipped a completely different god or pantheon of gods. Who is to say that it is we who are right and they who are wrong? I am convinced that any religion that is to be accessible to all people, irrespective of their cultural background, has to be built on that which is in common across all cultures. It has to be built on the rock of what it is to be human.

My second great hero is Philo the Jew.

In the nature of us all is a desire to reconcile conflicts and I desperately need to reconcile my commitment to Judaism and the Holy Scripture with my commitment to science and philosophy. I have taken to the writings of Philo like an infant takes to its mother's milk.

7th year of Nero's reign (61 CE)

Alexandria is not just a center of learning. It is a thriving trading port and a city of commerce. The fertile valley of the Nile is the empire's granary. During the harvest season, grain is transported by canal to the city and shipments regularly leave the port for Rome. In return come ornately carved wooden items and, of course, slaves. Also, in the wake of Alexander's conquests, trading routes to the east were established. Merchants come from India laden with silks, spices, incense, pearls and precious stones.

The agora is a sensuous delight, a place where people from all nations, people of all races, people of all classes rub shoulders - Greeks, Jews, Egyptians, Romans, Persians, Carthaginians, Syrians, Nubians, people from countries and regions nearby such as Judea, Galilee, Samaria, Idumea, Cyprus, Crete and Cyrene and people from places as far away as India. There is a constant hubbub of activity as buyers and sellers barter for an acceptable price. Often striving to communicate in a language that is not their own, they still manage, somehow, to be understood. All manner of goods can be bought and sold. There are perfumes and cosmetics, aromatic oils and incense. There are glass objects, ornate bottles and jugs and exquisite yet fragile vessels in a range of colors of wonderful translucence produced by the Alexandrian glass blowers. There are ceramic vessels, storage vessels like pots and jars as well as crockery such as plates and dishes and cups. There are cooking pots and pans with their associated utensils. There are small wooden items such as intricately carved bowls and jewelry boxes and the more mundane spoons and boxwood combs. There are robes, cloaks and shawls made from cotton or wool. There are horsehair brushes and mirrors and bronze razors and strigils used to scrape sweat off the body. There are leather bags, cloth bags and small woolen bags and there are baskets of all shapes and sizes. There is a plethora of terracotta figurines used for decoration or as children's toys.

And there is food, lots and lots of food.

There are rows and rows of all sorts of fish, freshly caught this morning. The delicious freshwater fish, the tilapia and perch, come from the Mareotis but these are outnumbered by the saltwater varieties. There are small fish such as anchovies, sardines, smelt, mackerel and squid as well as the larger fish such as mullet, sea bass

PART I

and bream. The live shellfish that are kept in large jars of salt water are not destined for the traditional Jewish palate.

There is some meat but no beef nor lamb. There is no grazing land around Alexandria so beef and lamb have to be imported but chickens and piglets are sold. These can be reared locally and are reasonably priced, the latter again being avoided by most Jews.

There are plenty of seeds, nuts and grains for sale. There are lentils and fava beans, broad beans and chick peas. There are carob seeds, sesame seeds, walnuts, almonds and pecans and there is wheat and barley brought in from the Nile valley.

The fruit and vegetables vary from season to season. In these summer days, there are figs, plums, watermelons, tiger nuts, colocynth, lettuces, leeks and fenugreek. In the autumn these will be joined by dates, pomegranates, grapes, olives and ziziphus. As autumn turns to winter, cabbage, celery, radishes, coriander and garlic become available and these will be joined by onions, peas and sycamore figs in the spring.

Some of the fruit can be preserved by drying. The fish and meat can be preserved for a short time by salting and salt that has been extracted from the sea in the shallow lagoons to the west of the city is sold as well.

Bread of course is sold. It is a staple. It is made usually of wheat but some Egyptians hanker after the more exotic variety made from pounded lotus roots. Of course, there is the papyrus root, cheap and plentiful; to be enjoyed at its best, baked in a hot oven.

Honey is sold as well, of course, and prepared foods such as tahini and hummus and oils – olive oil and sesame seed oil used in cooking and, of course, there are the wonderfully exotic spices, seeds and roots. I don't know them all but they include ginger, black pepper, cinnamon and cassia and many, many more.

And there is drink. The jugs contain the beer that is the staple of the Egyptians and the amphorae and skins contain the full bodied wines that are produced in the vineyards of the Mareotis and are favored by the Greeks.

Rows of shops can be found along the main street away from the Agora with signs advertising their wares. There's the cobbler who will make sandals, slippers and shoes to the size and shape of your feet. There's the barber with his scissors and razor who will provide you with a haircut and shave. There are the clothes shops selling tunics and cloaks and togas and stola and palla and many linen garments and undergarments including kilts for the men and long dresses with straps for the women. The fabric can also be bought by the measure to be fashioned as one sees fit. There are the jewelers selling brooches, buckles and bangles, necklaces, ear rings, anklets and pendants often embedded with colored glass or precious stones such as emeralds, malachite and lapis lazuli. There is the shop selling house furnishings such as mirrors and marble and mosaics of numidian stone. There is the eating place with its tables and benches and aromas which, especially on the cooler days, stimulate the appetite and entice the customers.

And there is the shop that sells the scrolls. This is a city where knowledge and ideas are highly valued. There are many works that can be freely purchased - the mathematical writings of Euclid, Archimedes and Erastothenes, the philosophical writings of Plato, Aristotle and Philo, the plays of Aristophanes and the stories of Homer. By virtue of my status as a teacher in the Musaeum, I have access to these works in the library. However, there are other works that are not stored there – those many and varied religious and mystical works.

Parchment copies can be purchased by those who can afford them; papyrus copies are available to the rest. I obtained the letters easily enough.

There were the letters from Paul, of course, who described James, Peter and John as the *"pillars of the church"* and there was the letter from James himself. Some letters are pseudonymous. It is a lucrative trade. There is good money to be made in passing off a letter as a work of one of the apostles. I don't know the apostles personally, of course, but from their writing I gained some insight into their characters. Their letters would come to suit my purpose beautifully.

22nd Year of Tiberius' reign (35 CE) - 1

I'd studied Aristotle. Aristotle taught the principles of rhetoric and that any persuasive argument should appeal to credibility (ethos or faith), emotions (pathos or spirit) and reason (logos).

I'd studied Philo and his Plato-influenced writing of a tripartite divine soul with divine reason as being the image of God.

And I'd studied Plato. Plato saw the soul as containing three parts in a hierarchy with reason being the most valuable; as if reason could somehow exist in a vacuum. In this he was wrong. The soul had three parts – faith, spirit and reason – but they were of equal value.

But Plato was also influenced by astronomical discoveries. He wrote of the world or divine soul bounded by two bands comprising the solar ecliptic path (the path on which the sun orbits the earth) and the celestial equator. These cross each other like the two arms of the letter *"chi"*. The rotation of the cosmos around the celestial equator gives us day and night. The ecliptic path of the sun gives us our seasons.

Just like Plato, I have been influenced by science. I have studied the works of the astronomers and mathematicians and their measurements of the three dimensions of space and the dimension of time. And I believe that although both Plato and Philo were right to draw the parallel of the cosmic soul with the human soul, they both missed the obvious parallel.

Consider the first dimension of space. It is like a line, drawn so infinitely thin, it cannot be defined but just is. In a similar way are my feelings. Feelings are neither good nor bad; they are amoral; they just are.

Consider the second dimension. Running at a right angle to the first, it gives definition. It makes visible that which is hidden. In a similar way are my thoughts. When I think there is I and there is the object of my thoughts – that which is being defined.

Consider the third dimension. Running outwards at a right angle to the second, it is not a two dimensional picture but is real. It is in the world. In a similar way are my actions. When I do, I give physical expression to my thoughts and feelings.

Consider the dimension of time. The universe changes with the passage of time. In a similar way, I change. My experiences shape the person I am.

The force that creates the stars and planets, courses through my veins. This energy fused with my feelings gives me the spirit that inspires me to create, to destroy, to express myself.

But energy creates mass and the stars and planets around which other bodies rotate. Similarly, with experience, spirit fuses to create faith and our feelings, thoughts and actions are pulled towards that which is created.

Spirit gives purpose and drives us to challenges. Faith gives purpose and encourages us to commitment. And life without purpose is empty.

It is from the fusion of thoughts and faith that reason is born. Reason interprets faith. Action is the expression of spirit.

And reason, faith and spirit are the aspects of the psyche. And behavior is the aspect of the body.

This is a dynamic model. Our faith dies and is reborn. Spirit challenges faith and faith supports spirit.

Divide this model horizontally through the center and you can see a representation of the youth-age polarities. Young people, like my sons, tend to be active; driven by spirit but without the faith commitment. Older people find purpose in their faith.

Divide this model vertically through the center and you can see a representation of the male-female polarities. Like my wife, women tend to be more emotional and more intuitively understanding. Men tend to work things out rationally.

But we have male and female and young and old characteristics within us all.

This is what it is to be human; this is what we are.

After several years I had come to the realization of something which on reflection was obvious.

The tendency of philosophers is to value reason above all else because it is the nature of philosophers to express themselves through reason alone. That is why the writings of philosophers are often regarded as dull and lifeless. We are not beings of pure reason. We are emotional beings as well.

Myth, on the other hand, such as that related in the books of the prophets, in the works of Homer and in the various stories of the pagan gods, touches people's emotions. It is myth that is most highly valued by people. It is myth that can challenge and inspire. It is myth that can break down divisions, that can bring people together, that can change people's behavior for the good.

22nd Year of Tiberius' reign (35 CE) - 2

On the far side of the Mareotis, far enough away from the stress and distractions of city life, live the mixed sex monastic community of the therapeutae. The members of the community are dedicated to reducing their needs by freeing themselves from their own desires and training their bodies to subsist on the minimum of nourishment.

I was inspired to join the community, as many were, by the stories of John the Baptist that reached us from Judea. John himself reduced his needs to a minimum and, in acts of spiritual healing, symbolically washed away the sins of those who repented.

Each of us lives in our own small dwelling with a separate holy sanctuary and enclosed courtyard. Most of the week, we spend alone. Much of my time is taken up in the composition of hymns of praise, in solitary prayer and in the study of scripture.

There is much that I have learned through discussion with others and in that simple solitary reflection. We are social animals. We need to live with others. Yet in Alexandria, and in many other cities, living side by side with those of a different culture often causes conflict.

It is conflict that is born through the expression of egos. Although it is both natural and healthy, as we are growing up, to develop a strong sense of our own self, the lives of those who are unable to move beyond this stage are in a state of constant conflict. Our forefathers regarded the number seven as the holy number. People have different interpretations of why this should be but for me, we come to God in six steps grouped as follows:

- o We are infused with divine spirit when our own spirit is attuned to both divine reason and faith in the divine.
- o We are infused with divine reason when our own reason is attuned to both divine spirit and faith in the divine.
- o We are infused with faith in the divine when our own faith is attuned to both divine reason and divine spirit.

For those who achieve this the seventh step is putting into practice what they have become and to truly embody the logos.

It seems to me that when relationships break down, each of the three aspects of our individual psyche break their connection with the common tripartite psyche. This is when we are in conflict.

In Jewish scripture the number twelve, as in the twelve tribes of

Israel, is another significant number. It refers to reconciliation. It seems to me too that reconciliation between people is achieved when the three aspects of the individual psyche of both parties break their connection with their old tripartite and social psyche, their old faith, and re-establish a connection with a new tripartite and social psyche, a new faith.

Irrespective of the reason for the mystical significance of the number, reconciliation requires a commodity that is in short supply in Alexandria. It requires trust.

Healing

3rd Year of Tiberius' reign (36 CE) - 1

It is a bizarre theory and even my lecturer cautioned against giving it too much credence. Nevertheless, it is highly influential and is certainly better than some traditional beliefs that diseases are caused by evil spirits or are God's punishment on the wicked. Hippocrates promoted the theory that the human body was filled with four basic substances or humors - black bile, yellow bile, phlegm, and blood – and our health resulted from a balance in these humors. Conversely, all diseases and disabilities, he argued, resulted from an excess or deficit of one of these four humors.

There are medical practitioners in Alexandria who are followers of Hippocrates who make a good living from those who can afford their services. Their customers are mainly women, and I can't help but think that the improvements in the health of their patients is often down to the fact that the practitioners are prepared to listen and take them seriously.

Nevertheless, there is something in the theory that does tell us about the psychological temperament of people. It is in people's nature for them to gravitate toward a particular aspect of being.

People of sanguine temperament are often courageous but are often unreliable. These are people of spirit. People of choleric temperament are dynamic doers but become easily angered and bad tempered. These are people of action. People of melancholic temperament are deep reflective thinkers who need time alone and can become despondent and irritable. These are people of reason. People of phlegmatic temperament are calm and unemotional and can be reluctant to try new experiences. These are people of faith.

Hippocrates was right in this respect. Our psychological health comes from a balance of these temperaments.

The medical practitioners in Alexandria are not without competition. Members of the therapeutae community may not be skilled in healing bodies, but many are certainly skilled in healing souls and they often receive gifts of food in exchange for their services. There are many who make the journey from the city to seek their help.

After many months in the community, I have been permitted, with the assent of the ones who had come to be healed, to sit on some of the counseling sessions.

For Jews, there are particular difficulties in having to adhere to the strict, sometimes incomprehensible constraints that our religion demands while living alongside Greeks and Egyptians who have no such constraints. The types of experiences that people relate are common to many.

Some young Jews are torn between the demands of their religious elders and the seemingly innocent pleasures enjoyed by their gentile friends; whether it is the eating of pork or shellfish, the participation in the games at the Gymnasium or simply larking around on the Sabbath. Many who do succumb to temptation are subsequently stricken with guilt, fearful of the judgment of others.

There is an unwillingness of some of the elders to countenance any relaxation of the Jewish law and this causes friction between them and the younger Jews, many of whom regard the law as asinine.

Some young Jews, with no commitment to their traditions and little commitment to their families, are disrespectful to their parents but still make demands when they want something. Families often break apart as the same rehearsed arguments are repeated over and over.

Some gentiles have an utterly irrational fear of Jewish people that is stoked by slanderous and malevolent tales and this distrust is itself a cause of anxiety. Some Jews on hearing these slanders and themselves being raised with tales of the barbarism of Antiochus have an irrational fear of the Greeks.

Then there are those disaffected Jews who relinquish their Jewish identity and live independent and often materially successful but isolated lives, apart from the community.

The spiritual counselors do not dictate nor pass judgment but simply act as a sounding board, gently asking those probing questions that allow the sufferer to come to an understanding of their situation themselves. They see their role simply as enabling people to hear that inner voice of authority. For many, it helps put their problems in perspective when they discuss their relationship problems with people who are both celibate and chaste and their financial problems with people who have nothing.

23rd Year of Tiberius' reign (36 CE) - 2

On each seventh day with the therapeutae there is no counseling. Instead we celebrate simply together. On each seventh week, we come together, clothed in white garments, for a special celebration. When we enter the place of congregation, men and women diverge to sit separately, men on one side, women on the other.

After we sit down, the ephemereutae, with eyes raised to heaven, pray publicly to God that the entertainment may be acceptable, and welcome, and pleasing. Then the entertainment starts.

It begins with a discourse from one of the elders of the community that involves an interpretation of a passage of scripture, delivered in allegories. It may be difficult to believe it but it really is a most moving experience. The stark reading of the scripture passage resembles the visible body but the invisible meaning concealed under and lying beneath the plain words resembles the soul. As the speaker unfolds and explains the symbols within the scripture, bringing the secret meaning to light, my own rational nature contemplates my own soul.

After the discourse, someone will stand up and sing a hymn or recite a psalm made in the honor of God. Others will follow, sometimes in chorus. Everyone listens in respectful silence until such time as they are asked to join in. Then when all singing has finished, the food is brought in.

The meal is simple and symbolic, spring water and coarse bread flavored with salt and sometimes hyssop. The bitter taste of the hyssop reminds us of our past misdeeds. The bread is the healing food bringing us to humility. There are no slaves in the community and I am expected, together with the other novices, to wait on the others. This is not something that I am used to doing but this is the practice. Irrespective of the background that we have come from, irrespective of our previous position in society, we serve the other members. There are people from privileged backgrounds and people from humble ones; those who are Roman citizens and those who had been slaves; those who are lifelong Jews and those who are converts; those of unblemished reputation and those who had once been rogues or thieves. It is a simple act but a highly symbolic one. It feels right.

Conflict

4th Year of Caligula's reign (40 CE)

I know him through the Musaeum. He is an easy, fluent and eloquent speaker and an expert on the works of Homer. He was appointed head of the grammar school and teaches rhetoric there. I

PART I

had attended one of his lectures myself.

He is a man who is happy to blur the distinction between history and fiction in a most self-aggrandizing manner. He seems to crave the attention and adulation of the gullible.

For those familiar with the Odyssey, he claims to have received from Kteson, an inhabitant of Ithaca, during his stay there, an exact description of Penelope's suitors' game of draughts.

He claims to have heard from Egyptian sages the true account of Moses and the Exodus.

He claims to have been an eye-witness of the scene at the Circus Maximus when the runaway slave Androclus tended to the wounded lion and tamed him so he became like a domesticated dog.

He claims to have received information about the Homer's place of birth and parentage which he is not permitted to disclose.

His name is Apion. He is an Egyptian by birth, his name derived from the bull-god Apis and he is known both for his love of all things Greek and his utter detestation of all things Jewish.

He teaches rhetoric and uses it with effectiveness for his own malicious ends. He spreads ludicrous tales about the Jewish people that poisons the minds of the Greeks. He alleges that the term *"Sabbath"* originated during the Jewish exodus from Egypt. After walking for six days, he claims, the Jews developed buboes in their groins, a malady that was termed *"sabbatosis"* by the Egyptians, and it was because of these buboes that they had to rest on the seventh day.

He asserts that when Antiochus Epiphanes desecrated the temple, he found there in the most sacred of places, an ass's head made of pure gold, as if Jewish people worshipped an ass.

He is known to narrate in detail a fable of how Antiochus, after entering the Jerusalem temple, found a man in some distress who told the King that he was a Greek who had been captured and imprisoned and provided with the most exquisite food. However, he had found out from the servants that he was being fattened for sacrifice and that every year, at Passover, a Greek is killed and his entrails tasted.

After mocking the Jewish faith and ridiculing and then demonizing the Jewish people, he will stir up the Greek crowd by demanding to know why Jews worshipped apart from others and why they alone refused to worship the Emperor. By portraying the Alexandrian Jews as the enemy within, he blasphemes against the Holy Spirit.

Apion is a man who has considerable influence within the Greek community and depressingly, in the fourth year of Gaius Caligula's reign, he was chosen to head the Greek delegation to the Emperor to present the formal charge of disloyalty against the Alexandrian Jews. It was Philo himself who headed the Jewish delegation.

Regrettably, despite Philo's superior moral character and greater intellect, good sense did not prevail.

1st Year of Caligula's reign (37 CE)

Plato described the best society as the one ruled by a philosopher king and the worst as the one ruled by a tyrant.

Ever since Julius installed himself as the first Caesar, the empire had been ruled by an autocrat but the Emperors were not philosopher kings and, with one exception, they were not tyrants. Some of them, however, did suffer from that most common of human failings - an insufferable vanity.

Julius was a brilliant general and a great statesmen and he introduced the much needed reform of the calendar that brought some regularity to our measurement of the seasons. The calendar was exquisite in its simplicity, comprising as it did twelve months of alternate 30 and 31 days, except for February where there was 29

PART I

days and 30 days on a leap year. Unfortunately, Julius felt the need to assent to the proposition of having a month named after him.

So Julius was created, a month of 31 days.

Augustus was also a brilliant general and great statesman and if Julius was to have a month named after him then so was he. Of course, Augustus could not possibly have a month of fewer days than Julius. That would, surely, imply that he was somehow less significant.

So Augustus was created, following Julius, a month of 31 days and the duration of September, October and November were amended and an extra day removed from February and as a consequence that exquisitely simple calendar was exquisitely simple no longer.

Tiberius was a contrary character. Augustus named him successor and he dealt brutally with his rivals and yet, when his position was secured, he gave every impression of having no desire for it.

Nevertheless, to his credit, Tiberius refused to countenance a month being named in his honor. When it was suggested, he famously replied:

"What will you do when there are 13 Caesars?"

In his later years, the empire suffered as a result of his indifference. However, even at his worst, Tiberius was far superior to the self-obsessed young man who was to follow him. Power corrupts. It allows free rein to the most excessive of narcissistic tendencies and Gaius Caligula had those in spades.

For the first few months of Gaius' reign, he seemed to rule well and energetically but he was then struck with an illness. He was laid low for a number of months but eventually recovered. Some Alexandrian Jews offered sacrifices in the temple at Leontopolis in thanks for the Emperor's return to health.

However, since the illness, Gaius has lost all self-restraint.

Within months he squandered the vast wealth amassed by Tiberius and he showed great cruelty to those who were close to him. He ordered the killing of his co-heir, Tiberius' grandson. He ordered the killing of his father in law, Silanus, who would do no more than attempt to influence the extreme behavior of his son in law. Even now he takes pleasure in boasting of his adulteries.

His words and actions make little sense. He often appears in public dressed as a god or demigod, whether Hercules, Venus, Mercury or Apollo and unlike all previous Emperors he has those in Rome, even Senators, worship him as a physical living god.

Some attribute his extreme behavior to a troubled childhood.

Some put it down to an irresponsible young man, little older than a boy, being granted unrestrained power.

Some attribute it to his epilepsy that causes him sleepless nights and wild delusions.

Whatever the reason, Gaius has no sense of justice and he persists in ignoring the advice of wiser counsel. And when those in authority govern unjustly then that injustice is pervasive, infecting all those over whom they have authority.

2nd Year of Caligula's reign (38 CE) - 1

The appalling events started with *"a bit of fun"*. In truth it was an act of callous insensitivity. That poor soul, Carabbas was accosted and marched to the gymnasium. There he was stood in plain view on the podium and dressed mockingly as a king. In place of a diadem, a flattened papyrus leaf was put on his head. A door mat instead of a cloak was draped over his shoulders and instead of a scepter; a small stick of papyrus was placed in his hand. Then, in imitation of royal bodyguards, young men bearing sticks stood either side of him while, in mock deference, others approached him, some as if to salute him, some as if to plead their case, some as if to consult him about the affairs of the state.

PART I

Then the calls came from the assembled throng. They knew that Agrippa was by birth a Syrian so, with much laughter, they shouted *"Maris"*, which is Syrian for *"Lord"* and *"All hail, King of the Jews"*.

Flaccus could have openly chastised those ring leaders for daring to insult a king and a friend of Caesar. He could have imprisoned Carabbas, giving him protection from the excesses of the mob. Instead, he turned a blind eye and a deaf ear and in his tolerance of this open ridiculing of Jewish authority, he was complicit in it and his complicity gave the mob license for the events that followed.

A call came from the crowd for statues to be erected in the synagogue. There were statues to the Emperor in the Serapeum. The Emperor demanded it. It was a reminder to the public of who was in charge and a demonstration of public loyalty. There were no such statues in the synagogues, however. There were no graven images. Jewish law forbids it.

The crowd reasoned that if they accepted statues as a demonstration of their loyalty then so should the Jews. Through force, the synagogues were entered. Those Jews who did protest were beaten and the statues were erected. Flaccus could have sent soldiers to stop this desecration of our places of worship. He could have had the ring-leaders arrested. Instead, he did nothing and in his inertia, he was complicit in the actions of the mob and his complicity gave the mob further license.

There was a call from the crowd for Jews to be evicted from all but *"their"* district of the city. There were five districts and two of these were predominantly populated by Jews. Some Jews lived in the other districts scattered among the Greeks and Egyptians.

The crowd, fuelled by antipathy toward these *"alien people"*, were determined that they be ghettoized; that families be driven out. Properties were looted, businesses plundered and all booty carried aloft as trophies. The actions were unlawful and Flaccus could have ordered the troops to protect the homes and businesses of the Jewish people. Instead, he stayed silent and his silence gave the mob further tacit support and encouragement.

There were further atrocities from those in the crowd as Jews who dared to raise a voice or were slow in obeying these unjust demands, were beaten with sticks or stoned or kicked. Some took up more efficient weapons and Jews, including whole families, were slain, killed with swords, clubs or by fire.

Jewish women were dragged away to be displayed as a public spectacle in the theatre. They were commanded to eat the flesh of pigs and, if they refused, were tortured.

It was utterly unbelievable. It was utterly terrifying. There were those who inflicted acts of brutal torture on people who had done no wrong and there were those, some of whom I knew, some of whom I had previously respected, who, far from doing all they could to prevent these atrocities, were watching, applauding, jeering and cheering. These were ordinary, previously law-abiding people who were taking a vicarious pleasure in seeing others being brutally tortured. The mob had descended into barbarism.

Flaccus could have instructed his troops to defend those being attacked. Instead, he instructed them to side with the oppressors.

Thirty eight of the Jewish elders were rounded up and led in chains through the agora and into the theatre. There, they were stripped and scourged in front of the crowd. They were flogged with such severity that many died of their wounds, while others were rendered incapacitated for months.

Those Jews for fought to defend themselves were themselves arrested, scourged and tortured as Flaccus responded to the demands of the mob and in that cruel and murderous final act of humiliation they were publicly crucified – their visible agonies deterring those who would dare to raise a voice of protest.

I lost many friends during those days and I grieve for them all but the one that I grieve for most was that gentle, vulnerable and trusting soul who took no sides, Carabbas himself, for in those godless atrocities, he too was killed.

PART I

Judas

2nd Year of Caligula's reign (38 CE) - 2

There was much wailing and sobbing throughout the days of the uprising and during the days that followed. The battered and bloodied corpses were retrieved by surviving family members or friends and washed in preparation for burial. Jews and Greeks, as if for the first time aware of the enormity of what had happened, avoided each other. The depth of the shame felt by the majority of the Greeks, those who held no blame for the atrocities, was exceeded only by the depth of the loss experienced by the Jews. Greeks and Jews would look away quickly if there was any chance of catching the eye of another.

Except for the grieving and the occasional shouted taunt from those involved in the perpetration of those godless acts, the city was unnaturally quiet. Any noise seemed an intrusion on the grief of the bereaved. As I walk through the city, I see it with new eyes. Those public buildings, that so impressed me when I first arrived, have lost their magnificence. The Caesareum, commissioned by Cleopatra, I see now for what it is – a monument to hubris and greed.

I was brought up to respect authority but those who had authority were corrupt, unjust and irresponsible. Their actions were divisive. The Jewish leaders were the same. Herod the Great massacred all whom he regarded as a threat to his rule. His successors with their insatiable appetite for wealth enjoyed a life of luxury and indolence as they commanded us to respect the authority of Rome.

The message of Judas the Galilean is that power corrupts and distorts social relations and authority is not to be trusted. This is a message that strikes a chord with many and the events in Jerusalem shows what can be achieved. When Pilate ordered the standards of Caesar to be erected within the city walls, 50,000 Jews protested. When Pilate ordered his soldiers to unsheathe their swords, 50,000 necks were bared. Our people are prepared to die as witness to what is right. Confronted with a choice of mass slaughter of those who did no wrong or acquiescence to their request, Pilate relented. The standards were removed.

In this mass action of civil disobedience, the followers of the Galilean were allied with the Pharisees who were motivated by the traditional Jewish prohibitions on worship of images. However, although allied in action, they differed in philosophy. The Pharisees implore us to stay true to our faith by strict adherence to the letter of the law. This is a madness that will drive a wedge through social relations. We live and work side by side with Greeks and Egyptians. We need to bring people together, not drive them apart. The only choices seem to be to either follow the Herodians or to follow the Pharisees and neither is a palatable choice.

2nd Year of Caligula's reign (38 CE) – 3

Civil disobedience is only one part of the message from the Galilean. He was disparaging of those who awaited a Messiah from the House of David arguing that the Messiah is to be found in our own hearts. After the atrocities, the Galilean's message attracted many.

Across the city, communities have been established where individuals pool their money into community funds. The money is used to provide for the basic needs of community members with the surplus used to help those widowed and orphaned as a result of the atrocities. Many of the individuals who have joined our community are disaffected Jews, both men and women who have relinquished their Jewish faith but are called to do what is right.

On a daily basis, we meet and eat together. On a weekly basis we celebrate with an agape meal and interpretation of the scriptures, much like I did with the therapeutae. Community decisions are made by vote. We truly believe that power has a corrosive influence and we are endeavoring to establish a community that avoids the structures of power.

PART I

4th Year of Vespasian's reign (73 CE) - 1

There are many of us who were inspired by the teachings of the Galilean who was executed under Pontius Pilate. Judas taught that there are laws given by God and there are laws given by man. The laws of God are written in our hearts and are sacrosanct. The laws given by man are designed to benefit some at the expense of others. He argued that taxation was no better than an introduction to slavery. He called on the Jewish people to assert their liberty and said that God was to be our only Ruler and Lord.

It is a subversive message that threatens the state whatever its nature but in these days it is a threat to Roman authority.

Many of us look for Christ within our own hearts and tried to live quietly and equitably within communities, holding property in common and being generous to others.

Others, who are fuelled by the idealism of Judas, agitate for a more equitable society and have done so even in Rome itself.

Others again, utterly pervert the message of peace and liberation. These are the Sicarii who first became known in the third year of Nero's reign with their murder of the High Priest Jonathan. Their name is derived from the small assassin's dagger that they keep about their person. Their aim is to intimidate or kill those Jews who, under Roman rule, hold positions of authority over others. In the eyes of the Sicarii, these Jews are servants of the laws of man. They feel no inhibitions in removing these *"cancers"* on the Jewish faith.

Alexandria has recent experience of the Sicarii. Three years after the fall of Jerusalem, Masada, that last remaining bastion of Sicarii resistance, finally succumbed to Roman military might. We heard that the defenders had taken their own lives, each having drawn lots to kill each other in turn. The last man was the only one who killed himself.

On the fall of the fort, many of those Sicarii who were still active in

Judea migrated to Alexandria and here they founded their liberation movement. The council of the elders summoned a mass meeting where the philosophy of the Sicarii was explained. Once informed of the danger, the authorities wasted no time in arresting them. Those of the Sicarii who were grown men and women had made their choice and I confess that I felt little sympathy for their plight. Some of the children though were as young as eight or nine and they too were indoctrinated. It was heart-rending to witness. Like many other bystanders, I urged them to relent but despite all the tortures inflicted on their young bodies, none could be made to confess that Caesar was their Lord. They chose suffering and death over life. Those responsible for instilling this blind, ignorant faith into the minds of those little ones would have been better thrown into the sea with great millstones around their necks.

Their philosophy is a madness that has spread like a toxin throughout the Empire and the dagger is not the only weapon they bear. The injustices in Cyrene were initiated by Jonathan. Known as a weaver, he was, in truth, a weaver of tales and his slanderous lies poisoned the hitherto tolerant environment of my home city. With devastating consequences for those that I loved, the governor Catullus was all too ready to listen.

James

6th Year of Claudius' reign (46 CE)

The atmosphere in the agora these days is more solemn than joyous. Although there is still plenty of locally produced fish, pork, fruit and vegetables, the cereal foods including grain and bread are very expensive and this pushes up the price of everything else. Last year the Nile flooded later than usual. This meant that crops were sown late and the harvest was poor.

Whatever force caused the late flooding of the Nile seemed to have the same detrimental impact on harvests throughout all countries that border the Eastern Mediterranean. In Judaea there is famine.

PART I

Reports from Jerusalem tell of the civil unrest in the city and how hundreds of emaciated bodies, more skeletons than flesh and blood human beings, line the streets begging those of means for scraps of food or money to buy it.

Tons of grain have been taken from local grain stores and shipped to Caesarea for distribution among the people. It is grain that we can ill-afford to lose but the needs of the Judean people are more pressing than our own.

Our community, and many others like ours, is in crisis. The youthful idealism and optimism of the early years has been replaced by a more pessimistic outlook. I am not the only one fed up with the constant wrangling and interminable debates. We spend more time arguing than doing.

In creating a community where all are equal, we have created a culture where people regard all opinions as equally valid and they are not. There are some who think that, irrespective of whether or not they are knowledgeable, they not only have the right, but the duty to proffer their opinion on any topic. Those who speak are often not those who have the best judgment but those who are the most forthright.

It is not just the discussions, of course. We are asked to look for the voice of Christ within ourselves but many can only hear the yearnings of their own heart. There has been more than one adulterous affair that has poisoned social relations.

And of course, there is the food shortage. In Judaea it is worse but even here, there are those who hoard food for themselves and their families that should be shared amongst the whole community. Then, when challenged, they brazenly deny doing any such thing. Empty bellies and moral values make bad bedfellows.

With the benefit of hindsight, many of us can see that what united us in the early days was opposition to an authority that we all saw as unjust. Under Claudius, however, there has been good governance. Alexandria is a far less divided city than it had once been and although there were some in Judaea who preferred to starve rather than take charity from authority, most were grateful. How then can they truly be opposed to those that they rely on for sustenance? If we are to grow, we now need to be united not in opposition but under a respected authority.

There is one man who fills this role. This is a man who is well versed in scripture, authoritative in word, holy in deed, who has a vision of how things could be. And many of the disparate and fragmented communities of the nascent church, such as it is, are coming together under his vision.

1st Year of Nero's reign (55 CE)

There are two forms of the Golden Rule:

> *"Do unto others as you would have them do unto you"*

And

> *"Do not do unto others that which you would not have them do unto you."*

What a society we could create if people followed these principles.

I thought of my family. We were more than a collection of individuals. We were an entity in itself as my wife and I helped direct the high spirited nature of our children and our children found security within the family unit. We did things together, we overcame problems together and we were committed to each other. Each individual had faith in the family.

In a similar way the community is more than just a collection of individuals and families. Despite the personality differences, the community was an entity in itself as the community did things together, each contributing their individual talents and individuals and families celebrated together, they overcame problems together and they were committed to each other. Each individual and each family had a sense of community spirit.

How much better would it be if society was more than just a collection of communities but if different communities worshipped together and overcame problems together and if the different communities – Jew, Greek, Egyptian and Roman were committed to each other with a sense of social spirit.

And humanity, of course, is more than just a collection of different societies. It is an entity in itself as different societies interacted with each other; traded with each other, discussed issues with each other and overcame the problems of humanity with a shared understanding and a common spirit.

And, as Plato explained, the world, bounded as it is by the two bands crossing each other as in the letter chi, is more than just a collection of living entities. It is an entity in itself endowed with a soul and intelligence and comprising all living entities which are all related.

And although I cannot, with any sound logic, prove, deep in my heart I know – the parallels are so striking – that the cosmos itself is more than just a collection of stars and planets, it is an entity in itself as cosmic bodies and cosmic forces interact with each other in creating its form.

And that which works through the cosmos and the world and humanity and society and community and family and the individual is a universal spirit, and in this God is to be found, an entity in itself, for love is God and God is love.

6th Year of Nero's reign (60 CE)

We have dined and cleared away, the boys are asleep in their bedroom and as my wife has taken up her sewing, I've retired to my study. The oil lamp that hangs on the stand next to my desk casts a shadow on the scroll as I lay it on the desk, unroll it, place weights on either end and start to read.

I treasure this scroll above all others. This is James' letter and his teaching has made a great impression on me. He has a deep understanding of human nature and writes with great authority. James condemns those who profit from the labors of others. He writes of the law of freedom but he also urges restraint.

The Jesus Christ of James is a divinity that speaks to our humanity – a God of spirit, that internal authority within us, through whom the divine reason or *"logos"* is revealed and a God of faith, that external authority that sets boundaries; a God of freedom and a God of restraint. It is a powerful combination with a dynamic tension.

Regrettably there are some of a much more fundamentalist temperament who corrupt James' teachings by putting too much emphasis on the lawgiver and too little on the logos.

Joseph

15th Year of Nero's reign (69 CE) - 2

The boys are asleep in their bedroom and I've retired to my study. The light from the oil lamp reflects off the purple colored fruit in the basket in front of me. The fruit look ripe and ready for eating. Instinctively, I reach out and take one. As I roll it around my hand, the plump and tender flesh yields slightly with the pressure of my fingers. I gaze at it for a moment and then return it to the basket. My wife would have disapproved but I have no appetite. Translating these writings makes me feel queasy. The authors sanctify the Torah; one dismisses those who fail to insist on strict adherence to the letter of the law as *"boundary shifters";* another writes disparagingly of efforts to unite Jews and gentiles as making *"men as the fish of the sea"* as if this was somehow a bad thing.

This is what religion now means for many Jews - slavish adherence to ludicrous laws and unquestioning prejudice.

It didn't use to be like this. The scriptures were inspired by God. Now more than ever we need some of that inspiration. Christ is the divine intermediary between faith and spirit. He is the personification of divine reason in the same way as Moses is the personification of divine authority and Elijah is the personification of divine spirit. At this point in time we needed inspiration not prescription. We needed Elijah not Moses.

I remember those passages in Hosea when Yahweh spoke:

> *When I found Israel, it was like finding grapes in the desert; when I saw your ancestors, it was like seeing the early fruit on the fig tree.*

And

> *Ephraim is blighted, their root is withered, they yield no fruit.*

It is Judah that is now like an old fig tree that has ceased producing fruit. It will wither and die. There needs to be space for a new and more vibrant alternative.

8th Year of Claudius' reign (48 CE)

Philosophically, the Jesus Christ of James personifies a divine reason that speaks to our humanity. It is beautiful in its simplicity. Nevertheless, the movement is not as popular as we had hoped. Even in our own congregation there are some who identify Christ with Serapis, a god who is so overladen with culturally different traditions, that it is difficult to know what he represents.

Many educated Christians despair of the situation and some have spent many, often fruitless, hours explaining to others the nature of the divine reason. However, there is no use lamenting the fact. This Jesus Christ is too abstract a notion for most that look to a god with whom they can identify. The truth is that there is value in myth that even the brightest and most educated of people fail to recognize.

Eratosthenes, for instance, is a hero of mine. He was a learned man of science and a committed humanist as well. For a period of time, three hundred years ago, he was chief librarian of the same Alexandria library where I had once studied. A statue of the great man is positioned next to the ground floor staircase. It was Eratosthenes who calculated the circumference of the earth. It was Eratosthenes who derived a formula for obtaining prime numbers. It was Eratosthenes who wrote a comprehensive treatise on geography. It was Eratosthenes who developed a method of measuring global position using latitude and longitude. Eratosthenes was the complete scientist.

I am a huge admirer of the man. However, it is extraordinary how someone like Eratosthenes, regarded as one of the most intelligent and learned of men could be so dismissive of the importance of the arts. Eratosthenes stated that the *"aim of the poet was not to instruct but to give pleasure"*. This is wrong. The poet should not be constrained by either of these options. People can *"know"* things through reason. That is plain. People can also *"know"* things through feeling. That is not so plain. Nevertheless, empathy and sympathy, a sense of belonging and a sense of loss are very important emotions that needed to be exercised.

There are many parts of Plato's Timaeus that I find distasteful but on one point I do agree. In his dialogue with Socrates, the title character explains that:

> *there are three kinds of soul located within us, having each of them motions, and …. one part, if remaining inactive …., must necessarily become very weak, but that which is trained and exercised, very strong. Wherefore we should take care that the movements of the different parts of the soul should be in due proportion.*

PART I

Plato did not elaborate on the consequences if one kind of soul was exercised at the expense of another but it was something that was of great interest to me.

We need to exercise our feelings and it these feelings that religion, at its best, can invoke. Egyptian mythology was thousands of years old, the old gods were still worshipped and the stories re-enacted and of these stories there was none more popular than the myth of Osiris. Osiris was King and ruled with his sister Isis with whom he had fathered a child Horus. His brother Set, jealous of his brother's position, hatched a plot to kill him. He secretly arranged for the manufacture of a wooden sarcophagus that matched the dimensions of his brother. Then at a feast that ostensibly he organized to honor him, the sarcophagus was offered to whoever could fit inside. There were many who made an attempt but it fitted none until Osiris was persuaded to try. It fitted perfectly but as soon as he lay down, the lid was slammed shut and locked and the box was sealed with lead and thrown into the Nile.

When she heard that Osiris was lost, Isis set out to look for him. She searched far and wide and eventually found the sarcophagus in the palace of the king of Lebanon. Isis retrieved the sarcophagus but while returning home, she left it by an area of marshland by the banks of the Nile. Set was hunting in the area and he came across the sarcophagus and recognized it at once. He prized the box open and tore the body apart, scattering the pieces across Egypt.

Once again Isis searched for his body. Her search took her all across the country. She found all the body parts and arranged them in order, connecting all the pieces with wax. Then she wrapped the body in a linen cloth and buried it.

Osiris went to the place of the dead. As his son, Horus, was growing up, however, the spirit of Osiris visited him often. Egyptians interpret the troubles of life as a battle between Horus, armed with the spirit of Osiris, and Set. When Horus wins, the world is at peace. When Set wins, the world is in turmoil. In the last days, Horus and Set will fight one last time. Horus will defeat Set forever, and Osiris will return to the land of the living. On that day, the Day of Awakening, all the tombs shall open and the just dead shall live again and all sorrow shall pass away forever.

Osiris is depicted as a green figure representing rebirth, Horus as a falcon headed sun god. Although I am yet to meet an Egyptian in Alexandria who believes in the literal truth of the myth, there is something wonderful in its re-enactment of the story of suffering, death and resurrection that speaks to the human heart. There is something in the story of Horus' eventual triumph that gives hope.

Over time, most educated Christians changed their outlook. They learnt the value of myth and the wisdom of arguing a case from another's perspective. Jesus Christ needed to be meaningful both to our intellect and to our emotions.

9th Year of Claudius' reign (49 CE)

Many of us are surprised by the news. In the main the Jews of Alexandria are well disposed toward Claudius. His letter following the uprising guaranteed us our long held rights. Certainly, Claudius did not discriminate against Jews on the grounds of our faith alone. However, over the years, the Jewish population in Rome has multiplied to such an extent that they have become a sizeable minority within the city and with their strength in numbers comes an increased readiness to protest. The protests were initiated by the followers of the Galilean, he who asked people to look for Christ within their own hearts.

All those Jews who were identified as protesters and their families were expelled from Rome as were many who had no involvement at all. Roman soldiers ensured that all so identified were evicted from their houses with no more than that which they could carry. Thousands were transported by boat to cities across Greece, Macedonia, Asia and Syria.

Those few Jews that remain are under strict orders not to assemble. It is time of considerable tension within the heart of the Roman Empire and this is something of enormous concern to Jews of wealth and standing throughout all its territories.

10th Year of Claudius' reign (50 CE)

There is a both a widespread desire and a pressing need to see Jews and gentiles united and the Council of Jerusalem was called to discuss how this could be achieved.

Some look for a conquering Messiah, a Son of David, to usher in an era of peace and prosperity.

Some follow the teachings of the Galilean and argue that we should look for the Messiah in our own hearts.

Some see Jews and gentiles united under a shared commitment to the law with Damascus being used as a symbol of a New Jerusalem for Jewish people who see themselves as reaching out to gentiles.

Some of us who follow James try to promote a theology of the logos personified by the composite figure of Jesus Christ.

But the conquering Messiah is too confrontational, the teaching of the Galilean too idealistic, commitment to the law too dogmatic and the Jesus Christ of James too abstract. None of these appeal to gentiles.

What do appeal are the myths of suffering, death and resurrection that are prevalent throughout the countries bordering the eastern Mediterranean and beyond. While Osiris-Serapis is worshipped by the Egyptians and Alexandrian Greeks, Adonis is worshipped by the Phoenicians, Tammuz by the Babylonians and Attis by the Phrygians. In Greek mythology too, the cult of Demeter and Persephone holds great attraction.

There is one man by the name of Paul who, on the road to Damascus, had a different vision of Jesus Christ than that shared by James and his followers. This is a vision of a faith based not on commitment to laws, but on a shared culture and common identity.

It is a vision that is highly influential.

Despite the protestations of many who were zealous for the law, the judgment of the Council is of historical significance. What is being created is not just an offshoot of Judaism. It is an entirely new religion.

Simon

3rd Year of Nero's reign (57 CE)

I know the shop owner well. Indeed, when I was a student I worked for him. If he thought scrolls would sell, he would employ scribes to copy them for him. He paid more for translations. It allowed me to earn a few extra denarii when I needed it.

The recently composed papyrus scrolls are kept on the shop front in wooden buckets, visible to prospective customers. Each bucket contains several copies of the same scroll and is labeled with a description of the content. Older works and the more valuable parchment copies are stored on gently sloping shelves within the shop. Any work can be ordered on request. The shop keeper has more than one contact in the library that will, for a fee, be only too happy to oblige.

Much of his business is done on trust. If he knows the customer, he allows them to read the scroll themselves before purchase. Otherwise he asks an assistant to read out passages.

Every week or so, I go there to see what is new. The shop owner knows my interests and today he was eager to tell me of Galatians, the latest letter from Paul.

The letter is enlightening because it explains so much about Paul's early life. It is surprising as well. If it is true, that which he wrote, about the actions of Peter under the influence of James, then it is understandable that Paul became angry. If we are creating a single faith for Jews and gentiles alike then there cannot be one rule for one group and one rule for the other. There cannot be two classes of Christians. I have the highest regard for James but it may be that he has developed a fear that the faith of the Jewish Christians can be corrupted by fraternizing with gentiles. This would be absurd and self-defeating. We can only change people's behavior by treating them with respect.

However, although I share Paul's sentiments, I disagree with his actions. He seems hell-bent on isolating himself. Writing so publicly about the incident impairs his chances of any reconciliation with the other apostles.

13th Year of Nero's reign (67 CE)

The letters from the apostles allude to that which the cognoscenti already know. Christ was the personification of the divine reason - the logos of Philo, the one worshipped by the true followers of Judas the Galilean. However, this Christ, to be found in people's hearts, was often a threat to authority.

James fused Christ, the internal authority with Jesus, an external authority; one that asked for obedience to the law and took that law to the gentiles.

This Jesus Christ was too abstract a notion for many and at the Jerusalem Council that was held shortly after the expulsion of Jewish Christians from Rome and following discussions with Paul, Jews of influence requested a Jesus Christ with whom people could identify.

This was something that Paul provided. He preached of an incarnate Jesus Christ who was crucified and resurrected. Amazingly, those gentiles, to whom he preached this message, responded to this Christ in their thousands.

But Paul, like James, was now dead. Their followers were in turmoil like sheep without a shepherd, arguing over the interpretation of this Christ and clamoring, as the more rationally minded Greeks were wont to do, for information on this incarnate son of God. All that they *"knew"* of the life of Christ, from the letters, was that he was crucified and resurrected and that is a flimsy basis on which to establish a new faith.

The task for me is to create that story. The superficial story will be easy to understand and I hope that it inspires many but for those who seek a deeper meaning, what I am writing is designed to be interpreted. There are plenty of clues. I have used the pointers for identifying allegorical interpretation that I have learnt both from the writings of Philo and from my time with the therapeutae.

Peter will be the personification of spirit. Andrew will be the personification of action. If we are to *"make men as fish of the sea"* then these will be the fishers who will energetically proselytize this new faith. James is the one who created Jesus Christ as the fusion of divine reason and lawgiver. James will be the personification of faith. John will be the personification of reason. Together they are the voice of conviction. Their Father represents Judaism and those familiar with the Latin alphabet will surely see the significance of that faith coming to a natural conclusion with Zebedee. James and John will leave their father in the boat with the men he employs.

There will be another James, a son of Alphaeus, a Greek word meaning *"changing"*. This will be a James for the Greeks for whom a monotheistic faith will be introduced for the first time; supplanting Greek philosophy and polytheistic worship.

And as Levi for the Jews was the only son of Jacob who did not head one of the twelve tribes but instead performed the priestly functions for all tribes, so there will be a Levi for the Greeks, another son of Alphaeus, who will not be one of the twelve disciples but instead will perform the priestly functions for all disciples. This Levi will leave the custom house to take on his new role and concern with financial dealings will be replaced by concern for the spiritual.

PART I

War

8th Year of Nero's reign (62 CE)

I thought of Jerusalem, the *"City of Peace"*, and I permitted myself a wry smile. Never was there a city more inappropriately named.

News from that city always travelled fast, brought by traders and returning pilgrims.

We heard that the king, Agrippa, in an act of political interference in religious affairs, replaced the High Priest and in this action he had but one motive.

That man called *"the Just"* and *"the Righteous"*, that good and innocent man preached against the rich, the privileged, and powerful. In Judaea there was no one richer, more privileged or powerful than the king himself. For Agrippa, James was a thorn in the flesh. He was determined to rid himself of that troublesome teacher.

Agrippa was no doubt mindful of the response of the people to his father's uncle Antipas following his execution of the Baptist. A popular backlash would surely have resulted if he was seen to have a direct involvement in James' execution. Instead, the king directed the High Priest to carry out his bidding. Even with his assent, the approval of the Roman procurator was needed before the death penalty could be passed, but Joseph son of Simon gave no such assent. He was unwilling to be a party to an act that was no more than legitimized murder. On the death of the Roman procurator Festus, however, Agrippa, blatantly demonstrating his political opportunism, removed Joseph son of Simon as High Priest and installed in his place Ananus son of Ananus, someone who had no such qualms.

Ananus assembled a council of judges and they passed judgment. From all accounts, the trial was a sham, a parody of justice. A sinless man of God died because he challenged political authority.

As James was executed by stoning, the people wept.

10th Year of Nero's reign (64 CE)

News came from Rome of the great fire that burned for over five days and completely destroyed three districts of the city and seriously damaged seven more. There were some hot headed Christians who celebrated this devastation, believing it presaged the coming of the end days and the rise of a new society from the ashes.

Once the fire had been controlled, those who were seen celebrating the destruction were arrested, not because they were suspected of starting the fire (there was no evidence for that) but simply because they were suspected of harboring a desire for the collapse of Roman society. Those arrested were tortured and in their torture they implicated others. All who were implicated were killed.

The tortures were a barbaric cruelty, ordered by an Emperor who, like Gaius Caligula, was allowed free rein to indulge his narcissistic tendencies. There was no justice in his actions, no due process, no discernment, no identification of the *"guilty"*, although none were proven guilty of anything more than a foolish hope for the end of the dominion of Rome.

12th Year of Nero's reign (66 CE) – 1

It is a time of chaos. Social order throughout the Jewish world has completely broken down. The spark that ignited that powder keg of pent up antagonism occurred in Caesarea Maritima, the port previously known as Tower of Strato. Much of the blame for the calamity can be apportioned to Gessius Florus, the Roman governor of Judaea. It didn't take long for news of his injustices to reach Alexandria. Driven by greed, disdainful of truth, he is the most heartless of men.

In Caesarea, the Jews have a synagogue alongside a piece of ground

PART I

belonging to a Greek citizen. Reportedly, this man has repeatedly refused generous offers to purchase the land. He further antagonized the Jewish people by beginning the construction of factory right at the boundary that separated them leaving the worshippers with a narrow path through which it was impossible to gain access. After failing in their attempt to stop the work by force, the leading Jews attempted to influence Florus by bribing him with eight silver talents. In exchange for the money, Florus promised full cooperation. On the next Sabbath, as the Jews gathered at the synagogue, a Greek partisan placed a chamber pot upside down at the entrance and was sacrificing birds on it. On seeing their place of worship desecrated in such a manner, the Jews were furious and the leading men among them went to plead their case to the governor and to remind him of his promise. Instead of intervening in the dispute, however, Florus had the men arrested and thrown into prison.

News of this outrage caused anger in Jerusalem and Florus succeeded in fanning the flames even more by having seventeen talents taken from the Temple treasury on the pretext that Caesar needed it.

Uproar followed and the people rushed into the Temple. Many called aloud to Caesar to free them from Florus' misrule as if many hundreds of miles away in Rome the Emperor could hear their pleas. Some made mockery of the governor by circulating a basket and requesting donations for the *"impoverished"* man. Some felt free to call him all sorts of names. When Florus heard of these insults he left for Jerusalem with his soldiers and there demanded of the Jewish leaders that they give up those who had abused him. The leaders protested that there were bound to be some impudent juveniles within a mass of people but it was impossible to identify the miscreants. This response enraged Florus and he ordered the soldiers to sack the area known as the Upper Market place and kill all they met. 3,600 were killed that day. The numbers included women, children and even infants.

This attack on innocent people was the most extreme provocation. For very many Jewish people, war seems to be the only option.

Some think it inevitable for since the beginning of the year, a comet has appeared in the night sky that many have taken to be a sign from God.

12th Year of Nero's reign (66 CE) – 2

Some attributed the current turmoil to James' killing, some to the actions of Florus. Whatever the reason, the whole of the Jewish world, it seems, is in revolt. Rebel forces have taken Masada, killed the Roman garrison and gained access to the King's armory. These same rebels have now taken Jerusalem itself and the Roman garrison there have been killed too.

At the same time, the Greeks of Caesarea massacred their Jewish neighbors, killing 20,000 in less than an hour. The news of this outrage spread like wildfire and infuriated the whole nation. In response, Jews sacked many of the Syrian cities and neighboring villages.

In Scythopolis the local Jews defended the local population against attack from Jewish outsiders but the Syrians persuaded them to demonstrate their fidelity by relocating themselves and their families into a nearby grove. Later, in a cowardly act of betrayal, armed Syrians slaughtered them all and looted the property of the whole colony. 13,000 were killed.

The slaughter in Scythopolis encouraged other cities to take up arms against their Jewish inhabitants. 2,500 were killed in Ascalaon and 2,000 in Ptolemais. In Damascus too, the Jews were herded like cattle into the Gymnasium, before being slaughtered. 10,500 were killed there in one hour.

They say that the first casualty of war is truth and certainly, in Alexandria, there were conflicting interpretations of the causes of the conflict. The Jews blamed both the Greek citizens of Caesarea and Florus, the Roman governor of Judaea. The Greeks blamed the Jewish people and their expectation of a Messiah and those such as Menahem, the leader of the bandits that took Masada and

Jerusalem, that were inspired by Judas the Galilean.

Whatever the reasons for the conflict elsewhere, the conflicting interpretations, the historical animosity and messianic expectations of many of the Jews have all contributed to the febrile atmosphere in Alexandria.

15th Year of Nero's reign (69 CE) - 3

The meeting was held at the Imperial palace. The speaker was a target for the zealots and his security was paramount. Josephus' arrival caused quite a stir and I was privileged along with other community leaders to have been invited to meet him. I did so with some trepidation. It was my first visit since that fateful night and it did bring back painful memories. Nevertheless, it was well worth it.

Josephus is a thin-faced, clean-shaven man with short curly hair and a long and somewhat crooked nose. He speaks easily and evidently has a sharp mind. He is no doubt a proficient organizer but I can't imagine him as a leader who would inspire his charges. He is too ready to boast of his own exploits.

During his talk he spoke of his youth and his training for the priesthood. He spoke of the time he was commander of the rebel forces in Galilee. He gave his account of the siege at Jotapata and the anxiety he felt when his hiding place was discovered by the victorious Roman soldiers. He also spoke of the mercy shown to him by Vespasian. What struck me, during the talk, was his attitude toward the general. His faith did not just result from a fawning gratitude that the general spared his life but from a genuine belief that the general was a force for good. Whatever it was that caused a leader of forces that were rebellious to Rome to champion Roman authority, it was not just a desire to save his own skin and it was not just a desire to further his own interests.

15th Year of Nero's reign (69 CE) - 1

Only after taking Jericho did Vespasian learn of Nero's death and his succession by Galba. After waiting in vain for confirmation of his command, Vespasian sent Titus to pay homage to the new Emperor and seek his instructions. Agrippa travelled along with the same objective. While they were travelling, Galba was assassinated after a mere seven months and was succeeded by Otho. On this news, Titus decided to terminate his journey and return to his father. Agrippa continued. Shortly after, Otho himself was killed and was succeeded by Vitellius.

The empire had need of good and strong leadership but Vitellius was a man who was disliked and distrusted by many. Vespasian was persuaded by his own troops to make a bid to become Caesar himself.

Vespasian wrote to Tiberius Alexander informing him of the army's enthusiasm and requesting his help and cooperation. After reading the letter aloud at the Caesareum, Alexander called on soldiers and civilians alike to swear allegiance to Vespasian. Almost without exception, they were happy to give their support.

We learned a great deal from the emissary. We learned how following the news of the Emperor's death the general endeavored to cut off Jeruslaem from the North and East. He sent Lucius Annius and his cavalry squad to capture the surrounding settlements. One, overlooking the northern end of the Dead Sea was the home to a community of several hundred religious fanatics, zealous for the law. Between sixty and seventy of these men surrendered immediately and were taken captive.

The others held firm, ensconced in their stronghold until Lucius ordered the undermining of the walls. When the walls collapsed, the Roman troops were merciless.

From interrogation of the prisoners, they learned of the nature of the community in which these people had lived; they learned of the extraordinarily stringent requirements for membership and the hatred of both the Romans and the temple priesthood that was instilled into them; they learned how dwelling places were fashioned in the soft stone near to the site and they learned of the scrolls they kept and studied. The emissary had brought with him as a gift for the library those scrolls that had been found. I was asked to translate them. They were written in Hebrew and Aramaic so were unintelligible to the Romans.

Of the captives, those who had surrendered without a fight were spared. Those who didn't were less fortunate. Vespasian amused the troops by ordering them to be trussed up like pigs and tossed into the sea to see how they floated.

The others, fearing of the consequences should their collaboration with the Romans become known, pleaded with the general to allow them to stay with him. Instead, they were released with strict instructions to pass on the news of the consequences of armed resistance, the news of the destruction of this zealot stronghold and the mercy shown to those who resisted the temptation to take up arms.

It is regrettable but necessary. Only after the disease of zealotry has been expunged can the Jewish people truly start to live in harmony with their neighbors.

The everlasting name

12th Year of Nero's reign (66 CE) – 4

It was the stories of John the Baptist that inspired me to join the therapeutae. This was the start of my journey of faith and I was not the only one inspired by this charismatic preacher.

John commanded us to exercise virtue and he was virtue's model. As a public declaration of their commitment to virtue, those who renounced their sins were baptized by John in the river Jordan and they were numbered in their thousands.

I remember that passage in Isaiah.

> *A voice of one calling:*
>
> *In the wilderness prepare the way for the Lord; make straight in the desert a highway for our God.*

John preached that which all of us knew, in our heart of hearts, was right. He was the living embodiment of the Galilean's teaching that the Christ is to be found within us. It was through John that the God of Abraham spoke. It is with John that the story truly starts.

1st Year of Vespasian's reign (70 CE) - 1

It is a glorious time; a time of celebration. The news has arrived that Vitellius has been defeated. Vespasian is Emperor and the people are joyful.

Envoys have come from far and wide to greet the new sovereign and the city is filled to bursting with people. The Governor has arranged the festivities. There are to be events in the theatre and gymnasium but the main event is the procession from the Caesareum to the Serapeum. I have come with my sons and we have positioned ourselves on the left hand side of Soma Street a hundred meters or so down from the junction with Canopic Way. Like many others, we find ourselves being pushed about as people jostle for position in the huge crowd. The crowd is in very good humor. The arrival of the parade was announced by the fanfare of trumpets and there followed gymnasts and jugglers and a troupe of girl dancers and their musicians, the drummers and pipe players. After them came some mime artists carrying their props and dressed up as Greek gods. On the far side of the street, walking gracefully and using her hand mirror to confirm her beauty, was a young, attractive woman dressed as Aphrodite. She was accompanied by a child dressed as Eros holding a bow in his hand and with a quiver over his shoulder. With chest puffed out like a cockerel, spear in hand and dressed as a gladiator, a young man portraying Ares walked on our side of the street. Alongside him,

PART I

holding amphorae of wine and staggering comically from side to side whilst waving to the crowd was a young actor dressed as Dionysus. In a chariot behind them sat an actor portraying Zeus with a child dressed as Hermes sitting next to him.

Using her womanly charms, Aphrodite desperately sought the attention of Ares but he showed more interest in strutting about with spear held aloft and mockingly confronting the soldiers stationed alongside the road. The goddess sent Eros, bow in hand to shoot him with a love dart, but the dart hit Dionysus instead. At this point Dionysus stopped waving to the crowd and gazed with infatuation at Aphrodite. He skipped over to her and knelt on the ground, proffering her his amphorae of wine. Of course, she looked on him with disdain but that didn't stop him making comically exaggerated gestures of love. He clasped his hands across his chest and with eyes closed, reached out an arm as if reciting an ode to love. Aphrodite carried on walking, her face betraying her increasing frustration. When Dionysus realized she had moved on, he scampered after her and grabbed her hand. In response Aphrodite slapped him across the face.

At this point Hermes dismounted the chariot and ran across to them. He poked them both with a stick to get their attention and pointed to Zeus, now standing up in the chariot and waving an admonishing finger. Suitably chastised, both Dionysus and Aphrodite shrugged their shoulders and returned to the positions in which they started.

After a time, Eros was sent on his mission once again and this time the love dart hit Ares. However, when Ares turned around the first person he saw was Dionysus and his love fell on him. Ares approached Dionysus in a familiar manner and Dionysus gave a surprised but accepting look and they shared his amphorae of wine. With arms around each other's shoulders, they both drank and made fun of those in the crowd.

Then Hermes dismounted the chariot once more and ran across to them. He once again poked the players to get their attention and pointed to Zeus who was again waving his admonishing finger. This time it was Ares who with Dionysus accepted the chastisement and returned to the positions in which they started.

This mime was repeated for the duration of the procession. It was very, very funny and put the crowd in good spirits.

After these actors came more musicians and more dancers and then came the cohort of soldiers, in full military attire marching slowly with eyes focused straight ahead. The chariot carrying Vespasian and Tiberius came next. As they passed, the General waved and the crowd cheered.

When they reached the Serapeum, the temple doors were open and one could just make out the statue of the great god inside. Vespasian prostrated himself on the ground before the doors for what seemed like an age, but in reality was only a minute or so. It was refreshing to see an Emperor worshipping a God instead of insisting that others worship him. The stories are widespread of his miraculous cures of the blind man and the one with the withered hand and the people are enthusiastic in their admiration.

He was a merciful general with whom people could identify. He had proved his mettle. He was steadfastly loyal to the empire and his achievements on the battlefield were without equal but there are no airs and graces with the man. He came from humble beginnings, and sought no honor for himself. Indeed, the story of how he fell asleep at one of Nero's recitals, incurring the Emperor's displeasure, is a source of some amusement.

Vespasian was used to leading and the empire needed a leader, not one who inherited the throne, as previous Emperors had done but one who, like Jacob, wrestled for it.

We really feel that this is a man who can help bring peace and stability. It is a new beginning and if I was to flatter him, surely it could do the cause no harm.

PART I

Sin

5th Year of Nero's reign (59 CE)

I do teach students and although the subject matter is difficult to grasp, I am happy to. I enjoy teaching. Much of the subject matter that I teach, I have learned from studies at the Musaeum and my time with the therapeutae.

I teach regularly in the Musaeum and Serapeum. Sometimes I teach in the courts of the Caesareum, other times on the steps or under the porticoes. There are many others who teach there. Some consider themselves sophists, inheritors of the tradition of Protagoras, some are stoics, followers of Seneca and some follow Apollonius of Tyana. Alexandria is a city that values learning. It is a city that values ideas.

I teach of the Golden Rule, that which instructs people to act in the best interests of each other and I teach of that which impedes such actions. It is not people's failure to follow laws that has given rise to our divided society but the failure to demonstrate respect for and commitment to each other. If our own souls are in align with the divine soul, all would be well and good but too often they are not.

When I teach formally it is in front of a group of about 15 to 20 young men. I split them up into groups of three or four to discuss questions I pose them such as what results if individual spirit is out of tune with divine reason or individual faith is out of tune with divine spirit or individual reason is out of tune with faith in the divine?

It requires abstract thinking. Some of them grasp it more readily than others.

I also ask them to imagine divine reason being personified. What would it say and what would it do?

After I teach of the psychological fractures that result if one aspect of the psyche is out of tune with an aspect of the divine soul, I teach of identity, the role of the state and the obligations of rulers and subjects. I teach of the abstract souls of social entities of which an individual is part – of family, community, society, and humanity.

I often ask my students what fracture in the social entity results if an out of tune aspect of the individual soul is exercised in a social context.

I enjoy the interaction. It is immensely satisfying to see young minds being challenged and the teaching is necessary. As well as living in an age of tremendous psychological trauma we also live in an age of terrible social conflict.

4th Year of Vespasian's reign (73 CE) - 2

Although the time frame is fixed, the storyline is not and I know how I have to use it. I reflected on the sins that I needed to portray and those whose manifestation of those sins had the most calamitous consequences.

I reflected on those who betrayed another's trust for their own ends and I thought of the Sicarii who were inspired by the teaching of Judas the Galilean. In particular, I thought of that weaver of tales, Jonathan, who connived with Catullus in bringing false accusations and so contrived the arrest and execution of those who were completely innocent of all charges.

I reflected on those who were intolerant of others and acted harshly when they felt threatened and I thought of Agrippa and the High Priest Ananus. James was a holy man who was to be found every day in the temple teaching and praying for the forgiveness of the sins of the people. However, Agrippa was so threatened by James' preaching against the rich and powerful that he imposed Ananus as High Priest to deal with the trouble maker. In a sham trial, in front of the entire Sanhedrin, Ananus arranged for James' execution.

I reflected on those who didn't listen and didn't explain and were dogmatic in their language and I thought of the leaders of the Essene community on the shores of the Dead Sea; those who recognized neither priestly nor Roman authority. They were stringent in their discipline as they awaited the coming of the prophesied Messiah. So convinced where they of the righteousness of their cause and so judgmental were they of others that they were determined to avoid being contaminated. They considered themselves to be children of light who lived by the law. Those who didn't live by the law were children of darkness.

I reflected on those who make a commitment that they fail to honor and I thought of my own guilt on that night of the massacre of the Jews on the order of Tiberius Alexander. I was called to the Imperial Palace and asked to make a stand. Yet while others went to talk to the rebels, I stayed in the palace courtyard warming myself at the fire. Out of ignorance, out of inertia and out of fear, I denied Christ by doing nothing.

I reflected on those who avoided their responsibility and I thought of Flaccus the governor of Alexandria. So aggrieved was he by the appointment of Caligula as Emperor and the elevation of Agrippa, that ingrate who betrayed the trust of Tiberius, that he abdicated all the responsibility that his position entailed. He afforded that gentle soul Carabbas no protection. Instead he encouraged the ridicule and abuse that subsequently led to the rampant persecution of the Jews by an inflamed and uncontrolled mob. To placate the mob, whose passions he himself had helped incite, he succumbed to their request that those Jews who protested against those outrages be scourged and crucified.

Finally, I reflected on those who acted impetuously with no regard for the consequences and I thought of the Alexandrian mob. Their feelings were understandable. Yet they had a free choice. They could have chosen to act in accordance with their human feelings to the detriment of others or they could have borne their slights with patience. Regrettably, they made the wrong choice. Already primed by the slanders of Apion, their passions were ignited by the inflammatory language and incendiary tone of the main agitators, Isidorus and Lampo. At the start of the uprising, they called for

Carabbas, dressed him as a faux king and ridiculed him with mock praise. Their behavior then degenerated into barbarism as Jewish families were murdered by swords and clubs and while Roman soldiers stood by watching, that gentle and innocent soul, who trusted everyone and took no sides, was killed. He had a nature like that of Isaac and, although his name was Carabbas, the name Bar-Abbas would have been more appropriate for truly, he was a son of the Father.

Divine reason

1st Year of Vespasian's reign (70 CE) - 2

Everyone knows what's going to come. It's the wait that's excruciating. Heaven knows what it's like in Jerusalem itself. I hope that others have the awareness that I failed to have. History would repeat itself. If some Jews fight to protect the temple then retribution will be inflicted on not just those that fight but on the whole community, as it was in Alexandria. I hope that when the temple is defiled, people flee the city.

I have spent a long time pondering the grief and death. I remembered the feelings I experienced at the calamity. 50,000 people were slaughtered for the sins of a few.

I wasn't prepared. I didn't believe what was happening; I was frightened and then angry at myself for not doing anything to stop it. And then there was that feeling of utter desolation.

It is those feelings that I want to evoke in my writing. It is those feelings that motivated me because I experienced it. I saw it. I was there.

I want others to see the same in their mind's eye. I want others to experience the same feelings. I want others to be similarly motivated.

PART I

I remember the anguished cry in the psalm. I remember the death of Elijah as told in the Book of Kings. Elisha, his disciple, was filled with Elijah's spirit because he saw Elijah being taken away from him up to heaven. Elisha then took up Elijah's mantle.

I want others to inherit my spirit – the spirit that is born from my experience.

It has to be dramatic.

It has to be believable.

It has to be *"real"*.

On the third hour they crucify him and the nails pierce divine spirit. On the sixth hour the taunts, with which they mock him, pierce divine reason. On the ninth hour faith in the divine is replaced by alienation, cynicism and despair as Christ utters that same anguished cry that he utters every second of every minute of every hour of every day as he cries out:

> *"My God, my God, why have you forsaken me?"*

I briefly scanned that passage in the Book of Wisdom that I keep close by, and then, once more, I picked up my pen.

3rd Year of Vespasian's reign (72 CE)

It is the tenth anniversary of James' death. Although I hadn't known James personally, I always had the greatest respect for him. James was thoroughly committed to doing what he believed was right. Every day he was to be found in the Jerusalem temple. Indeed he was permitted to enter the Holy place within the temple for he wore the linen garments of the priest. In his attitude to external authority he was like his Old Testament namesake Jacob who ignored his blind father's wishes and used subterfuge to obtain the blessing that was intended for his brother Esau. In the same way that Jacob usurped his brother, James usurped his spiritual *"brother"* Judas the

Galilean. Like Judas he did not respect external authority for its own sake. Unlike Judas he saw the need for external authority to restrain behavior.

Despite James' many admirable personal qualities, however, he didn't proselytize. Not like Paul.

Jacob's son Joseph was unlike his father. He was naturally outgoing and bore all his trials with fortitude. When thrown into a pit by his brothers, he uttered no complaint; when sold into slavery, he voiced no dissent; when unjustly accused and sentenced to prison, he did not protest. He accepted life as a slave; he accepted life as a prisoner. He found it no burden to be forced to leave his family to set up a life in Egypt. In contrast to Jacob, there was no subterfuge with Joseph. He needed external authority and respected it. He respected his father and obeyed his instructions to go to his brothers despite their animosity toward him, he respected his master Potiphar and rejected his master's wife attempts to seduce him. He respected Pharoah and was honest in his interpretation of Pharoah's dream and the advice he gave. Even when appointed governor of Egypt, he respected his father when, contrary to Joseph's wishes, he blessed his youngest son Ephraim before his elder son Mannaseh.

My sons exhibit those same types of personality. They have grown up to be fine young men and I love them both dearly but they are so different.

Alexander has an innate sense of what is right and what is wrong. Rufus is more influenced by others. They have both been through their share of trauma. They were young when their mother died. Rufus always used to listen to his mother. She was his external authority. After her death his behavior became difficult. He would respond aggressively to the slightest chastisement and would frequently keep company with trouble makers. Alexander became very quiet and would spend much time brooding on his own. He needed to be coaxed into engaging with others. People respond to loss in different ways.

PART I

4th Year of Vespasian's reign (73 CE) - 3

It is complete at last. It has taken eight years and has been a long and arduous process but I am proud of the work. It is a story that speaks to different people in different ways. To those directed by external authority, it is the story of Jesus of Nazareth, the Son of God who died on the cross for the sake of us all and rose again. To the cognoscenti it is an allegorical tale that provides a model of how we should live our lives. For both, I hope, it will be a source of inspiration. It didn't matter how people interpreted the gospel. What mattered was how people responded to it. Those who read the gospel allegorically must be tolerant of those who read it literally. Those who read the gospel literally must be tolerant of those who read it allegorically. We didn't need more division.

This will not be the end of the story, of course. Each age will produce its different challenges and no doubt, different gospels will be produced to reflect the times but this work contains a message that is timeless.

This is a Christ who didn't die *"for our sins"* in a sacrificial act of atonement but dies *"because of our sins"* every day in the here and now.

This is a Christ who didn't physically rise from the dead in a miraculous reconstitution of tissue and bone but is resurrected in healing and inspirational words and actions every day in the here and now.

This is a Christ who is part of a Holy Trinity, a unifying God of all that is not beyond all human understanding, but is instead born from an understanding of what it is to be human.

It is important that those who are to follow take no liberties with what has been created for any theology that is not ultimately rooted in humanity is worse than useless. It is divisive. I dearly hope that people will embrace the life enhancing myth and resist the temptation to graft meaningless fictions upon it.

Despite the reservations, I feel excited. What has been created is something that will unite different cultures. In spite of all the persecutions and injustices that will surely come, I really feel that this is the dawn of a new era. For the good of us all, this is a God that is well worth worshipping.

Part II

With many similar parables Jesus spoke the word to them, as much as they could understand. He did not say anything to them without using a parable. But when he was alone with his own disciples, he explained everything.

[Mark 4:33-34]

Christianity

In churches and chapels around the world, Christians are often asked to reflect on the life, death and resurrection of the person of Jesus Christ, the savior who sacrificed himself for our sins by dying on the cross at Calvary. Yet this dogma sits uneasily in our multi-cultural, scientific and secular society where we are encouraged to see all world religions as equally valid, where science dismisses any claims of the miraculous and where the necessity of a human sacrifice seems both baffling and barbaric.

In seminaries and colleges around the world, Christians are often asked to reflect on the life, death and resurrection of the historical person of Jesus Christ, the incarnate God. Yet there are those who, while pointing out the scarcity of references to the actual life of Jesus outside of the four canonical gospels, question whether such an historical figure existed at all.

In study groups and discussion groups and prayer groups around the world, Christians are often asked to reflect on the life, death and resurrection of the person of Jesus Christ whose story is related in the gospels. Yet in order to understand the gospels, it is surely more fruitful to try and understand what motivated the author of the earliest gospel to write his work and what influenced him. It is surely more fruitful to reflect on the social and political forces at work, the philosophical ideas that were influential and the historical events that occurred in the countries bordering the eastern Mediterranean during the first century of the Common Era.

PART II

Alexandria and Judaea

Alexander had reigned for twelve years when he died. Each of his officers established himself in his own region. All assumed crowns after his death, they and their heirs after them for many years, bringing increasing evils on the world.

[1 Maccabees 1: 9]

Eleazar the High priest sends greetings to King Ptolemy his true friend. ....

In the presence of all the people I selected six elders from each tribe, good men and true, and I have sent them to you with a copy of our law. It will be a kindness, O righteous king, if you will give instruction that as soon as the translation of the law is completed, the men shall be restored again to us in safety. Farewell.

[Letter of Aristeas: 41 & 46]

Alexandria

As a young man, Alexander was taught by the best. His father, Philip of Macedon employed Aristotle as his tutor. Aristotle was the most learned man of his time and a great philosopher. One of Alexander's best friends who came to be one of his most trusted generals was Ptolemy. On Alexander's death, Ptolemy took control of Egypt and founded the Ptolemaic dynasty, centered on its capital Alexandria. This man, the first of the Ptolemys, was given the epithet *"Soter"* which means *"Savior"*.

Ptolemy was keen that the Greek and Egyptian communities in Alexandria worshipped the same deity and to this end he commissioned the building of the Serapeum, a temple to the syncretic Hellenistic-Egyptian god, Serapis. This deity was an amalgam of the Egyptian bull god, Apis with the god of the underworld, Osiris, and he was portrayed as Greek-style anthropomorphic figure, completely different to the bull-like statues of Apis and the heavily stylized, two dimensional pictures of the resurrected and green-colored god, Osiris.

Ptolemy had a high regard for knowledge and this was something he instilled into his son. Indeed it was either during the life of Ptolemy I Soter (323–283 BCE) or his son Ptolemy II Philadelphus (283–246 BCE) that the famous library of Alexandria and the associated Musaeum (or temple of the muses) was constructed. The latter was the equivalent of a modern day university and it attracted the best scholars of the ancient world.

Often referred to as the *"Father of Geometry"*, Euclid was one of the early scholars. In about 300 BCE, he wrote his hugely influential work, *"Elements"*, a compendium of thirteen books on geometry and number theory. The work was a compilation of the discoveries of many ancient mathematicians and explained the deduction of (what is now called) Euclidean geometry from a small set of axioms. It was still used as a textbook in academic institutions at the beginning of the twentieth century.

It is said that in reply to King Ptolemy's request for an easier way to understand this material, Euclid answered:

> *Oh King, in the real world there are two kinds of roads, roads for the common people to travel upon and roads reserved for the King to travel upon. In geometry there is no royal road.*
>
> [Proclus (410-485) Eudemiarz Summar]

The third chief librarian of the Great Library was Eratosthenes. He invented the discipline of geography including a system of latitude and longitude. To measure the circumference of the earth, he took a reading of the length of the shadow cast at noon on the summer solstice at Syene a city in the south of Egypt that straddled the Tropic of Cancer. At the same time on the same day in a different year, he took a measurement of the length of the shadow cast in Alexandria. Using the distance between the two cities and the difference in the length of the shadows, he calculated that the earth's circumference was about 40,000 kilometers, a remarkably accurate figure that is within 1% of the true value.

Under the patronage of the Ptolemys, the library itself became well stocked. Scrolls were collected from the book fairs of Rhodes and Athens and every ship that came into port was searched for scrolls that were then taken and copied, with the copies being returned to the owners.

From the earliest times there were many Jews in the city. After the first King Ptolemy conquered Judea, Josephus claims, he led 120,000 Jewish captives to Egypt. An inscription recording a Jewish dedication of a synagogue to Ptolemy and his wife Berenice was discovered in the 19th century near Alexandria. Josephus also claims that, soon after, these 120,000 captives were freed of their bondage by Philadelphus.

Greek became the first language of the Jewish people and there was a pressing demand for a translation of the Hebrew Scriptures so that the literature of their ancestors became once more accessible to the Alexandrian Jews.

There is a tradition, based on the *"Letter of Aristeas"* composed in the 3rd century BCE, that 72 Jewish translators were enlisted by Ptolemy II Philadelphus to complete the translation of the Torah, the first five books of the Old Testament. Even though they were kept in separate chambers, they all produced identical versions of the text in seventy-two days.

Further books were translated over time and the complete text or Septuagint, as it became known, was completed in the 2nd Century BCE.

Ptolemy II Philadelphus is also credited with commissioning the building of the lighthouse of Alexandria on the island of Pharos. With a height variously estimated at between 393 and 450 feet (120 and 140 meters), it was for many centuries among the tallest man-made structures on Earth and one of the Seven Wonders of the Ancient World.

The Ptolemaic dynasty came to an end in 30 BCE with the suicide of Cleopatra VII, the most famous female head of state of the ancient world. Known for her love affairs, first with Julius Caesar and then with Mark Anthony, Cleopatra was the most Machiavellian of leaders, being both highly manipulative and ruthless with those who threatened her pre-eminence. On the death of her father, Ptolemy XII, in March 51 BCE, the eighteen year old Cleopatra was installed as co-ruler with her younger brother Ptolemy XIII. She soon made it clear that she had no intention of sharing power. By August of the same year, Cleopatra dropped Ptolemy's name from official documents and the coins of that period featured her face alone. Her sole reign was ended, by a cabal of courtiers, in 48 BCE and Cleopatra was forced to flee Alexandria with her elder half-sister, Arsinoe.

During this time, the Roman civil war was raging and in the autumn of that same year, Julius Caesar arrived in Alexandria in pursuit of his rival, the general Pompey, who had fled to the city in search of sanctuary. Two days earlier, Ptolemy who was still only thirteen, in an attempt to curry favor with the Emperor, had ordered Pompey's beheading. On his arrival, the severed head was presented to Caesar.

Instead of gratitude, Caesar was enraged that the thirteen year old King had taken it upon himself to execute his rival. He seized control of the city and took up residence in the palace overlooking the harbor. Legend has it that to avoid Ptolemy's guards, Cleopatra had herself smuggled into the palace within a rolled up carpet. In any event, the twenty one year old Queen became mistress to the fifty two year old Emperor and nine months later bore him a son who became known as Caesarion or *"little Caesar"*.

PART II

After Caesar and Cleopatra became lovers, the Emperor backed Cleopatra's claim to the throne and Caesar's Roman troops and the forces of Ptolemy with his sister Arsinoe joined in battle.

That Caesar emerged victorious was in no small part due to the arrival of reinforcements from Judea under the command of Antipater I, sent with the consent of Hyrcanus, the last of the Hasmonean High Priests.

After the victory, Ptolemy XIII was drowned in the Nile and Caesar restored Cleopatra to her throne, with another younger brother Ptolemy XIV as her new co-ruler.

Arsinoe was transported to Rome where, in 46 BCE, she was forced to appear in Caesar's triumphal parade. Despite usual traditions of prisoners in such parades being strangled when the festivities were at an end, Caesar spared Arsinoe and granted her sanctuary at the temple of Artemis in Ephesus.

In recognition of the help he received, Caesar returned Hyrcanus to the high-priesthood and granted Antipater Roman citizenship and made him chief minister of Judea, with the right to collect taxes. He issued a decree registered in both Greek and Latin on a table of brass granting Hyrcanus and the Jews certain privileges. He gave Judea the right of *"status clientis"*—the broadest autonomy that countries subject to Rome could enjoy.

Caesar was assassinated on 15 March, 44 BCE. Cleopatra was with him in Rome at the time. After his murder she returned to Alexandria and following the death of Ptolemy XIV, allegedly poisoned by his older sister, Cleopatra made Caesarion her co-regent and successor.

The assassination of Caesar was followed by a period of instability within the empire. By 41 BCE Antony and Octavian, Julius Caesar's great nephew and named heir (who would later change his name to Augustus) shared the leadership of Rome and had divided the Empire into two regions - the western portion including Spain and Gaul ruled by Octavian, the eastern region including Greece and the

Middle East ruled by Antony whose first meeting with Cleopatra is described in a biography of the man written by Plutarch:

> *As he was getting ready for the Parthian war, he sent to Cleopatra, ordering her to meet him in Cilicia in order to make answer to the charges made against her of raising and giving to Cassius much money for the war. But Dellius, Antony's messenger, when he saw how Cleopatra looked, and noticed her subtlety and cleverness in conversation, at once perceived that Antony would not so much as think of doing such a woman any harm, but that she would have the greatest influence with him. He therefore resorted to flattery and tried to induce the Egyptian to go to Cilicia "decked out in fine array" (as Homer would say), and not to be afraid of Antony, who was the most agreeable and humane of commanders. She was persuaded by Dellius, and judging by the proofs which she had had before this of the effect of her beauty upon Caius Caesar and Gnaeus the son of Pompey, she had hopes that she would more easily bring Antony to her feet. For Caesar and Pompey had known her when she was still a girl and inexperienced in affairs, but she was going to visit Antony at the very time when women have the most brilliant beauty and are at the acme of intellectual power. Therefore she provided herself with many gifts, much money, and such ornaments as high position and prosperous kingdom made it natural for her to take; but she went putting her greatest confidence in herself, and in the charms and sorceries of her own person. Though she received many letters of summons both from Antony himself and from his friends, she so despised and*

PART II

laughed the man to scorn as to sail up the river Cydnus in a barge with gilded poop, its sails spread purple, its rowers urging it on with silver oars to the sound of the flute blended with pipes and lutes. She herself reclined beneath a canopy spangled with gold, adorned like Venus in a painting, while boys like Loves in paintings stood on either side and fanned her..............

.... Accordingly, she made such booty of Antony that, while Fulvia his wife was carrying on war at Rome with Caesar in defense of her husband's interests, and while a Parthian army was hovering about Mesopotamia (over this country the generals of the king had appointed Labienus Parthian commander-in-chief, and were about to invade Syria), he suffered her to hurry him off to Alexandria.

There, indulging in the sports and diversions of a young man of leisure, he squandered and spent upon pleasures that which Antiphon calls the most costly outlay, namely, time.

[Plutarch: Antony 25-28]

In Alexandria, Cleopatra and Antony formed a society of *"inimitable livers"* whose members lived what some historians have interpreted as a life of debauchery and folly and others have interpreted as lives dedicated to the cult of the god Dionysus.

To safeguard herself and Caesarion, in 41 BCE, Cleopatra persuaded Mark Antony to order the execution of Arsinoe. She was killed on the steps of the temple, a gross violation of the temple sanctuary and an act which scandalized Rome.

Antony also received two dispatches, one from Rome gave the news that his brother Lucius and his wife Fulvia had joined in war against Caesar; the other that Labienus, at the head of the Parthian army, was overrunning Asia. Action was needed and Antony left Alexandria in 40 BCE. For four years, he and Cleopatra were separated. Antony first travelled to Rome to make peace and rekindle the alliance with Octavian. From there he sent forces to Asia under the command of Venditius to check the advance of the Parthians. It was also there that in 39 BCE, he married Octavia, a noble Roman lady.

With Octavia's help, a treaty between Octavian and Antony was signed in 38 BCE. In 37 BCE, he set sail for Syria, leaving in Caesar's charge his wife and children. In Judea, Parthian forces had taken Jerusalem and installed Antigonus as King. Venditius had great success in conquering Parthian forces and he sent, at Antony's instruction, reinforcements to Herod. In that year Antigonus was defeated and Herod took up the office that was bestowed on him by the Roman senate three years earlier, and became King.

Antony himself felt the need to join battle but as he arrived in Syria, Plutarch states:

> *But the dire evil which had been slumbering for a long time, namely, his passion for Cleopatra, which men thought had been charmed away and lulled to rest by better considerations, blazed up again with renewed power as he drew near to Syria. And finally, like the stubborn and unmanageable beast of the soul, of which Plato speaks, he spurned away all saving and noble counsels and sent Fonteius Capito to bring Cleopatra to Syria. And when she was come, he made her a present of no slight or insignificant addition to her dominions, namely, Phoenicia, Coele Syria, Cyprus, and a large part of Cilicia; and still further, the balsam-producing part of Judaea, and all that part of Arabia Nabataea which slopes toward the outer sea. These gifts particularly annoyed the Romans. And yet he*

PART II

> *made presents to many private persons of tetrarchies and realms of great peoples, and he deprived many monarchs of their kingdoms, as, for instance, Antigonus the Jew, whom he brought forth and beheaded, though no other king before him had been so punished. But the shamefulness of the honors conferred upon Cleopatra gave most offence. And he heightened the scandal by acknowledging his two children by her, and called one Alexander and the other Cleopatra, with the surname for the first of Sun, and for the other of Moon.*
>
> [Plutarch: Antony 36:1]

Josephus describes the very same events:

> *As for Antony, he was so entirely overcome by this woman, that one would not think her conversation only could do it, but that he was some way or other bewitched to do whatsoever she would have him; yet did the grossest parts of her injustice make him so ashamed, that he would not always hearken to her to do those flagrant enormities she would have persuaded him to. That therefore he might not totally deny her, nor, by doing everything which she enjoined him, appear openly to be an ill man, he took some parts of each of those countries away from their former governors, and gave them to her. Thus he gave her the cities that were within the river Eleutherus, as far as Egypt, excepting Tyre and Sidon, which he knew to have been free cities from their ancestors, although she pressed him very often to bestow those on her also.*
>
> [Josephus: Antiquities 15:4:1]

Plutarch was critical of Antony's first military engagement with the Parthians believing him to be preoccupied with other concerns. The campaign ended in disaster:

> *For so eager was he to spend the winter with her that he began the war before the proper time, and managed everything confusedly. He was not master of his own faculties, but, as if he were under the influence of certain drugs or of magic rites, was ever looking eagerly towards her, and thinking more of his speedy return than of conquering the enemy.*
>
> [Plutarch: Antony 37:4]

Later, in 33 BCE, Antony did successfully manage to annex Armenia. On return to Alexandria, there was a celebratory parade through the city before the whole city was summoned to the gymnasium. Surrounded by Cleopatra and her children, Antony distributed kingdoms between his children that were not his to distribute: Alexander Helios was named king of Armenia, Media and Parthia, his twin Selene received Cyrenaica and Libya, and the young Ptolemy Philadelphus was awarded Syria and Cilicia. As for Cleopatra, she was proclaimed Queen of Kings and Queen of Egypt, to rule with Caesarion (Ptolemy XV Caesar, son of Julius Caesar), King of Kings and King of Egypt. Caesarion was declared legitimate son and heir of Caesar. These proclamations were known as the Donations of Alexandria and caused a fatal breach in Antony's relations with Rome.

September 2nd 31 BCE marked the start of the decisive battle of Actium, a battle between the naval forces of Octavian and those of Antony and Cleopatra. Octavian's navy was victorious and Antony and Cleopatra were forced to escape to Egypt with 60 ships. Octavian and his forces followed and in August of 30 BCE, Antony committed suicide by stabbing himself with his sword. Cleopatra was found dead shortly after, apparently poisoned. Surprisingly, no-one knew quite how she died, although suicide was assumed. Some thought it was from the bite of an asp, which had been hidden in a

PART II

basket of figs or a water jar (although no snake was found), or a scratch to which poison was applied from a pin used to fasten her hair or hidden in a hollow comb.

The death of Cleopatra marked the end of a dynasty and the life of the most manipulative of political leaders. In a hugely rich country, she led an opulent, luxurious and self-indulgent lifestyle but she wanted more and to get what she wanted, Cleopatra seduced those who were already married, slandered other leaders and killed her own family members whom she perceived were a threat to her position. Through the eyes of the Jewish population of Alexandria, the manner of her death may have seemed apposite – hers was a life that was poisoned by moral corruption.

The Book of Wisdom, a beautiful and fascinating work and one of the deuterocanonical books, may have been written with Cleopatra in mind.

The unnamed author is indicated to be Solomon. Indeed in Greek, the work is called the Wisdom of Solomon. Clearly, this is not the case. The book is written in Greek and contains many Hellenistic influences. That the author makes use of the Septuagint version of Isaiah dates the work to sometime after the end of the 3rd century BCE.

The author's extended reference to the events of Exodus, his contrast of Egyptians with Israelis and his attacks on animal worship, shows that he lived in Alexandria. He makes no reference to the works of the hugely influential Philo which may suggest that the work predates him. The author is writing primarily for those Jews whose faith is shaken by the cultural life of Alexandria but he does also hope to encourage gentiles to God.

The book starts with a call to the leaders of the world to seek wisdom and love uprightness. It warns:

> *Wisdom will never enter the soul of a wrong-doer, nor dwell in a body enslaved to sin;*

> *for the holy spirit of instruction flees deceitfulness, recoils*
> *from unintelligent thoughts, is thwarted by the onset of*
> *vice.*
>
> [Wisdom 1:4-5]

In a short section still directed at the leaders of the world that may possibly be read as a posthumous reference to Cleopatra, the author refers to death simultaneously as both a spiritual and physical demise:

> *Do not court death by the errors of your ways, nor invite*
> *destruction through the work of your hands.*
> *For God did not make Death, he takes no pleasure in*
> *destroying the living.*
> *To exist -- for this he created all things; the creatures of the*
> *world have health in them, in them is no fatal poison, and*
> *Hades has no power over the world:*
> *for uprightness is immortal.*
>
> [Wisdom 1:12-15]

The work contains a proto-Christian theology with Wisdom being personified as female and the love that the author declares for her stands in stark contrast to Antony's infatuation with Cleopatra:

> *Wisdom I loved and searched for from my youth;*
> *I resolved to have her as my bride.*
> *I fell in love with her beauty.*
> *She enhances her noble birth by sharing God's life,*
> *for the master of all has always loved her.*
> *Indeed, she shares the secrets of God's knowledge,*
> *and she chooses what he will do.*
>
> [Wisdom 8:1-4]

PART II

In truth, there is no consensus in dating the composition of the work. Some scholars suggest a date as early as 221-204 BCE during the reign of Ptolemy IV Philopator or 145-117 BCE during the reign of Ptolemy VII Physicon. Others suggest a date as late as 37-41 CE during the reign of Gaius *"Caligula"*.

What is clear is that the author inhabited the same cultural milieu as both Philo and the author of the earliest of the canonical gospels.

As Philo makes reference to the geometrical works of Euclid, the author of the Book of Wisdom makes reference to other scientific discoveries:

> *He it was who gave me sure knowledge of what exists,*
> *to understand the structure of the world and the action of the elements,*
> *the beginning, end and middle of the times,*
> *the alternation of the solstices and the succession of the seasons,*
> *the cycles of the year and the position of the stars*
> *the natures of animals and the instincts of wild beasts,*
> *the powers of spirits and human mental processes,*
> *the varieties of plants and the medicinal properties of roots.*
> *And now I understand everything, hidden or visible,*
> *for Wisdom, the designer of all things, has instructed me.*
>
> [Wisdom 7:17-26]

The female personified Wisdom described in this work is one and the same as the male personified divine reason described in New Testament writings. This book describes Wisdom as follows:

> *She is a reflection of eternal light, a spotless mirror of the working of God, and an image of his goodness.*
>
> [Wisdom 7:26]

The letter to the Hebrews describes Christ in a similar fashion:

> *The Son is the radiance of God's glory and the exact representation of his being, sustaining all things by his powerful word.*
>
> [Hebrews 1:3]

The Book of Wisdom is perhaps best well known for its passage that contrasts life with and without spirituality and describes the lives of the godless as driven by self-indulgence. It is in this passage that we have a *"prediction"* of the Passion:

> *But the godless call for Death with deed and word, counting him friend, they wear themselves out for him; with him they make a pact, worthy as they are to belong to him.*
> *And this is the false argument they use, 'Our life is short and dreary, there is no remedy when our end comes, no one is known to have come back from Hades.*
> *We came into being by chance and afterwards shall be as though we had never been. The breath in our nostrils is a puff of smoke, reason a spark from the beating of our hearts; extinguish this and the body turns to ashes, and the spirit melts away like the yielding air.*
> *In time, our name will be forgotten, nobody will remember what we have done; our life will pass away like wisps of cloud, dissolving like the mist that the sun's rays drive away and that its heat dispels.*
> *For our days are the passing of a shadow, our end is without return, the seal is affixed and nobody comes back.*
> *'Come then, let us enjoy the good things of today, let us use*

PART II

created things with the zest of youth:
take our fill of the dearest wines and perfumes, on no account forgo the flowers of spring but crown ourselves with rosebuds before they wither, no meadow excluded from our orgy; let us leave the signs of our revelry everywhere, since this is our portion, this our lot!
'As for the upright man who is poor, let us oppress him; let us not spare the widow, nor respect old age, white-haired with many years.
Let our might be the yardstick of right, since weakness argues its own futility.
Let us lay traps for the upright man, since he annoys us and opposes our way of life, reproaches us for our sins against the law, and accuses us of sins against our upbringing.
He claims to have knowledge of God, and calls himself a child of the Lord.
We see him as a reproof to our way of thinking, the very sight of him weighs our spirits down;
for his kind of life is not like other people's, and his ways are quite different.
In his opinion we are counterfeit; he avoids our ways as he would filth; he proclaims the final end of the upright as blessed and boasts of having God for his father.
Let us see if what he says is true, and test him to see what sort of end he will have.
For if the upright man is God's son, God will help him and rescue him from the clutches of his enemies.
Let us test him with cruelty and with torture, and thus explore this gentleness of his and put his patience to the

> *test.*
> *Let us condemn him to a shameful death since God will rescue him -- or so he claims.'*
> *This is the way they reason, but they are misled, since their malice makes them blind.*
> *They do not know the hidden things of God, they do not hope for the reward of holiness, they do not believe in a reward for blameless souls.*
> *For God created human beings to be immortal, he made them as an image of his own nature;*
> *Death came into the world only through the Devil's envy, as those who belong to him find to their cost.*
>
> [Wisdom 1:16 – 2:24]

Judaea

Alexander the Great conquered Judaea in 332 BCE. The 1st Book of Maccabees relates:

> *Alexander of Macedon son of Philip had come from the land of Kittim and defeated Darius king of the Persians and Medes whom he succeeded as ruler, at first of Hellas. He undertook many campaigns, gained possession of many fortresses and put the local kings to death. So he advanced to the ends of the earth, plundering nation after nation; the earth grew silent before him, and his ambitious heart swelled with pride. He assembled very powerful forces and subdued provinces, nations and princes, and they became his tributaries. But the time came when Alexander took to his bed, in the knowledge that he was dying. He*

PART II

summoned his officers, noblemen who had been brought up with him from his youth, and divided his kingdom among them while he was still alive. Alexander had reigned for twelve years when he died. Each of his officers established himself in his own region. All assumed crowns after his death, they and their heirs after them for many years, bringing increasing evils on the world.

[1 Maccabees 1: 1– 9]

On his premature death in 323 BCE, Alexander's empire was divided into four separate power blocks headed by former generals. Of these the largest was the Seleucid empire, founded by Seleucus I, that extended from the eastern shores of the Mediterranean sea in the west to the Indus river in modern-day Pakistan in the east and encompassed most of modern day Turkey and Syria.

Egypt was part of the Ptolemaic kingdom, founded by Ptolemy I Soter, which, at its height stretched from Cyrene in modern day Libya to southern Syria. This kingdom was centered on its capital Alexandria, which came to be the greatest city of the western world.

Between these great power blocks lay the disputed territory of Judea, homeland to the Jewish people, with its capital, Jerusalem, home to the great Jewish temple. From 305 BCE to 198 BCE, Judea was part of the Ptolemaic kingdom. From 198 BCE to 141 BCE, it was part of the Seleucid Empire.

One of the most historically reviled of the Seleucid kings was Antiochus IV Epiphanes whose interference in the affairs of the Jews had the most enormous repercussions. The problem started with internal rivalries between Jewish factions, one of whom supported the incumbent High Priest Onias, the other who pressed the claims of a rival named Jason. In 173 BCE, the latter faction caused Onias to be deposed and Jason was appointed as successor. To ingratiate himself with the king, Jason established an arena for public games close by the Temple. However, a rival to Jason, named Menelaus bribed the King and in 171 BCE was himself appointed as Jason's successor. In order to fund his bribes, Menelaus seized the sacred vessels in the Temple stores, an act that came to the attention of Onias, who publicly accused Menelaus of robbing the Temple. Menelaus, afraid of the consequences of this accusation, arranged to have Onias murdered.

While Antiochus was on a military campaign in Egypt, a rumor spread in Jerusalem that he had died. Jason took this opportunity to usurp Menelaus, forcing him to flee to Egypt.

In fact, Antiochus had been compelled by the Romans to leave Egypt and the news of Jason's uprising was a further challenge to his authority. He marched against Jerusalem, massacred the inhabitants, and plundered the Temple; in this he is said to have been assisted by Menelaus:

> *When these happenings were reported to the king, he thought that Judea was in revolt. Raging like a wild animal, he set out from Egypt and took Jerusalem by storm. He ordered his soldiers to cut down without mercy those whom they met and to slay those who took refuge in their houses. There was a massacre of young and old, a killing of women and children, a slaughter of virgins and infants. In the space of three days, eighty thousand were lost, forty thousand meeting a violent death, and the same number being sold into slavery.*
>
> [2 Maccabees 5:11-14]

Antiochus imposed strict laws prohibiting any expression of Jewish culture. The possession of Jewish scripture was an offence that was punishable by death. Circumcision was made illegal, sacrifice to the Jewish god was forbidden and the traditional Jewish observances of the Sabbath and feast days were banned. The worship of Greek gods was promoted and a statue of Zeus was erected in the temple.

PART II

This attempted extermination of Jewish identity had predictable consequences.

An altar to Zeus was erected in the small city of Modin and the king's soldiers ordered the most influential of the city's citizens, a man named Mattathias, to make sacrifice. He pointedly refused, proclaiming:

> *Though all the nations that are under the king's dominion obey him, . . . yet will I, and my sons, and my brethren, walk in the covenant of our fathers.*
>
> [I Maccabees 19-20]

Moreover, when another Jew was about to take his place, Mattathias, in outrage, killed the offender and destroyed the altar, while his sons killed the king's officer. Then Mattathias called out:

> *Whoever is zealous for the law, and maintaineth the covenant, let him follow me.*

Many responded to his call and followed him to the mountains and desert places of Judea. Although Mattathias died soon after, his son Judas known as the *"Maccabee"* or *"hammer"* led the followers in a series of guerrilla attacks upon the occupying forces of Antiochus and his Hellenist sympathizers.

Their eventual triumph resulted in the recapture of the Jerusalem Temple. It was cleansed, refurnished, and rededicated exactly three years to-the-day of its desecration, that is, on the 25th of Kislev, 165/4 BCE. The rededication of the temple is celebrated as the Jewish feast of Hanukkah.

Although after the revolt, Jews had gained some autonomy over their own affairs, Judaea was still part of the Seleucid Empire until the death of Antiochus VII in 129 BCE. This brought in a period of Jewish independence under the Hasmonean dynasty that lasted until the conquest by the Roman general Pompey in 63 BCE.

The last of the Hasmonean High Priests was Hyrcanus, the eldest son of Alexander Jannaeus who was both High Priest and King. After the death of Alexander in 76 BCE, his widow, Alexandra Salome, succeeded him as ruler of Judea and installed Hyrcanus as High Priest.

When Salome died in 67 BCE, she named Hyrcanus as successor to the Kingship as well. After three months there started a bitter battle for the kingdom between Hyrcanus and his brother Aristobulus II, a feud that was to only end with the death of Aristobulus. During the political machinations that the feud entailed, Hyracanus was deeply indebted to his Idumean adviser, Antipater.

The diplomacy and artful politics of Antipater, as well as his insinuation into the Hasmonean court, paved the way for the rise of his son Herod the Great, who used this position to marry the Hasmonean princess Mariamne, endear himself to Rome and become king of Judea under Roman influence. He was bestowed with the title *"King of the Jews"* by the Roman senate in 40 BCE. It was only in 37 BCE, however, after victory over his Hasmonean rival Antigonus who was supported by the invading Parthian forces, that Judea was secured and the Herodian dynasty established – a dynasty that was to last for over a hundred years.

The reign of Herod the Great lasted until 4 BCE and was notable for both outstanding architectural achievements and brutal murders of his own family members.

He strengthened the fortifications of the hill forts of Machaerus and Massada that overlooked the Dead Sea and transformed Massada into a luxurious palace complex. In the eighteenth year of his reign, he rebuilt the Temple.

Most impressively, he arranged for the construction of an artificial harbor at Caesarea Maritima. This was an action designed to benefit the whole country. If Judea could use the Mediterranean, it could become a great trading nation with a port to rival Alexandria, but the country had no natural harbor large enough to cater for the great trading ships so Herod arranged for the construction of an artificial harbor using vast quantities of volcanic ash cement that hardened in sea water. The harbor was named Sebastos, which is Greek for Augustus. Around the harbor, on the site known as Strato's Tower, was built the city. It was constructed on a Greek grid plan, renamed as Caesarea Maritima and, in an official ceremony in 9 BCE, dedicated in honor of the Emperor. It became home to a largely gentile population that looked outward to the sea for their livelihood.

However, despite his many significant achievements, Herod was always conscious of his Idumean background and the parts played by both he and his father in the usurping of the Hasmonean dynasty, who many saw as the rightful heirs to the kingdom. He was a deeply insecure man. With his marriage to Mariamne, of course, he hoped to gain some legitimacy in the eyes of the Jews but, because of his actions, Mariamne came to deeply resent him.

Firstly, Herod executed his wife's grandfather, Hyrcanus, who had previously been taken prisoner by the Parthians, but on release, had ventured back to his homeland. Herod executed Hyrcanus not because he presented a threat but because Hyrcanus' claim to the throne was stronger than his own.

Next, he bestowed the position of High Priest on Mariamne's seventeen year old brother, Jonathan but when Jonathan put on the sacred vestments and approached the altar during a feast, the whole crowd burst into tears. Fearful of Jonathan's popularity, Herod had him drowned in a swimming pool.

Then embittered by jealousy after hearing rumors of an affair between his young wife and Mark Antony, Herod ordered Mariamne's execution.

Herod fathered two sons by Mariamne, Alexander and Aristobulus, who were both schooled in Rome. Despite an apparent reconciliation between Herod and his sons after Mariamne's death, Herod was too ready to listen to rumors of treachery. He sent them both to Sebaste with orders that they be strangled.

Antipater was the only son that Herod's fathered by his first wife, Doris, and on the death of his half-brothers Alexander and Aristobulus, he became heir to the throne. However, in 5 BC Antipater was brought before the Roman governor of Syria, charged and found guilty of the intended murder of his father. Antipater was imprisoned and executed 5 days before his father succumbed to a debilitating illness.

During his reign, Herod had killed his wife's grandfather, his seventeen year old brother in law, his young wife and their two sons and his son by his first marriage. His successors to his kingdom were the sons from his fourth and fifth marriages. The elder son from his fourth marriage, Archelaus assumed the Tetrarchy of Judaea, the younger, Antipas, the Tetrarchy of Galilee and Perea. A son from his fifth marriage, Philip, became Tetrarch of the North East portion of his father's kingdom comprising the territories of Gaulanitis, Batanea and Trachonitis.

Archelaus proved an unpopular leader and he was deposed in 6 CE and banished to Vienne in Gaul. After Archelaus' banishment, the Roman province of Judaea was formed comprising Samaria, Judea proper, and Idumea and for the following 35 years, until the short reign of Herod Agrippa I, Judaea was governed by a Roman procurator and the seat of government located not in Jerusalem but in Caesarea.

PART II

The tripartite soul

No man ever had a distinct idea of the trinity. It is mere Abracadabra of the mountebanks calling themselves the priests of Jesus. If it could be understood it would not answer their purpose.

[Thomas Jefferson: Letter to Van der Kemp, 1816]

Plato and the tripartite psyche

Of all philosophers in the history of Western culture, it is perhaps Plato who is the most revered.

It was Alfred North Whitehead, the English mathematician and philosopher who, in his book *"Process and Reality"*, coined the famous phrase:

> *The safest general characterization of the European philosophical tradition is that it consists of a series of footnotes to Plato.*
> *I do not mean the systematic scheme of thought which scholars have doubtfully extracted from his writings. I allude to the wealth of general ideas scattered through them...*

[Process and Reality, Free Press, 1929]

It is Plato's writing on Forms that has influenced the Christian conception of God; a God of infinite power, infinite knowledge, infinite size, infinite love and ever present; a God who is omnipotent, omniscient, omnipresent, benevolent, eternal and unchanging.

It is these same writings that have influenced the Christian understanding of an immortal soul that is able to exist apart from the body and a belief that if we restrain ourselves from indulging the physical desires of this world then we train ourselves for the spiritual world of the next.

However, despite Plato's eminent status, many find his dialogues desperately dull and there is something disconcerting about his readiness to make judgments about others.

It is ironic that of the 16 portrait statues of eminent men that adorn the main reading room in the Library of Congress, a statue of Plato is one of only two philosophers.

Ironic because the Library of Congress was previously known as the Thomas Jefferson Library, in honor of the American President who was chief author of the Declaration of Independence, and who contributed to the library his personal collection of books.

The Declaration of Independence contains the ringing and memorable phrase, later used by Martin Luther King in his *"I have a dream"* speech of August 1963:

> *We hold these truths to be self-evident, that all men are created equal*

…. This is not a sentiment that Plato would regard as self-evident.

Thomas Jefferson was the third American President and one of the most intellectual and well read.

He was a man of his times – a man of the Enlightenment and his beliefs reflect the majority opinion of today's Western European Society – a deep sympathy for the moral teaching within the gospels mixed with disdain for those gospel stories involving the miraculous. In a letter to another former president John Adams on April 11 1823, he wrote:

> *And the day will come when the mystical generation of*

PART II

> *Jesus, by the Supreme Being as his father in the womb of a virgin will be classed with the fable of the generation of Minerva in the brain of Jupiter. But may we hope that the dawn of reason and freedom of thought in these United States will do away with this artificial scaffolding, and restore to us the primitive and genuine doctrines of this most venerated reformer of human errors.*

In an earlier letter to the same recipient dated October 12 1813, he described the moral teachings within the gospels as:

> *the most sublime and benevolent code of morals which has ever been offered to man.*

It is extraordinary how someone like Thomas Jefferson, regarded as one of the most intelligent and widely read of the American presidents could read the gospel so literally. So taken was he with the moral teachings and so dismissive was he of the *"miracle"* stories, that he composed a composite gospel of his own, taking pieces from each of the four canonical gospels and incorporating them into one, shorn of the miraculous. Jefferson looked at the gospels through purely rational eyes but scripture should not be read this way. It is designed to be interpreted. Needless to say the *"Life and Morals of Jesus of Nazareth"*, otherwise known as the *"Jefferson Bible"* has not achieved widespread appeal.

We don't need to guess as to the opinion Jefferson held of Plato. In a letter to John Adams on July 5th 1814, he wrote:

> *I am just returned from one of my long absences, having been at my other home for five weeks past. Having more leisure there than here for reading, I amused myself with reading seriously Plato's republic. I am wrong however in calling it amusement, for it was the heaviest task-work I ever went through. I had occasionally before taken up some*

of his other works, but scarcely ever had patience to go through a whole dialogue. While wading thro' the whimsies, the puerilities, and unintelligible jargon of this work, I laid it down often to ask myself how it could have been that the world should have so long consented to give reputation to such nonsense as this?

....

The Christian priesthood, finding the doctrines of Christ leveled to every understanding, and too plain to need explanation, saw, in the mysticisms of Plato, materials with which they might build up an artificial system which might, from its indistinctness, admit everlasting controversy, give employment for their order, and introduce it to profit, power and pre-eminence. The doctrines which flowed from the lips of Jesus himself are within the comprehension of a child; but thousands of volumes have not yet explained the Platonisms engrafted on them: and for this obvious reason that nonsense can never be explained. Their purposes however are answered. Plato is canonized; and it is now deemed as impious to question his merits as those of an Apostle of Jesus.

The frustration, Jefferson felt, is evident in his writing and it is easy to sympathize. However, despite the influence of Plato's writing on Forms had on the development of Christianity, it is his writing on the tripartite soul that has the most influence on the gospel of Mark.

Plato introduces this concept in the *Republic*. Later, in *Phaedrus*, he expands on this as he draws an allegory of the soul being like a chariot, drawn by two horses – one black and unruly, one white and well-tempered. The charioteer himself controls the horses as best he can. The black horse represents the appetitive part of the soul, the

PART II

white horse represents spirit and the charioteer represents reason:

> *Of the nature of the soul, though her true form be ever a theme of large and more than mortal discourse, let me speak briefly, and in a figure. And let the figure be composite–a pair of winged horses and a charioteer. Now the winged horses and the charioteers of the gods are all of them noble and of noble descent, but those of other races are mixed; the human charioteer drives his in a pair; and one of them is noble and of noble breed, and the other is ignoble and of ignoble breed; and the driving of them of necessity gives a great deal of trouble to him........*
> *The right-hand horse is upright and cleanly made; he has a lofty neck and an aquiline nose; his color is white, and his eyes dark; he is a lover of honor and modesty and temperance, and the follower of true glory; he needs no touch of the whip, but is guided by word and admonition only. The other is a crooked lumbering animal, put together anyhow; he has a short thick neck; he is flat-faced and of a dark color, with grey eyes and blood-red complexion; the mate of insolence and pride, shag-eared and deaf, hardly yielding to whip and spur*

Plato uses this allegory to illustrate, quite humorously, in a way that we can all recognize the desire, foolishness, remorse and self-torture of the psyche of the person in love.

But more generally, Plato makes qualitative distinctions between the different aspects of the soul that are completely unjustified.

Reason is the superior aspect and yet a charioteer without horses can do nothing at all. So in what way is reason superior?

The appetitive part of the soul is the inferior aspect (*"ignoble and of ignoble breed"* and *"a crooked lumbering animal"*). This is the part that instinctively acts according to the urges of the body. As well as being responsible for our sexual desires, it is the part that prompts us to eat when we are hungry. If we are to regard this as less worthy then we regard the body itself as being less worthy. But it is the body that houses our soul, without which it cannot exist. It is the well fed man who can make these philosophical speculations. The hungry man has more pressing concerns.

Spirit is superior to the appetitive part of the soul. He is *"noble and of noble breed"* and *"he is a lover of honor and modesty and temperance, and the follower of true glory"*. Yet there is something troubling about the relative merits of two horses so described, whether intentional or not. Countless atrocities have been committed for *"noble"* causes. Countless atrocities have been committed in the defense of pure breeding.

There is another analogy that can be used to understand the tripartite soul – one that dispenses with the qualitative distinctions between the different aspects that are perceived by Plato, but instead sees the parts of the soul working cooperatively as one.

Thomas Jefferson was a child of the Enlightenment but so are we all. There is a widespread tendency to see religious writings as claiming a literal truth when they do not.

However, if we are equipped with an understanding of what it is to be human, religious writings including the gospel of Mark, the earliest gospel in the New Testament canon can be understood allegorically rather than literally. The gospel can be shown to contain seeds of a Christianity that Thomas Jefferson would happily endorse and point to a God that many of us surely, would be happy to worship.

The universal psyche

For Thomas Jefferson and many others, Plato's works are heavy going. They can be long winded and, to the modern mind, illogical. No more so than the *Timaeus* where Plato relates his understanding of creation. However, within the fantastical, speculative and tedious pronouncements on the properties of the four elements (fire, air, earth and water) and their interactions, there are places where we can obtain a real insight into Plato's thinking.

Plato understood that the tripartite soul of man was replicated in the state so the state was composed of the philosophers (that acted in the best interests of the state) [REASON], the guardians (that protected the state) [SPIRIT] and the artisans and husbandmen that responded to the prompts of their own instincts [APPETITE]. In the *Timaeus*, he goes beyond this and speculates that this soul is present in the world itself:

> *This is in the truest sense the origin of creation and of the world, as we shall do well in believing on the testimony of wise men: God desired that all things should be good and nothing bad, so far as this was attainable. Wherefore also finding the whole visible sphere not at rest, but moving in an irregular and disorderly fashion, out of disorder he brought order, considering that this was in every way better than the other. Now the deeds of the best could never be or have been other than the fairest; and the creator, reflecting on the things which are by nature visible, found that no unintelligent creature taken as a whole was fairer than the intelligent taken as a whole; and that intelligence could not be present in anything which was devoid of soul. For which reason, when he was framing the universe, he put intelligence in soul, and soul in body, that he might be the creator of a work which was by nature fairest and best. Wherefore, using the language of probability, we may say that the world became a living creature truly endowed with*

soul and intelligence by the providence of God.

[Plato: Timaeus]

During the 1st century, the tripartite soul was certainly a topic of some thought. Within an eleven volume work entitled Lectures on Pythagoreanism, Moderatus of Gades (modern Cadiz in Spain), while accusing Plato of effectively plagiarizing Pythagoras' works, gives the following account of the divinity:

There is a first, a second and a third One. The first one is beyond all being and ousia. The second, i.e. that which is actually being and intelligible, equals ideas. The third One, viz. The psychical, participates in the first One and in the ideas.

[Ricken, Philosophy of the Ancients, University of Notre Dame Press]

Whereas Moderatus saw Plato as being influenced by Pythagoras, the Jewish theologian and philosopher, Philo of Alexandria (c.20 BCE—c.50 CE) saw in Plato's account of creation a similarity with the account of creation within Genesis. He thought Plato was influenced by Moses.

Philo was a man of some wealth and stature in the Jewish community and was greatly influenced by Greek (Hellenistic) culture. His works, in the main, provide an allegorical explanation of Jewish scripture. Although Philo did not formalize any allegorical rules, he certainly regarded the use of names, numbers and any peculiarity in a phrase or even individual words as being a justification for searching for an allegorical meaning. In New Testament scripture there are plenty of sections of text that cry out for an allegorical interpretation including:

1. Names – their meaning
2. Numbers – their symbolism
3. A chronological reversal

PART II

4. The doubling of a phrase
5. An apparently superfluous expression
6. Professions – their significance
7. A play upon words (pun)
8. A reference to an improbable geographical location
9. Noteworthy omissions
10. Repetition of statements previously made

Many scholars see the influence of Plato's *Timaeus* on Philo's model of creation narrated in *Legum Allegoriae*. It is in this work, that we find Philo attributing the authorship of the Book of Genesis to Moses.

Using the following description in the book of Genesis of the creation of the first day, Philo gives an allegorical interpretation of the creation story as the creation of divine nature:

> *In the beginning God created the heavens and the earth.*
> *Now the earth was formless and empty, darkness was over the surface of the deep, and the Spirit of God was hovering over the waters.*
> *And God said, "Let there be light," and there was light.*
> *God saw that the light was good, and he separated the light from the darkness. God called the light "day," and the darkness he called "night."*
> *And there was evening, and there was morning —the first day.*
>
> [Genesis 1:1-5]

Whereas Plato detected a tripartite soul in the individual and the state and then tentatively suggested a world soul based on the same model, in his *Legum Allegoriae*, Philo starts at the other extreme and uses these first five verses of the Old Testament to describe the world soul and implicitly sees this working through everyday life:

> *And, speaking symbolically, he calls the mind heaven, since the natures which can only be comprehended by the intellect are in heaven. And sensation he calls earth, because it is sensation which has obtained a corporeal and somewhat earthy constitution. The ornaments of the mind are all the incorporeal things, which are perceptible only by the intellect. Those of sensation are the corporeal.*

Here we have the first division of heaven and earth and (allegorically) mind and body.

There is a suggestion here of a subtle difference between Plato and Philo. Whereas Plato had incorporated the *"appetitive"* part of our nature into the psyche or mind, Philo classifies this as sensation and associates it with the body. He further goes on to draw analogies to divine spirit (air) and divine reason (light):

> *And air and light he considered worthy of the pre-eminence. For the one he called the breath of God, because it is air, which is the most life-giving of things, and of life the causer is God; and the other he called light, because it is surpassingly beautiful: for that which is perceptible only by intellect is as far more brilliant and splendid than that which is seen, as I conceive, the sun is than darkness, or day than night, or the intellect than any other of the outward senses by which men judge (inasmuch as it is the guide of the entire soul), or the eyes than any other part of the body.*

Using Plato's understanding of *"forms"*, he expands on the interpretation of *"air"* as divine spirit and contrasts it to the abyss of empty space that is life without spirit:

PART II

> *In the first place therefore, from the model of the world, perceptible only by intellect, the Creator made an incorporeal heaven, and an invisible earth, and the form of air and of empty space: the former of which he called darkness, because the air is black by nature; and the other he called the abyss, for empty space is very deep and yawning with immense width. Then he created the incorporeal substance of water and of air...*

He further expands on his interpretation of *"light"* as divine reason:

> *And the invisible divine reason, perceptible only by intellect, he calls the image of God. And the image of this image is that light, perceptible only by the intellect, which is the image of the divine reason, which has explained its generation.*

Here we see Philo referring to the third part of that divine trinity; that for whom the divine reason is an image – this is God himself. However, the three parts of the divine trinity themselves make up God and the dynamics between the three parts make this a dynamic and creative force.

The creation narrative for the seventh day states:

> *Thus the heavens and the earth were completed in all their vast array.*
> *By the seventh day God had finished the work he had been doing; so on the seventh day he rested from all his work.*

> [Genesis 2:1-2]

Philo comments on this verse, seeing creation as an ongoing process and God as the creative force:

> *First, therefore, having desisted from the creation of mortal creatures on the seventh day, he began the formation of other and more divine beings.*
> *For God never ceases from making something or other; but, as it is the property of fire to burn, and of snow to chill, so also it is the property of God to be creating. And much more so, in proportion as he himself is to all other beings the author of their working.*
> *Therefore the expression, "he caused to rest," is very appropriately employed here, not "he rested." For he makes things to rest which appear to be producing others, but which in reality do not effect anything; but he himself never ceases from creating.*
> *On which account Moses says, "He caused to rest the things which he had begun."*

He sees life as being ever-changing:

> *For all the things that are made by our arts when completed stand still and remain; but all those which are accomplished by the knowledge of God are moved at subsequent times. For their ends are the beginnings of other things; as, for instance, the end of day is the beginning of night. And in the same way we must look upon months and years when they come to an end as the beginning of those which are just about to follow them. And so the generation of other things which are destroyed, and the destruction of others which are generated is completed, so that that is true which is said that--*
> *And naught that is created wholly dies;*

> *But one thing parted and combined with others produces a fresh form.*

Those things that are *"accomplished by the knowledge of God"*, surely refer to family and community and society including those empires that are formed and destroyed. And the phrase *"For their ends are the beginnings of other things; as, for instance, the end of day is the beginning of night."*, surely resonated with those who awaited the end times whether it be the end times of Judaism and the formation of a new faith or the end times of the Roman Empire and the formation of a new society.

If this theology sounds familiar to us, then we are not the only ones. Based on these and the other surprisingly numerous written works of Philo still available, the 19th Century German philosopher and theologian, Bruno Bauer identified Philo as being the father of Christianity. While it is true that Philo provided much of the theoretical framework, there were others whose actions provided the catalyst.

Women

Women have a significant role in Mark's gospel and most are portrayed in a positive light. The Syro-phoenician woman, whose daughter was possessed by an unclean spirit, treats Jesus with the utmost respect:

> *The woman was a Greek, born in Syrian Phoenicia. She begged Jesus to drive the demon out of her daughter.*
>
> [Mark 7:26]

Jesus initially refuses her request:

> *"First let the children eat all they want," he told her, "for it is not right to take the children's bread and toss it to the dogs."*

[Mark 7:27]

Her response is to take Jesus' own metaphor and use it to argue her case:

> *"Lord," she replied, "even the dogs under the table eat the children's crumbs."*

[Mark 7:28]

Jesus struck by her reply, cures her daughter:

> *Then he told her, "For such a reply, you may go; the demon has left your daughter."*

[Mark 7:29]

So much of the meaning within the gospel is to be found in the interaction between characters. The women's daughter, surely, represents any child that is intent on pushing boundaries and the women's respectful but spirited dialogue with Jesus demonstrates how we should speak to those who push boundaries.

Later in the gospel, Jesus is in the temple watching people put money into the temple treasury:

> *Jesus sat down opposite the place where the offerings were put and watched the crowd putting their money into the temple treasury. Many rich people threw in large amounts. But a poor widow came and put in two very small copper coins, worth only a few cents.*
> *Calling his disciples to him, Jesus said, "Truly I tell you, this poor widow has put more into the treasury than all the*

PART II

others."

[Mark 12:41-43]

Here, Jesus contrasts the commitment of the widow[1] who gave two small coins with the commitment of the rich people who gave a fraction of what they could afford.

Ever since its creation the institutionalized church has held an ambivalent attitude toward women. Although comprising the vast majority of the laity, the Catholic Church does not permit women to become deacons or priests.

Instead women are invited to follow the role model of *Mary*, Christ's mother. Described in Luke's gospel as the *"handmaid of the Lord"*, *Mary* is popularly portrayed as meek, mild, chaste and subservient. This is not and never has been an attractive role model for all women.

Perhaps the last great intellectual who worked in the library of Alexandria was a woman named Hypatia. She was a mathematician, astronomer, physicist, head of the Neoplatonic School of philosophy and much admired teacher. In 415 CE she became a victim of an ongoing feud between Orestes, the governor of Alexandria, and Cyril, the patriarch of the Alexandrian church:

> *THERE WAS a woman at Alexandria named Hypatia, daughter of the philosopher Theon, who made such attainments in literature and science, as to far surpass all the philosophers of her own time. Having succeeded to the school of Plato and Plotinus, she explained the principles of philosophy to her auditors, many of*

---

[1] "And she is a widow; not meaning by that, as we generally use the word, a woman when she is bereft of her husband, but that she is so, from being free from those passions which corrupt and destroy the soul" [Philo: On the Unchangeableness of God XXIX (137)]

whom came from a distance to receive her instructions. On account of the self-possession and ease of manner, which she had acquired in consequence of the cultivation of her mind, she not unfrequently appeared in public in presence of the magistrates. Neither did she feel abashed in going to an assembly of men. For all men on account of her extraordinary dignity and virtue admired her the more. Yet even she fell victim to the political jealousy which at that time prevailed. For as she had frequent interviews with Orestes, it was calumniously reported among the Christian populace, that it was she who prevented Orestes from being reconciled to the bishop. Some of them, therefore, hurried away by a fierce and bigoted zeal, whose ringleader was a reader named Peter, waylaid her returning home, and dragging her from her carriage, they took her to the church called Caesareum, where they completely stripped her, and then murdered her with tiles[2]. After tearing her body in pieces, they took her mangled limbs to a place called Cinaron, and there burnt them. This affair brought not the least opprobrium, not only upon Cyril, but also upon the whole Alexandrian church. And surely nothing can be farther from the

---

[2] The Greek word is ostrakois, literally "oystershells," but the word was also applied to brick tiles used on the roofs of houses.

> *spirit of Christianity than the allowance of massacres, fights, and transactions of that sort. This happened in the month of March during Lent, in the fourth year of Cyril's episcopate, under the tenth consulate of Honorius, and the sixth of Theodosius.*

Although it was his supporters who were responsible, this atrocity did not impact on Cyril's career. He became a major player in a bizarre theological argument over the proper title for *Mary* that led to the first schism within the institutionalized church. Nestorius, the patriarch of Constantinople, objected to *Mary* being referred to as "*Mother of God*" or "*Theotokos*", arguing that when Christ was born, he had a human not a divine nature so the title "*Mother of Christ*" was more appropriate. Cyril, disagreed:

> *That anyone could doubt the right of the holy Virgin to be called the Mother of God fills me with astonishment. Surely she must be the Mother of God if our Lord Jesus Christ is God, and she gave birth to him! Our Lord's disciples may not have used those exact words, but they delivered to us the belief those words enshrine, and this has also been taught us by the holy fathers.*
>
> *In the third book of his work on the holy and consubstantial Trinity, our father Athanasius, of glorious memory, several times refers to the holy Virgin as "Mother of God." I cannot resist quoting his own words: "As I have often told you, the distinctive mark of holy Scripture is that it was written to make a twofold declaration concerning our Savior; namely, that he is and has always been God, and that for our sake in these latter days he took flesh from the Virgin Mary, Mother of God, and became man."*
>
> [Cyril of Alexandria, Divine Motherhood of Mary]

At the first Council of Ephesus in 431 CE, one hundred and six years after the Council of Nicaea, the matter was debated by the assembled bishops. Cyril won. The teachings of Nestorius were declared a heresy and Nestorius himself was ordered to recant or face excommunication. He refused. The churches supportive of Nestorius were severed from Western Christendom. Nestorius retired to a monastery. Hypatia was largely forgotten. Cyril was made a saint.

Surprisingly, throughout the gospel of Mark, *"Mary"* is one of only three women's names mentioned, the others being *Herodias*, a verifiable historical figure and *Salome*.

The name *"Mary"*[3] is derived from *"Miriam"* which in rabbinic literature is explained as meaning merum (bitterness).

Justification for this interpretation is to be found in the Old Testament.

In Genesis, Miriam is the sister of Aaron and Moses and she and Aaron speak out against Moses because of the assertion of his authority in taking a second wife:

> *Miriam and Aaron began to talk against Moses because of his Cushite wife, for he had married a Cushite. "Has the Lord spoken only through Moses?" they asked. "Hasn't he also spoken through us?" And the Lord heard this.*
>
> [Numbers 12: 1-2]

After speaking out against Moses, Miriam and Aaron were confronted by the LORD:

---

[3] Pay attention to the meaning of names

PART II

> *(Now Moses was a very humble man, more humble than anyone else on the face of the earth.)*
>
> *At once the Lord said to Moses, Aaron and Miriam, "Come out to the tent of meeting, all three of you." So the three of them went out. Then the Lord came down in a pillar of cloud; he stood at the entrance to the tent and summoned Aaron and Miriam. When the two of them stepped forward, he said, "Listen to my words:*
>
> *"When there is a prophet among you, I, the Lord, reveal myself to them in visions, I speak to them in dreams. But this is not true of my servant Moses; he is faithful in all my house. With him I speak face to face, clearly and not in riddles; he sees the form of the Lord. Why then were you not afraid to speak against my servant Moses?"*
>
> [Numbers 12: 3-8]

Despite both Miriam and Aaron speaking out against Moses, it is only Miriam who is punished:

> *The anger of the Lord burned against them, and he left them.*
>
> *When the cloud lifted from above the tent, Miriam's skin was leprous—it became as white as snow. Aaron turned toward her and saw that she had a defiling skin disease, and he said to Moses, "Please, my lord, I ask you not to hold against us the sin we have so foolishly committed. Do not let her be like a stillborn infant coming from its mother's womb with its flesh half eaten away."*
>
> *So Moses cried out to the Lord, "Please, God, heal her!"*
>
> *The Lord replied to Moses, "If her father had spit in her*

> *face, would she not have been in disgrace for seven days? Confine her outside the camp for seven days; after that she can be brought back." So Miriam was confined outside the camp for seven days, and the people did not move on till she was brought back.*
> *After that, the people left Hazeroth and encamped in the Desert of Paran.*
>
> [Numbers 12: 9-16]

In the gospel, as we can see later, physical afflictions are used as metaphors for *"spiritual"* ailments and the type of affliction gives some indication of the type of ailment. Leprosy is a skin disease that visibly corrodes the body. Bitterness and the associated resentment is a spiritual ailment that visibly corrodes the social body – the community. It is interesting to note, in this passage, that Miriam was not rejected. Indeed the community did not move on until she was reconciled with them.

Whereas the meaning of Mary is *"bitterness"*, the meaning of Salome is the opposite for Salome, from Shalom, means *"peace"*.

Numbers

Both Greeks and Jews saw symbolism and beauty in numbers. Indeed the fervent attachment to numbers of Pythagoras and his followers boarded on the religious. For the ancient Greeks, there was no sharp divide between religion and science that there is in current day Western society. Indeed, in many cases mathematics is used a rhetorical tool in philosophical and religious arguments. One example is in the *Legum Allegoriae* (Of the laws allegorical), where in several extraordinary passages, Philo gives praise to the number seven:

> *The number seven displays also another beauty which it possesses, and one which is most sacred to think of. For as it*

PART II

consists of three and four, it displays in existing things a line which is free from all deviation and upright by nature. And in what way it does so I must show. The rectangular triangle, which is the beginning of all qualities, consists of the Numbers three and four, and five {In Pythagoras' theorem; a right handed triangle where the sides at the right angle have a length of 3 and 4, the hypotenuse will be of length 5}; and the three and the four, which are the essence of the seven, contain the right angle; for the obtuse angle and the acute angle show irregularity, and disorder, and inequality; for one may be more acute or more obtuse than another. But a right angle does not admit of comparison, nor is one right angle more a right angle than another: but one remains similar to another, never changing its peculiar nature. But if the right-angled triangle is the beginning of all figures and of all qualities, and if the essence of the number seven, that is to say, the numbers three and four together, supply the most necessary part of this, namely, the right angle, then seven may be rightly thought to be the fountain of every figure and of every quality. And besides what has been already advanced, this also may be asserted that three is the number of a plane figure, since a point has been laid down to be, according to a unit, and a line according to the number two, and a plane superficies according to the number three. Also, four is the number of a cube, by the addition of one to the number of a plane superficies, depth being added to the superficies. From which it is plain that the essence of the number seven is the foundation of geometry and trigonometry; and in a word, of all incorporeal and corporeal substances. And it is also affirmed for the particular praise of the number seven, that it has a very admirable rank in nature, because it is composed of three and four. And if any one doubles the third number after the unit, he will find a square; and if he doubles the fourth number, he will find a cube. And if he doubles the seventh from both, he will find both a cube and a square; therefore, the third number from the unit is a square in a double ratio. And the fourth number, eight, is a cube. And the seventh number, being sixty-four, is both a cube and a square at the same time; so that the seventh number is really a perfecting one, signifying both equalities, the plane superficies by the square, according to the connection with the number three, and the solid by the cube according to its relationship to the number four; and of the numbers three and four, are composed the number seven.................................

[Philo: Legum Allegoriae]

Throughout the Old Testament there are many references to the number seven. In the Genesis creation story it was on the seventh day that God caused things to rest. In the story of Joseph, the first of Pharoah's dream was of seven fat cows and seven lean cows, the second of seven ripe ears of grain and seven that were withered and meager. In the story of Miriam and Aaron, Miriam is placed outside the camp until the seventh day. Of great significance, before the battle of Jericho, Joshua and his seven priests carrying rams horns walked around the city seven times before blowing the horns and causing the walls to collapse. This is a story about the people of Jericho coming to God.

Numbers also have significance in the gospel of Mark and there is also a connection to numbers three, four and seven.

PART II

Within the gospel, in the feeding of the four thousand gentiles, Jesus takes seven loaves. After the feeding, there are seven baskets remaining. This number indicates people coming to God.

The number twelve is the product of three and four and is used to refer to the reconciliation of those who have separated themselves from others. Most significantly, there are twelve apostles but the reference is in other places as well[4].

The woman with the hemorrhage had isolated herself before touching the hem of Jesus' garment. She had suffered with her affliction for twelve years. The words of Jesus, *"My daughter, your faith has saved you"* indicate a reconciliation.

The daughter of Jairus was twelve years old when Jairus rushed to Jesus to implore him to save his dying child. Jesus' words to Jairus *"Only have faith"*, are an instruction to show commitment to his child.

In the feeding of the five thousand, Jesus takes five loaves and two fishes; two being the number of division. After the feeding of the five thousand Jews, twelve loaves were left over – symbolic of Jews being reconciled with Greeks.

The number four is used to refer to man. The first disciples called, Simon, Andrew, James and John numbered four and they correspond to the aspects of being of man. The name *"Andrew"*, which within the gospel is the character that corresponds to the aspect of being of the body, is derived from the Greek for *"man"*.

The number three is the number of the aspects of the psyche and is of huge significance in the gospel where it is used to indicate the creation of new relationships (the temple is to be rebuilt in three

---

[4] Pay attention to numeral symbolism

days) but more powerfully it is used to illustrate the destruction of relationships.

When Peter denies Jesus three times, he does so first with ignorance, where divine reason is lacking:

> *While Peter was below in the courtyard, one of the servant girls of the high priest came by. When she saw Peter warming himself, she looked closely at him.*
> *"You also were with that Nazarene, Jesus," she said.*
> *But he denied it. "I don't know or understand what you're talking about," he said, and went out into the entryway.*
>
> [Mark 14: 66-68]

Then with indifference where faith in the divine is lacking:

> *When the servant girl saw him there, she said again to those standing around, "This fellow is one of them." Again he denied it.*
>
> [Mark 14: 69-70]

Finally with anger and remorse where divine spirit is lacking:

> *After a little while, those standing near said to Peter, "Surely you are one of them, for you are a Galilean."*
> *He began to call down curses, and he swore to them, "I don't know this man you're talking about."*
> *Immediately the rooster crowed the second time. Then Peter remembered the word Jesus had spoken to him: "Before the rooster crows twice you will disown me three times." And he broke down and wept.*
>
> [Mark 14: 70-72]

PART II

Jesus is mocked three times. In front of the chief priests where divine spirit is ridiculed:

> *Then some began to spit at him; they blindfolded him, struck him with their fists, and said, "Prophesy!" And the guards took him and beat him.*
>
> [Mark 14: 70-72]

In the Praetorium where divine authority is ridiculed:

> *The soldiers led Jesus away into the palace (that is, the Praetorium) and called together the whole company of soldiers. They put a purple robe on him, then twisted together a crown of thorns and set it on him. And they began to call out to him, "Hail, King of the Jews!" Again and again they struck him on the head with a staff and spit on him. Falling on their knees, they paid homage to him. And when they had mocked him, they took off the purple robe and put his own clothes on him. Then they led him out to crucify him.*
>
> [Mark 15: 16-20]

Finally on the cross where divine reason is ridiculed:

> *Those who passed by hurled insults at him, shaking their heads and saying, "So! You who are going to destroy the temple and build it in three days, come down from the cross and save yourself!" In the same way the chief priests and the teachers of the law mocked him among themselves. "He saved others," they said, "but he can't save himself! Let this Messiah, this king of Israel, come down now from the cross that we may see and believe." Those crucified with*

him also heaped insults on him.

[Mark 15: 29-32]

For extra emphasis, in multiples of three, Jesus was crucified on the third hour, taunted on the sixth and died on the ninth.

PART II

Healing

At that time Jesus came from Nazareth in Galilee and was baptized by John in the Jordan. Just as Jesus was coming up out of the water, he saw heaven being torn open and the Spirit descending on him like a dove. And a voice came from heaven: "You are my Son, whom I love; with you I am well pleased."

[Mark 1:9-11]

The Galilean healing miracles

Five of the six interlinked Galilean healing miracles are contained within the second section of the gospel.

These are:

- o Capernaum demoniac [1:21-28]
- o Simon's mother-in-law [1:29-31]
- o Leper [1:40-45]
- o Paralytic [2:1-12]
- o Man with withered hand [2:23-28]

The sixth interlinked miracle is the healing of the woman with a hemorrhage and is described in the section on commitment in [5:25-34].

These six miracles represent different types of unhealthy attitudes or *"fractures"* of the tripartite psyche.

The Capernaum Demoniac crying out *"Have you come to destroy us"* thinks the worst of others. He is fearful because he is not open-hearted. He represents spirit without faith in the divine.

Simon's Mother in law, suffering from stress, is unable to function. After Jesus talks to her gently and takes her by the hand, the fever leaves her. She represents spirit without divine reason.

The paralytic, paralyzed by guilt, cannot get to Jesus, *"because of the crowd"*. He represents faith without divine reason.

On the Sabbath, in contravention of Jewish law, Jesus heals the man with the withered hand - an infirmity symbolizing a small-minded intolerance of others. The watching and judgmental Pharisees represent faith without divine spirit

The woman with the hemorrhage isolated herself from others. *"She had spent all she had without being any better for it; in fact she was getting worse"*. She represents reason without divine spirit.

Of all these miracles, the healing of the leper, representing reason without faith in the divine, is of particular interest. This is the relevant passage in the 1984 version of the NIV Bible:

> *A man with leprosy came to him and begged him on his knees, "If you are willing, you can make me clean."*
> *Filled with compassion, Jesus reached out his hand and touched the man. "I am willing," he said. "Be clean!"*
> *Immediately the leprosy left him and he was cured.*
> *Jesus sent him away at once with a strong warning: "See that you don't tell this to anyone. But go, show yourself to the priest and offer the sacrifices that Moses commanded for your cleansing, as a testimony to them." Instead he went out and began to talk freely, spreading the news. As a result, Jesus could no longer enter a town openly but stayed outside in lonely places. Yet the people still came to him from everywhere.*

[Mark 1:40-45]

PART II

So much of the meaning in Mark is to be found in the interaction between characters. Although the leper *"begged him on his knees"*, his request, *"If you are willing, you can make me clean"*, seems rather aloof. There is no indication of a commitment from the leper in return. Indeed, after the healing, when Jesus instructs the leper to show himself to the priest and offer the sacrifices commanded by Moses, the leper disobeys him.

Nearly all modern Bibles state that Jesus was *"filled with compassion"* when seeing the leper. However, recent Biblical scholarship suggests that in the original wording Jesus was not filled with compassion but anger. Indeed this passage was changed in the 2011 New International Version of the Bible where Jesus is not compassionate but indignant:

> *A man with leprosy came to him and begged him on his knees, "If you are willing, you can make me clean."*
> *Jesus was indignant. He reached out his hand and touched the man. "I am willing," he said. "Be clean!" Immediately the leprosy left him and he was cleansed.*
>
> [Mark 1:40-42]

With a literal interpretation of the Bible, Jesus' attitude seems callous but with an allegorical interpretation it makes complete sense. Jesus' indignation results from the leper taking advantage of the good will of others.

Conflict

The tongue also is a fire, a world of evil among the parts of the body. It corrupts the whole body, sets the whole course of one's life on fire, and is itself set on fire by hell.

All kinds of animals, birds, reptiles and sea creatures are being tamed and have been tamed by mankind, but no human being can tame the tongue. It is a restless evil, full of deadly poison.

With the tongue we praise our Lord and Father, and with it we curse human beings, who have been made in God's likeness. Out of the same mouth come praise and cursing. My brothers and sisters, this should not be.

[James 3: 6-10]

The messianic secret

In certain passages within the gospel of Mark, Jesus explicitly forbids people from speaking and this recurring theme, known as the Markan (or Messianic secret) and debated by scholars at length, is remarkable because it is almost completely absent from the other gospels.

The motif is present throughout the Gospel but its significance is most clear in the Galilean healing miracles. Here there are four occasions where Jesus orders people to be quiet.

The Capernaum demoniac asks [1:24]:

> "What do you want with us, Jesus of Nazareth? Have you come to destroy us? I know who you are—the Holy One of God!"

PART II

Jesus gives a sharp response [1:25]:

> *"Be quiet!" said Jesus sternly. "Come out of him!"*

In chapter 1 verse 34, it states:

> *He also drove out many demons, but he would not let the demons speak because they knew who he was.*

After the healing of the leper [1:40-45], Jesus sternly ordered him:

> *"See that you don't tell this to anyone".*

After the cure of Jairus' daughter [5:43]:

> *He gave strict orders not to let anyone know about this*

On other occasions Jesus seems quite happy to publicize himself.

In the story of the healing of the paralytic that immediately follows the story of the healing of the leper, Jesus performs the healing in front of a crowd of people that fill the whole house.

The passage continues [2:10-12]:

> *But I want you to know that the Son of Man has authority on earth to forgive sins." So he said to the man, "I tell you, get up, take your mat and go home." He got up, took his mat and walked out in full view of them all. This amazed everyone and they praised God, saying, "We have never seen anything like this!"*

There's nothing secret about this miracle. There's nothing secret in the healing of the man with the withered hand, the healing of Peter's mother in law and the healing of the woman with the hemorrhage.

Why is there an insistence on secrecy in some passages, yet not in others?

Underpinning the gospel, although never made explicit, is a particular understanding that the human mind has a tripartite nature.

Throughout the gospel, whenever characters lack faith in the divine then Jesus instructs the characters to be quiet because an unrestrained tongue is the cause of conflict.

This was not something new. Included in the letter of James is a warning of the perils of the unrestrained tongue [James 3: 6-10].

The story of the Capernaum Demoniac demonstrates the emphasis of spirit at the expense of faith in the divine. The Demoniac is loud and vulnerable. It is the same scenario when Jesus cast out many devils. The story of the Leper demonstrates the emphasis of reason at the expense of faith in the divine. The leper is calculating and ungrateful.

The story of Jairus' daughter, a story of a young girl's depression, demonstrates the lack of both spirit and faith.

The author of the gospel has Christ calling us to be restrained in our language, to silence the sharp tongue and to refrain from using those verbal sticks and stones. He would have been well aware of the damage that the use of judgmental, slanderous and disparaging language could cause.

Flaccus

Flaccus was the governor of Alexandria, an intimate friend of the Emperor Tiberius and up until the time of Tiberius' death he ruled wisely.

However, he came to nurture a deep resentment toward both Tiberius' successor and the man who came to rule over the province of Judaea.

PART II

Agrippa was the son of Aristobulus and the grandson of Herod the Great. As a young man he lived a life of indolence and amassed huge debts that he had no possibility of repaying. To escape from creditors he went to Rome where he made accusations to the Emperor about his brother in law, Herod Antipas, Tetrarch of Galilee, the very same man who had John executed at Machaerus.

Tiberius rejected Agrippa's accusations but treated him courteously and allowed him to stay in Rome. While there Agrippa formed a good friendship with Gaius Caligula, the son of the general Germanicus who was himself the Emperor's nephew. In a moment of drunken indiscretion Agrippa expressed a wish that Tiberius were dead and that Gaius succeed him. It was an utterance that was conveyed to the ears of the Emperor who had Agrippa imprisoned for his impunity.

After six months, Tiberius did die and Gaius did accede to the position of Emperor. One of his first tasks was to release Agrippa and in time he granted him authority over the tetrarchy formerly ruled by Philip. When he was about to set out to take possession of his kingdom, Gaius advised him to avoid the long and difficult voyage from Brundusium to Syria and instead to take the shorter one by Alexandria, and to wait for the periodical winds.

Philo relates:

> *Accordingly, going down to Dicaearchia, and seeing some Alexandrian vessels in the harbor, looking all ready and fit to put to sea, he embarked with his followers, and had a fair voyage, and so a few days afterwards he arrived at his journey's end, unforeseen and unexpected, having commanded the captains of his vessels (for he came in sight of Pharos about twilight in the evening) to furl their sails, and to keep a short distance out of sight in the open sea, until it became late in the evening and dark, and then at night he entered the port, that when he disembarked he*

might find all the citizens buried in sleep, and so, without any one seeing him, he might arrive at the house of the man who was to be his entertainer. With so much modesty then did this man arrive, wishing if it were possible to enter without being perceived by anyone in the city.

For he had not come to see Alexandria, since he had sojourned in it before, when he was preparing to take his voyage to Rome to see Tiberius, but he desired at this time to take the quickest road, so as to arrive at his destination with the smallest possible delay. But the men of Alexandria being ready to burst with envy and ill-will (for the Egyptian disposition is by nature a most jealous and envious one and inclined to look on the good fortune of others as adversity to itself), and being at the same time filled with an ancient and what I may in a manner call an innate enmity towards the Jews, were indignant at any one's becoming a king of the Jews, no less than if each individual among them had been deprived of an ancestral kingdom of his own inheritance.

And then again his friends and companions came and stirred up the miserable Flaccus, inviting, and exciting, and stimulating him to feel the same envy with themselves; saying, "The arrival of this man to take upon him his government is equivalent to a deposition of yourself. He is invested with a greater dignity of honor and glory than you. He attracts all eyes towards himself when they see the array of sentinels and body-guards around him adorned with silvered and gilded arms. For ought he to have come into the presence of another governor, when it was in his power

PART II

to have sailed over the sea, and so to have arrived in safety at his own government? For, indeed, if Gaius did advise or rather command him to do so, he ought rather with earnest solicitations to have deprecated any visit to this country, in order that the real governor of it might not be brought into disrepute and appear to have his authority lessened by being apparently disregarded."

When he heard this he was more indignant than before, and in public indeed he pretended to be his companion and his friend, because of his fear of the man who directed his course, but secretly he bore him much ill-will, and told everyone how he hated him, and abused him behind his back, and insulted him indirectly, since he did not dare to do so openly; for he encouraged the idle and lazy mob of the city (and the mob of Alexandria is one accustomed to great license of speech, and one which delights above measure in calumny and evil-speaking), to abuse the king, either beginning to revile him in his own person, or else exhorting and exciting others to do so by the agency of persons who were accustomed to serve him in business of this kind. And they, having had the cue given them, spent all their days reviling the king in the public schools, and stringing together all sorts of gibes to turn him into ridicule. And at times they employed poets who compose farces, and managers of puppet shows, displaying their natural aptitude for every kind of disgraceful employment, though they were very slow at learning anything that was creditable, but very acute, and quick, and ready at learning anything of an opposite nature. For why did he not show his indignation, why did he not commit them to prison, why did he not chastise them for their insolent and disloyal evil speaking? And even if he had not been a king but only one of the household of Caesar, ought he not to have had some privileges and especial honors? The fact is that all these circumstances are an undeniable evidence that Flaccus was a participator in all this abuse; for he who might have punished it with the most extreme severity, and entirely checked it, and who yet took no steps to restrain it, was clearly convicted of having permitted and encouraged it; but whenever an ungoverned multitude begins a course of evil doing it never desists, but proceeds from one wickedness to another, continually doing some monstrous thing.

[Philo: Against Flaccus]

PART II

Judas

"Capital"... in the political field is analogous to "government"... The economic idea of capitalism, the politics of government or of authority, and the theological idea of the Church are three identical ideas, linked in various ways. To attack one of them is equivalent to attacking all of them . . . What capital does to labor, and the State to liberty, the Church does to the spirit. This trinity of absolutism is as baneful in practice as it is in philosophy. The most effective means for oppressing the people would be simultaneously to enslave it's body, it's will and its reason.

[Proudhon: 1809-1865]

Judas the Galilean

In his *Antiquities*, Josephus describes a character of considerable interest:

> *But of the fourth sect of Jewish philosophy, Judas the Galilean was the author. These men agree in all other things with the Pharisaic notions; but they have an inviolable attachment to liberty, and say that God is to be their only Ruler and Lord.*
> *They also do not value dying any kinds of death, nor indeed do they heed the deaths of their relations and friends, nor can any such fear make them call any man lord.*

[Josephus: Jewish Antiquities 18:1:6]

In the *Jewish War*, Josephus describes Judas as chiding the people:

> *... a certain Galilean, whose name was Judas, prevailed with his countrymen to revolt, and said they were cowards if they would endure to pay a tax to the Romans and would after God submit to mortal men as their lords.*
>
> *This man was a teacher of a peculiar sect of his own, and was not at all like the rest of those their leaders.*
>
> [Josephus: Jewish War 2:8:1]

For Josephus, Judas and his followers are a source of some bemusement. His claim, that they *"say that God is to be their only Ruler and Lord"*, suggests that they refuse to recognize not only Roman authority but any human authority. There is no indication from Josephus that Judas advocated violent action against the person and indeed, his campaign to persuade others not to pay taxes may be seen as an act of civil disobedience similar to that advocated, during a different era, by Mahatma Gandhi and Martin Luther King. However, Josephus attributes many of Judea's problems including the *"altering the customs of our fathers"* and the destruction of the temple itself to the pernicious influence of this man's teachings:

> *All sorts of misfortunes also sprang from these men, and the nation was infected with this doctrine to an incredible degree; one violent war came upon us after another, and we lost our friends which used to alleviate our pains; there were also very great robberies and murder of our principal men.*
>
> *This was done in pretense indeed for the public welfare, but in reality for the hopes of gain to themselves; whence arose seditions, and from them murders of men, which sometimes fell on those of their own people, (by the*

PART II

madness of these men towards one another, while their desire was that none of the adverse party might be left,) and sometimes on their enemies; a famine also coming upon us, reduced us to the last degree of despair, as did also the taking and demolishing of cities; nay, the sedition at last increased so high, that the very temple of God was burnt down by their enemies' fire.

Such were the consequences of this, that the customs of our fathers were altered, and such a change was made, as added a mighty weight toward bringing all to destruction, which these men occasioned by their thus conspiring together; for Judas and Sadduc, who excited a fourth philosophic sect among us, and had a great many followers therein, filled our civil government with tumults at present, and laid the foundations of our future miseries, by this system of philosophy, which we were before unacquainted withal, concerning which I will discourse a little, and this the rather because the infection which spread thence among the younger sort, who were zealous for it, brought the public to destruction.

[Josephus: Antiquities 18:1:1]

In the *Antiquities*, Josephus also states:

And it was in Gessius Florus's time that the nation began to grow mad with this distemper, who was our procurator, and who occasioned the Jews to go wild with it by the abuse of his authority, and to make them revolt from the Romans.

[Josephus: Antiquities 18:1.6]

This is a character who has a huge significance for Josephus but a minor role in scripture. He is mentioned in the Book of Acts, as Peter and the other apostles are brought before the High Priest and the Sanhedrin. The members of the Sanhedrin are furious with the apostles' disobedience:

> *But a Pharisee named Gamaliel, a teacher of the law, who was honored by all the people, stood up in the Sanhedrin and ordered that the men be put outside for a little while. Then he addressed the Sanhedrin: "Men of Israel, consider carefully what you intend to do to these men. Some time ago Theudas appeared, claiming to be somebody, and about four hundred men rallied to him. He was killed, all his followers were dispersed, and it all came to nothing. After him, Judas the Galilean appeared in the days of the census and led a band of people in revolt. He too was killed, and all his followers were scattered.*
>
> [Acts 5:34-38]

This is a passage that has intrigued many scholars for whereas Acts claims that Judas followed Theudas, Josephus makes it quite clear that Theudas came to prominence under the procurator Fadus from 44 CE - 46 CE, which is well after the time of Judas the Galilean who came to prominence during the census of 6 CE[5]. Most scholars attribute this to a mistake on the part of the author but is there not the possibility that by this chronological reversal, the author is purposefully drawing our attention to this passage and stating something significant about Judas? Acts states that the teachings of Theudas came to nothing but it does not say the same

---

[5] Pay attention to a chronological reversal

for the teachings of Judas. It is worth speculating on the nature of that *"fourth philosophy"* that particularly attracted *"the younger sort"*, that involved an inviolable attachment to liberty, that was hugely popular but particularly thrived when there was abuse of authority.

Society and spirit without faith in the divine

Eighteenth century Britain saw enormous social changes. First the passing of the enclosure acts allowed landowners to fence off common land previously used by the peasant class as grazing for their animals. Secondly, the rise of industrialization attracted the poorest to urban areas to work in factories or mines.

Mine and factory owners became extremely wealthy but during the nineteenth century, there was none wealthier than the 3rd Marquess of Bute whose father had paid for the building of the docks in Cardiff from which the steam coal extracted from underground seams in the South Wales valleys was exported. The 3rd Marquess of Bute was believed to be the richest man in the world.

The class of people who worked in the factories and mines did not see much of these riches. The work was hard and pay was pitiful. Men, women and children all worked and before 1842, there were no limits for the age of child labor. Children as young as six years old were employed.

There were many people who, reflecting on the economic prosperity of the owners and the poverty and hard labor endured by their workers, saw not just a colossal disparity in wealth; they also saw a colossal injustice. The situation of the proletariat was akin to slavery.

These social inequalities were not just peculiar to Britain. The same phenomenon was common across all industrializing countries. It was these social conditions that motivated the German activist and philosopher Karl Mark and gave birth to the *Communist Manifesto* of 1848 with its ringing call to revolution:

The Communists disdain to conceal their views and aims. They openly declare that their ends can be attained only by the forcible overthrow of all existing social conditions.

Let the ruling classes tremble at a communist revolution.

The proletarians have nothing to lose but their chains.

They have a world to win.

Working Men of All Countries, Unite!

[Marx & Engels: Communist Manifesto (1848)]

Marx was not the first to speak out about the appalling economic injustices in society. Some years previously, the French parliamentarian Pierre-Joseph Proudhon outlined his vision of a peaceful, anarchistic society of self-governing individuals. In his book, *What Is Property? Or, An Inquiry into the Principle of Right and of Government*, published in 1840, he famously declared that *"Property is theft"*.

By property he did not mean simple possessions, but the property from which the owner gains income without expending any effort.

Proudhon was the first to refer to himself as an anarchist and he defined anarchy as *"the absence of a master, of a sovereign"*. In The General idea of the Revolution (1851) he urged a *"society without authority"* and gave an eloquent critique of government:

To be GOVERNED is to be watched, inspected, spied upon, directed, law-driven, numbered, regulated, enrolled, indoctrinated, preached at, controlled, checked, estimated, valued, censured, commanded, by creatures who have neither the right nor the wisdom nor the virtue to do so. To be GOVERNED is to be at every operation, at every transaction noted, registered, counted, taxed, stamped, measured, numbered, assessed, licensed, authorized, admonished, prevented, forbidden, reformed, corrected,

PART II

> *punished. It is, under pretext of public utility, and in the name of the general interest, to be place[d] under contribution, drilled, fleeced, exploited, monopolized, extorted from, squeezed, hoaxed, robbed; then, at the slightest resistance, the first word of complaint, to be repressed, fined, vilified, harassed, hunted down, abused, clubbed, disarmed, bound, choked, imprisoned, judged, condemned, shot, deported, sacrificed, sold, betrayed; and to crown all, mocked, ridiculed, derided, outraged, dishonored.*
>
> *That is government; that is its justice; that is its morality.*
>
> [Proudhon: "What Is Government?" General Idea of the Revolution in the Nineteenth Century, translated by John Beverly Robinson]

Proudhon was also scathing in his comments on man-made laws:

> *Laws: We know what they are, and what they are worth! They are spider webs for the rich and mighty, steel chains for the poor and weak, fishing nets in the hands of the government.*

Dismissed by Marx as an idealist, Proudhon was neither a capitalist nor a communist. Instead he advocated mutualism, a school of thought that when labor or its product is sold, in exchange, it ought to receive goods or services embodying *"the amount of labor necessary to produce an article of exactly similar and equal utility"*.

Proudhon and Marx were just two intellectuals of the time who envisioned a different and better society. They were just two of many who articulated a widespread disaffection for the social order best described by the German word *"zeitgeist"* which means *"spirit of the times"*.

This zeitgeist was most visibly expressed in 1848 when a wave of popular rebellion swept across continental Europe. There was rebellion in France, Italy, Germany, Denmark, Austria, Hungary, Poland, Belgium, Switzerland and Wallachia. The demands of the rebels varied from country to country, but the zeitgeist was fuelled by the possibilities of change.

National governments were being reshaped either by revolution, as in France where the ruling elite where violently overthrown or by reform as in Britain where the vote was gradually extended to more and more of the populace. The life of the working class was transformed by the industrial revolution. Also, the popular press extended political awareness, and new values and new ideas such as those promoted by Proudhon and Marx became known. In addition, due to crop failure and economic downturn, particularly in the year 1846, there was starvation among peasants and the working urban poor.

These rebellions led to tens of thousands of people being tortured and killed, and in France led to the establishment of the Second Republic. Otherwise it came to nothing. Proudhon expressed his despair:

> *. . We have been beaten and humiliated . . . scattered, imprisoned, disarmed and gagged. The fate of European democracy has slipped from our hands.*
>
> [Pierre Joseph Proudhon: quoted in The Age of Revolution and Reaction, 1789 – 1850 by Charles Breunig (1977)]

The fourth philosophy

Within the whole of Josephus' writings there is no record of the account of the death of Judas the Galilean. This is an astonishing omission from an author who is usually so fastidious in his recording of the deaths of historical figures and is particularly significant given the importance that Josephus attributes to him.

Judas called the people to refuse to comply with the *"Census of Quirinius"* that was taken for tax purposes between 6-7 CE. There is no indication from Josephus that Judas advocated violent action against the person and indeed, his campaign to persuade others not to pay taxes may be seen as an act of civil disobedience.

It seems entirely plausible that Judas the Galilean, the one who advocated non-violent civil disobedience to Roman authority was crucified. From the Roman perspective there was reason enough to crucify him.

There are similarities between Judas and the Jesus of the gospel. Both are associated with Galilee. Both had a dedicated band of followers. One was born during the time of the census. The other's message became known during the time of the census. The teachings of both, according to Josephus, was received with *"pleasure"* by the people, although the latter reference to Jesus, indeed the sole reference in the existing Greek version of Josephus' works, is considered a Christian interpolation by many scholars:

Judas:

> *so men received what they said with pleasure*
>
> [Josephus: Antiquities 18:1:1]

Jesus:

> *Now there was about this time Jesus, a wise man, if it be lawful to call him a man; for he was a doer of wonderful works, a teacher of such men as receive the truth with pleasure.*
>
> [Josephus: Antiquities 18:3:3]

Both Judas and Jesus emphasized that people's actions should be guided by what people knew to be right. In the gospel, however, we can see a significant difference between them regarding the issue that animated Judas:

> *Later they sent some of the Pharisees and Herodians to Jesus*

to catch him in his words. They came to him and said, "Teacher, we know that you are a man of integrity. You aren't swayed by others, because you pay no attention to who they are; but you teach the way of God in accordance with the truth. Is it right to pay the imperial tax to Caesar or not? Should we pay or shouldn't we?"

But Jesus knew their hypocrisy. "Why are you trying to trap me?" he asked. "Bring me a denarius and let me look at it." They brought the coin, and he asked them, "Whose image is this? And whose inscription?"

"Caesar's," they replied.

Then Jesus said to them, "Give back to Caesar what is Caesar's and to God what is God's."

And they were amazed at him.

[Mark 12:13–17]

The gospel is a work of Realpolitik. Political authority was inevitable; so too the taxes that went with it. Any movement that chose to challenge that reality would be crushed. Judas, however, was an idealist. He was uncompromising. His message was a source of inspiration to many although the interpretation put on his message was not always one with which he would have agreed.

Judas Iscariot

Although Proudhon did not advocate violent activity against the person, there were many who followed him who called themselves anarchists but did not share this commitment. Toward the end of the nineteenth and the beginning of the twentieth centuries there was a tide of violent anarchist activity across Europe and the United States that targeted people of influence. These were actions of individuals who had lost all faith in the social order and for whom violent action was justifiable.

PART II

Judas encouraged people to reject external authority. However, there was a fine line between rejecting external authority and punishing those Jews who had that authority. There were some who were prepared to cross that line:

> *When the country was purged of these, there sprang up another sort of robbers in Jerusalem, which were called Sicarii, who slew men in the day time, and in the midst of the city; this they did chiefly at the festivals, when they mingled themselves among the multitude, and concealed daggers under their garments, with which they stabbed those that were their enemies; and when any fell down dead, the murderers became a part of those that had indignation against them; by which means they appeared persons of such reputation, that they could by no means be discovered. The first man who was slain by them was Jonathan the high priest, after whose death many were slain every day, while the fear men were in of being so served was more afflicting than the calamity itself; and while everybody expected death every hour, as men do in war, so men were obliged to look before them, and to take notice of their enemies at a great distance; nor, if their friends were coming to them, durst they trust them any longer; but, in the midst of their suspicions and guarding of themselves, they were slain. Such was the celerity of the plotters against them, and so cunning was their contrivance.*
>
> [Josephus: Jewish War 2:13:3]

The curse of the Sicarii did not just infect Jerusalem:

> *AND now did the madness of the Sicarii, like a disease,*

reach as far as the cities of Cyrene; for one Jonathan, a vile person, and by trade a weaver, came thither and prevailed with no small number of the poorer sort to give ear to him; he also led them into the desert, upon promising them that he would show them signs and apparitions. And as for the other Jews of Cyrene, he concealed his knavery from them, and put tricks upon them; but those of the greatest dignity among them informed Catullus, the governor of the Libyan Pentapolis, of his march into the desert, and of the preparations he had made for it. So he sent out after him both horsemen and footmen, and easily overcame them, because they were unarmed men; of these many were slain in the fight, but some were taken alive, and brought to Catullus. As for Jonathan, the head of this plot, he fled away at that time; but upon a great and very diligent search, which was made all the country over for him, he was at last taken. And when he was brought to Catullus, he devised a way whereby he both escaped punishment himself, and afforded an occasion to Catullus of doing much mischief; for he falsely accused the richest men among the Jews, and said that they had put him upon what he did.

Now Catullus easily admitted of these his calumnies, and aggravated matters greatly, and made tragical exclamations, that he might also be supposed to have had a hand in the finishing of the Jewish war. But what was still harder, he did not only give a too easy belief to his stories, but he taught the Sicarii to accuse men falsely. He bid this Jonathan, therefore, to name one Alexander, a Jew (with whom he had formerly had a quarrel, and openly professed

PART II

that he hated him); he also got him to name his wife Bernice, as concerned with him. These two Catullus ordered to be slain in the first place; nay, after them he caused all the rich and wealthy Jews to be slain, being no fewer in all than three thousand. This he thought he might do safely, because he confiscated their effects, and added them to Caesar's revenues.

[Josephus: Jewish War 7:11:2]

The assassination by the Sicarii of those Jews who held positions of authority was anathema to most Jewish people. It was contrary to the Law of Moses. It was a betrayal of people's trust and a betrayal of Judas' message. Many scholars regard the name "*Iscariot*" as meaning "*of the Sicarii*". In the gospel, of course, it was Judas Iscariot who betrayed Jesus.

For very many people, the term "*anarchy*" is synonymous with disorder but this was neither the case for Proudhon or Judas. The problem with the anarchic philosophy that they promoted, however, is that it requires a highly optimistic view of human nature. For if people lose faith in external authority, if they abandon the laws, discard the rules, jettison the regulations, bin the conventions and rid themselves of any commitment to the social order, what is left in its place to tell them what is right and what is wrong? To whom do they turn should they feel that their rights have been infringed and what prevents them from reacting to the slightest provocation?

James

But it has also happened that Jacob had his name changed to Israel; and this, too, was a felicitous alteration. Why so? Because the name Jacob means "a supplanter," but the name Israel signifies "the man who sees God." Now it is the employment of a supplanter, who practices virtue, to move, and disturb, and upset the foundations of passion on which it is established, and whatever there is of any strength which is founded on them. But these things are not brought about without a struggle or without severe labor; but only when any one, having gone through all the labors of prudence, then proceeds to practice himself in the exercises of the soul and to wrestle against the reasonings which are hostile to it, and which seek to torment it; but it is the part of him who sees God not to depart from the sacred contest without the crown of victory, but rather to carry off the prize of triumph. And what more flourishing and more suitable crown could be woven for the victorious soul than one by which it will be able acutely and clearly to behold the living God?

[Philo: On the Change of Names]

The decline of an ideology

Acts is a book whose authorship has traditionally been ascribed to Luke, the author of the third canonical gospel but whoever wrote the work used the same name and number symbolism that is used

PART II

in the gospel of Mark.

It is a book about the early church community. What is perhaps not often recognized is that it is a book about an evolving church that was born at Pentecost with the descent of the Holy Spirit. The nature of the first community was admirably democratic and equitable. Matthias was nominated and then chosen by lot to replace Judas in the twelve [1:23-26] and seven were elected to be responsible for distributing food to the poor [6:1-7]. The members of the community held all possessions in common:

> *All the believers were one in heart and mind. No one claimed that any of their possessions was their own, but they shared everything they had......*
> *there were no needy persons among them. For from time to time those who owned land or houses sold them, brought the money from the sales and put it at the apostles' feet, and it was distributed to anyone who had need.*
>
> [Acts 4:32 & 34-35]

In the early part of Acts, (Simon) Peter as the personification of that spirit of the early church community has a significant role.

It is Peter who preached to the assembled crowd of *"Jews and proselytes alike"* about Jesus Christ after they heard the apostles "speaking in their own language".

It is Peter together with John, the personification of reason, who in an act of empowerment cures the lame beggar with the words:

> *"Silver or gold I do not have, but what I do have I give you. In the name of Jesus Christ of Nazareth, walk."*
>
> [Acts 3:6]

Before the Sanhedrin, in the only place where John makes a contribution in speaking with Peter, they profess that they cannot stop their actions and they call for the response of the Sanhedrin to be based on reasoned judgment:

> *Then they called them in again and commanded them not to speak or teach at all in the name of Jesus. But Peter and John replied, "Which is right in God's eyes: to listen to you, or to him? You be the judges! As for us, we cannot help speaking about what we have seen and heard."*
>
> [Acts 4:18-20]

James, however, the personification of faith, is listed with the other disciples at the start of the book and not mentioned again until chapter 12. The verse in which he is mentioned is preceded by a passage on the famine in Judaea:

> *During this time some prophets came down from Jerusalem to Antioch. One of them, named Agabus, stood up and through the Spirit predicted that a severe famine would spread over the entire Roman world. (This happened during the reign of Claudius.)*
>
> [Acts 11:27-28]

The name Agabus means locust, and is purposefully reminiscent of the story within Exodus of the plague of locusts inflicted on the Egyptian people that laid waste to all their crops.

The poorest would have been those most affected by the famine. If people could only get food from the authorities then it would be to the authorities that they would submit. The passage mentioning James follows directly after:

> *It was about this time that King Herod arrested some who belonged to the church, intending to persecute them. He had James, the brother of John, put to death with the*

PART II

sword. When he saw that this met with approval among the Jews, he proceeded to seize Peter also.

[Acts 12:1-3]

In the gospel story the names James and (Simon) Peter represent faith and spirit respectively and the references to James and Peter in the above passage are unlikely to be a coincidence. What died during that famine was commitment to the cause. What was imprisoned was enthusiasm for it.

If this seems a fanciful theory then consider the equivalent reference in Josephus.

In the only reference to two of the sons of Judas the Galilean, Josephus records their deaths at the time of the famine when they were arrested and crucified on the orders of Tiberius Julius Alexander, the same Tiberius who was later to become governor of Alexandria:

Then came Tiberius Alexander as successor to Fadus; he was the son of Alexander the alabarch of Alexandria, which Alexander was a principal person among all his contemporaries, both for his family and wealth: he was also more eminent for his piety than this his son Alexander, for he did not continue in the religion of his country. Under these procurators that great famine happened in Judea, in which queen Helena bought corn in Egypt at a great expense, and distributed it to those that were in want, as I have related already. And besides this, the sons of Judas of Galilee were now slain; I mean of that Judas who caused the people to revolt, when Cyrenius came to take an account of the estates of the Jews, as we have showed in a foregoing book. The names of those sons were James and Simon, whom Alexander commanded to be crucified.

[Josephus: Antiquities 20:5:2]

Although Josephus gives us, by and large, historical accounts of the events of the 1st Century, he must certainly have relied on other material in the compilation of his works.

Tiberius may well have crucified people in the movement but in the whole of his works there is no other biographical detail on these James and Simon characters mentioned by Josephus. Their names, however, seemingly added as an afterthought, are laden with symbolism. Whereas Acts has James killed and (Simon) Peter imprisoned at the time of the famine, Josephus has both James and Simon killed.

If this is still seems far-fetched, then consider how else one makes sense of an otherwise baffling passage in Acts on Peter's imprisonment immediately following James' beheading:

> *The night before Herod was to bring him to trial, Peter was sleeping between two soldiers, bound with two chains, and sentries stood guard at the entrance. Suddenly an angel of the Lord appeared[6] and a light shone in the cell. He struck Peter on the side and woke him up. "Quick, get up!" he said, and the chains fell off Peter's wrists.*

---

[6] "If, therefore, you consider that souls, and demons, and angels are things differing indeed in name, but not identical in reality, you will then be able to discard that most heavy burden, superstition. But as men in general speak of good and evil demons, and in like manner of good and evil souls, so also do they speak of angels, looking upon some as worthy of a good appellation, and calling them ambassadors of man to God, and of God to man, and sacred and holy on account of this blameless and most excellent office" [Philo: On the Giants IV (16)]

PART II

Then the angel said to him, "Put on your clothes and sandals." And Peter did so. "Wrap your cloak around you and follow me," the angel told him. Peter followed him out of the prison, but he had no idea that what the angel was doing was really happening; he thought he was seeing a vision. They passed the first and second guards and came to the iron gate leading to the city. It opened for them by itself, and they went through it. When they had walked the length of one street, suddenly the angel left him.

Then Peter came to himself and said, "Now I know without a doubt that the Lord has sent his angel and rescued me from Herod's clutches and from everything the Jewish people were hoping would happen."

[Acts 12:6-11]

There are two soldiers in this passage, double chains and two guard posts. Two is the number of division and indicative of a society polarized between Romans and bandits, Herodians and Pharisees, faith and spirit, restraint and freedom. Until the angel of the Lord appeared, Peter was sleeping, a term that is used in Mark's gospel to indicate lack of awareness. When the angel appeared, Peter became aware of a third way. The passage continues:

When this had dawned on him, he went to the house of Mary the mother of John, also called Mark, where many people had gathered and were praying. Peter knocked at the outer entrance, and a servant named Rhoda came to answer the door. When she recognized Peter's voice, she was so overjoyed she ran back without opening it and exclaimed, "Peter is at the door!"

"You're out of your mind," they told her. When she kept insisting that it was so, they said, "It must be his angel."

> *But Peter kept on knocking, and when they opened the door and saw him, they were astonished. Peter motioned with his hand for them to be quiet and described how the Lord had brought him out of prison. "Tell James and the other brothers and sisters about this," he said, and then he left for another place.*
>
> [Acts 12:12-17]

In this passage, shortly after the death of one James, we have Peter asking the servant girl Rhoda to inform another James of Peter's release. This is a James that has not been previously introduced. This is a James we know nothing of. This other James represents a new faith, replacing the faith of old. It is tempting to suggest that in this passage *"John Mark"* is a reference to the author of the earliest canonical gospel and the servant girl Rhoda (one who came from Rhodes) is a *"signature"* reference for the author of Acts.

James

The central message in the letter of James is the call for restraint. The value of patience in the face of trials is emphasized at the start of the letter. This message is re-emphasized at the end with an exhortation to be patient until the Lord's coming:

> *Brothers and sisters, as an example of patience in the face of suffering, take the prophets who spoke in the name of the Lord. As you know, we count as blessed those who have persevered. You have heard of Job's perseverance and have seen what the Lord finally brought about. The Lord is full of compassion and mercy.*
>
> [James 5:10-11]

In addition to this call for restraint, James implores the reader to perform good deeds, to resist temptation, to curb the tongue, to

PART II

have respect for others and to not judge them on the grounds of appearance or wealth.

The letter of James was written by a man of great personal authority and it seems likely that it was written by the James who was head of the church in Jerusalem.

James is a man who is clear about what is right and what is wrong and, in his letter, when he feels he needs to emphasize a point, he pulls no punches. The following passage resonates with the argument of Proudhon that any wealth gained without labor is stolen from those who labored to create it:

> *Now listen, you rich people, weep and wail because of the misery that is coming on you. Your wealth has rotted, and moths have eaten your clothes. Your gold and silver are corroded. Their corrosion will testify against you and eat your flesh like fire. You have hoarded wealth in the last days. Look! The wages you failed to pay the workers who mowed your fields are crying out against you. The cries of the harvesters have reached the ears of the Lord Almighty. You have lived on earth in luxury and self-indulgence. You have fattened yourselves in the day of slaughter. You have condemned and murdered the innocent one, who was not opposing you.*
>
> [James 5:1–6]

In addition and despite the emphasis on restraint, James gives a one line sound-bite on freedom that could come straight from the voice of Proudhon:

> *Speak and act as those who are going to be judged by the law that gives freedom*
>
> [James 2:12]

James seems to be the spiritual heir of Judas the Galilean.

The Letter of James was only gradually accepted by the Church and was probably not universally recognized until the end of the fourth century. If it was indeed written by James the head of the Jerusalem church then it is surprising that it took so long to be recognized as inspired scripture.

A reason for this may be that, astonishingly, within the whole letter there is little reference to Christ.

James introduces the letter as follows:

> *James, a servant of God and of the Lord Jesus Christ, to the twelve tribes scattered among the nations: Greetings.*
>
> [James 1:1]

At the start of chapter two, there is a second reference to Christ:

> *My brothers and sisters, believers in our glorious Lord Jesus Christ must not show favoritism.*
>
> [James 2:1]

.. and that's it! No crucifixion. No resurrection. No reference to a bodily Christ at all.

What is regarded as a reliable account of James' death is reported in Josephus' *Antiquities*. A radically different account is recorded by Eusebius who quotes from an otherwise lost passage from Hegesippus (c.110 - c.180 CE). As Josephus is thought to have written his works toward the end of the 1st Century and Hegesippus would have written his works no earlier than the middle of the 2nd Century, his account is probably less historically reliable. Nevertheless, it does prompt intriguing questions. A significant passage is given below:

> *They came, therefore, in a body to James, and said: "We*

PART II

entreat thee, restrain the people: for they are gone astray in their opinions about Jesus, as if he were the Christ. We entreat thee to persuade all who have come hither for the day of the Passover, concerning Jesus. For we all listen to thy persuasion; since we, as well as all the people, bear thee testimony that thou art just, and showest partiality to none. Do thou, therefore, persuade the people not to entertain erroneous opinions concerning Jesus: for all the people and we also, listen to thy persuasion. Take thy stand, then, upon the summit of the temple, that from that elevated spot thou may-est be clearly seen, and thy words may be plainly audible to all the people. For, in order to attend the Passover, all the tribes have congregated hither, and some of the gentiles also."

The aforesaid scribes and Pharisees accordingly set James on the summit of the temple, and cried aloud to him, and said: "O just one, whom we are all bound to obey, forasmuch as the people is in error, and follow Jesus the crucified, do thou tell us what is the door of Jesus, the crucified." And he answered with a loud voice: "Why ask ye me concerning Jesus the Son of man? He Himself sitteth in heaven, at the right hand of the Great Power, and shall come on the clouds of heaven."

The scribes and Pharisees approached James to clarify for the people the nature of Jesus. Why would they come to James? He is surely, a member of the Church as well as being a hugely respected figure.

Although invited to clarify the nature of *"Jesus the crucified"*, James instead gives his interpretation of the nature of *"Jesus, the Son of man"*. He does not make any concession at all to a Christ who was once human.

Rather than recording an historical event, Hegesippus seems to be telling us something about a divergence of opinion between James and others, particularly Paul, on something as fundamental as the nature of Jesus Christ himself.

In Paul's second letter to the Corinthians, a passage of evident bitterness seems to corroborate this:

> *But I am afraid that just as Eve was deceived by the serpent's cunning, your minds may somehow be led astray from your sincere and pure devotion to Christ. For if someone comes to you and preaches a Jesus other than the Jesus we preached, or if you receive a different spirit from the Spirit you received, or a different gospel from the one you accepted, you put up with it easily enough.*
>
> [2 Corinthians 11: 3-6]

The name James is a derivation of Jacob and refers to the story in the Book of Genesis. Jacob and Esau were twin boys of Isaac and Rebekah. Esau was born first and as such was entitled to privileges above that of his sibling. However, Jacob succeeded in first obtaining his brother's birth right as his exhausted brother swapped it for some lentil stew. Then with the connivance of his mother, Jacob succeeded in the obtaining the blessing on the first born from his blind father.

The story is reminiscent of the evolution of mankind from a nomadic hunter – gatherer lifestyle to one of agricultural settlement. Esau was a skilled hunter and *"a man of the open country"*, Jacob stayed at home *"among the tents"*. Esau was hairy – symbolic perhaps, of being primitive, Jacob was smooth. Jacob went on to father twelve sons who established the twelve tribes of Israel.

The name *"Jacob"* means *"He who supplants"*. It is clear from his letter that James, described as the *"Brother of the Lord"*, in the same way as

PART II

Jacob supplanted his brother Esau, *"supplants"* the understanding of the Christ preached by Judas the Galilean and there is no doubting James' understanding of Christ.

He was not the son of Mary born in a stable in Bethlehem. He was not the miracle worker who healed the sick and disabled. He was not the wise preacher who attracted the multitudes. He was not the radical who overturned the tables of the money changers. He was not the figurehead for a group of twelve disciples. He was not God incarnate who died on the cross at Calvary. He was not the supernatural being who rose from the dead. This Jesus Christ was something else entirely.

Jesus

The letter of James is a masterful piece of writing. The letter is addressed to the twelve tribes of the dispersion. The Old Testament scriptures recount how there were twelve tribes of Israel ten of which were located in the northern part of Israel. These were the ten lost tribes, the people having been killed during the Assyrian conquest of about 720 BCE or integrated and assimilated into the pagan culture.

The word *"Jew"* refers to a person from one of the tribes that was not conquered – the tribe of Judah. The letter is an open invitation to all – whether they belonged to the tribe of Judah or simply held some sympathy for the faith.

In his section on faith and good deeds, James does not refer to Jesus and his healing miracles or even to the parable of the Good Samaritan. Instead he makes reference to the works of two characters from Old Testament scripture to argue his case that faith without good deeds is worthless. Interestingly, these characters were neither Jewish nor Israeli. The first was Abraham, the father of all nations and the one who, as Philo explained, followed the instruction of God. Of Abraham, James wrote:

Was not our father Abraham considered righteous for what

> *he did when he offered his son Isaac on the altar? You see that his faith and his actions were working together, and his faith was made complete by what he did. And the scripture was fulfilled that says, "Abraham believed God, and it was credited to him as righteousness," and he was called God's friend.*
>
> *You see that a person is considered righteous by what they do and not by faith alone.*
>
> [James 2:21-23]

The second was Rahab, a prostitute of Jericho and scripturally a fairly insignificant figure who is mentioned in the Book of Joshua:

> *In the same way, was not even Rahab the prostitute considered righteous for what she did when she gave lodging to the spies and sent them off in a different direction?*
>
> [James 2:25]

In the Book of Joshua, Rahab, an inhabitant of Jericho at a time before the Israelites conquered the land, grants refuge to two spies sent from Joshua. When an envoy from the king arrives and requests that she surrender the men, Rahab tells the man that those who he sought had already departed. Later, using a rope, she lets the spies escape through a window.

In other Bible translations of James' letter, the men are not described as spies but as messengers. If so, what would their message be?

The significance of the story lies in the significance of Joshua. Joshua was the son of Nun of the tribe of Ephraim. Nun is an Egyptian name meaning *"God of the Ocean"*. Ephraim was Egyptian born, the grandson of a pagan priest. Joshua's original name was Hoshea meaning *"salvation"* but Moses gave him the name Joshua

PART II

meaning *"God is our salvation"*.

Joshua was Moses' apprentice and he accompanied Moses part of the way when he ascended Mount Sinai to receive the Ten Commandments [Exodus 32:17]. Eventually Moses appointed Joshua to succeed him as leader of the Israelites. [Joshua 1:1-9]

While Moses was the lawgiver to the Jewish people, Joshua was tasked with taking the law to the gentiles. This is surely significant for James who set great store on compliance with the law:

> *For whoever keeps the whole law and yet stumbles at just one point is guilty of breaking all of it. For he who said, "You shall not commit adultery," also said, "You shall not murder." If you do not commit adultery but do commit murder, you have become a lawbreaker.*
>
> [James 2:10-11]

Christ is the divine reason or logos or Word; that voice of internal authority for which James has great regard. He implores us to:

> *….. get rid of all moral filth and the evil that is so prevalent and humbly accept the word planted in you, which can save you.*
>
> [James 1:21]

However, too often that voice of internal authority is drowned out by the clamor of selfish thoughts and feelings. As James states:

> *Do not merely listen to the word, and so deceive yourselves. Do what it says. Anyone who listens to the word but does not do what it says is like someone who looks at his face in a mirror and, after looking at himself, goes away and immediately forgets what he looks like. But*

> *whoever looks intently into the perfect law that gives freedom, and continues in it—not forgetting what they have heard, but doing it—they will be blessed in what they do.*
>
> [James 1:22-25]

James balanced the logos with the lawgiver. The result was a composite figure that supplanted the Christ of the early church. Christ as the logos and Joshua as the lawgiver. The Greek name for Joshua is Jesus.

There is other external evidence that far from being a flesh and blood itinerant preacher, Jesus Christ was originally created by James as an archetype for divine reason.

In 367 CE, forty two years after the council of Nicaea, a council that he had himself attended, Athanasius, the powerful Archbishop of Alexandria, warned of the dangers of "*heretical*" works:

> *They have fabricated books which they call books of tables, in which they shew stars, to which they give the names of Saints. And therein of a truth they have inflicted on themselves a double reproach: those who have written such books, because they have perfected themselves in a lying and contemptible science; and as to the ignorant and simple, they have led them astray by evil thoughts concerning the right faith established in all truth and upright in the presence of God.....*

His letter contains the earliest recorded listing of the books that comprise the New Testament canon:

> *.....it is not tedious to speak of the [books] of the New Testament. These are, the four Gospels, according to*

PART II

> *Matthew, Mark, Luke, and John. Afterwards, the Acts of the Apostles and Epistles (called Catholic), seven, viz. of James, one; of Peter, two; of John, three; after these, one of Jude. In addition, there are fourteen Epistles of Paul, written in this order. The first, to the Romans; then two to the Corinthians; after these, to the Galatians; next, to the Ephesians; then to the Philippians; then to the Colossians; after these, two to the Thessalonians, and that to the Hebrews; and again, two to Timothy; one to Titus; and lastly, that to Philemon. And besides, the Revelation of John.*

Athanasius made it quite clear that other books were inadmissible:

> *These are fountains of salvation that they who thirst may be satisfied with the living words they contain. In these alone is proclaimed the doctrine of godliness. Let no man add to these, neither let him take ought from these. For concerning these, the Lord put to shame the Sadducees, and said, 'Ye do err, not knowing the Scriptures.' And He reproved the Jews, saying, 'Search the Scriptures, for these are they that testify of Me'.*

[From Letter XXXIX.—(For 367.) Of the particular books and their number, which are accepted by the Church. From the thirty-ninth Letter of Holy Athanasius, Bishop of Alexandria, on the Paschal festival]

The "*Gospel of Thomas* may very well have been one of the books that Athanasius had in mind when he issued his warning about those "*fabricated*" books of the "*heretics*".

This work is contained in a collection of thirteen ancient codices containing over fifty texts that were discovered near the upper Egyptian town of Nag Hammadi in 1945. The works are commonly referred to as *"gnostic gospels"*, the word *"gnostic"* being derived from *"gnosis"* or *"insight"*. These works are thought by many to have been buried shortly after Athanasius issued his letter.

The language of many of the texts is strange, alien and impenetrable. The *"Gospel of Thomas"* is one of the more accessible books and it is generally regarded as one of the earliest. Within its collection of sometimes enigmatic sayings attributed to Jesus, it makes reference to James in what may be interpreted as a message to those who fail to recognize an historical Christ:

> *The disciples said to Jesus, "We know that you will depart from us. Who is to be our leader?"*
> *Jesus said to them, "Wherever you are, you are to go to James the righteous, for whose sake heaven and earth came into being."*
>
> [The Gospel of Thomas, 12]

PART II

Joseph

The Egyptians, whom you are pleased to commend to me, I know thoroughly from a close observation, to be a light, fickle, and inconstant people, changing with every turn of fortune. The Christians among them are worshippers of Serapis, and those calling themselves bishops of Christ scruple not to act as the votaries of that God.

The truth is, there is no one, whether Ruler of a synagogue, or Samaritan, or Presbyter of the Christians, or mathematician, or astrologer, or magician, that does not do homage to Serapis. The Patriarch himself, when he comes to Egypt, is by some compelled to worship Serapis, and by others, Christ.

[Emperor Hadrian: Letter to Servianus (134 C.E.)]

Qumran

The Dead Sea is an extraordinary natural feature. It is replenished constantly by the river Jordan but has no outlet to the sea. Indeed, its surface lies approximately 1400 feet below sea level. Water only leaves the Dead Sea through evaporation. The result is a body of water with extremely high concentrations of salt. This is not an environment that is conducive to life, hence its name.

Fortresses on the bank of the Dead Sea were built or rebuilt by King Herod the Great. These included Masada to the South, where, in 70-73 CE, a small group of Jewish Zealots held out against the might of the Roman legion, and Machaerus on the Eastern shore where, according to Josephus, John the Baptist was imprisoned by Herod Antipas and died.

Also about a mile inland from the north western shore, fourteen miles south of Jericho, are ruins of the settlement of Qumran. These ruins are located in a high mountainous region that is pockmarked by numerous caves, either created naturally or through manual excavation of the soft marl stone.

It is in one of these caves in 1947 that a Bedouin shepherd made a discovery of an ancient scroll. It was the first of many. Over the following nine years, the remains of approximately 825 to 870 separate scrolls were found in eleven of literally hundreds of these caves. Written mostly in Hebrew and Aramaic but with some texts in Greek and mostly on parchment (animal skin) but with some written on papyrus, the scrolls are a mixture of copies of Old Testament books, apocryphal manuscripts, psalms and sectarian manuscripts of relevance only to the community that produced them.

The site is strategically located. Facing eastwards, the panoramic view encompasses both the mouth of the Jordan River and the entire northern half of the Dead Sea. The site would have provided an ideal vantage point for the observance of any military threat to Jerusalem from the east. Within the ruins themselves, there are the remains of a heavily fortified tower that would have once dominated the site. This has walls up to 1.5 meters thick and the original building would have had two levels.

Most of the scrolls that have been found are from caves that are very near to the remains of this settlement and it seems very likely that they are associated with the community that lived there. Each scroll that was found was given a label that included the number of the cave in which the scroll was found. Any scroll prefixed with 4Q was found in cave 4, the *"Q"* signifies *"Qumran"*.

Of the Old Testament works discovered in the caves, there are fragments from every book except Esther and there were multiple copies of many of these books. The finds included twenty four copies of Genesis, eighteen copies of Exodus, seventeen copies of Leviticus, eleven copies of Numbers and thirty three copies of Deuteronomy. These books comprise the Torah, otherwise known as the Pentateuch – the first five books of the Old Testament which according to rabbinic literature contain the 613 commandments, divided into 365 restrictions and 248 positive commands.

These people were steeped in their history, mythical or otherwise.

Despite the archaeological investigation and research undertaken at Qumran, the population figure of the settlement at the time of its destruction is still uncertain. Recent scholars have put the estimate of the numbers of inhabitants of the buildings to less than fifty.

This sits at odds with both the size of what has been termed the *"assembly hall"*, estimated at being able to house between 120 and 150 people and the number of dining dishes (over 1000) that were discovered in the remains of what has been termed the *"pantry"*. To resolve this discrepancy, there have been suggestions that the majority of the community lived outside the settlement, coming together for worship, meetings and communal meals.

The latest Jewish coins found at the site were from the Spring of 68 CE to the Spring of 69 CE. The earliest Roman coins were minted in Caesaria in 67 CE - 68 CE. From the archaeological evidence it is clear that the Qumran ruins are the remains of a fortified settlement that was taken forcibly by the Romans sometime between CE 68 and CE 70.

What is also noticeable from the coin records is that there was an active community at Qumran between 103 BCE to 76 BCE and from 6 CE to 44 CE. No Jewish coins were found at all between 45 CE and 66 CE, a time frame that correlates with the start of the famine. Then in the single year of 67 CE (the second year of revolt), 83 coins were discovered, far more than had been discovered for any other single year. Several other coins were found that date from 68 CE.

The coin record suggests that during the second year of the revolt, Qumran became heavily populated, a population increase that was surely due to an influx of refugees fleeing the Roman advance. Although evidence has yet to be found, it is possible that many slept in the nearby artificially hewn caves.

The consensus of scholars is that although some of the scrolls may have been written in the second half of the first century, they relate to events in the Hasmonean period. This is a consensus that has been challenged, most notably and controversially, by Robert Eisenman, an American Biblical scholar, who believes the scrolls relate to events in the Herodian era (35 BCE – 70 CE) and later and sees in the scrolls evidence of a pre-Pauline Christianity.

It does seem inconceivable to many of those who oppose the consensus view that those who occupied the site in 67 CE did not create their own writings that commented on the lawlessness and banditry and irrepressible march of the Roman legions in the political, religious and social turbulence of their times. Certainly the evidence seems strong for a composition date around this time of the *Pesher Habakkuk*, a commentary on the Book of Habakkuk which itself is dated to about the 7th Century BCE. The pesher was among the original seven Dead Sea scrolls discovered in 1947 and published in 1951. The Book of Habakkuk starts with the following four verses:

> *The prophecy that Habakkuk the prophet received.*
> *How long, Lord, must I call for help,*
> *but you do not listen?*
> *Or cry out to you, "Violence!"*
> *but you do not save?*
> *Why do you make me look at injustice?*
> *Why do you tolerate wrongdoing?*
> *Destruction and violence are before me;*
> *there is strife, and conflict abounds.*
> *Therefore the law is paralyzed,*
> *and justice never prevails.*
> *The wicked hem in the righteous,*
> *so that justice is perverted.*
>
> [Habakkuk 1:1-4]

No doubt the author of the pesher saw parallels between the book and events of his time with the law becoming less and less influential. The pesher is very fragmented yet it is possible to piece together some phrases and gain a feel of the age in which the author is writing. The Romans are seen as a threat, ones who *"destroy many by the sword"* and the work would have been written either as a response to the invasion of Pompey in 63 BCE or the invasion of Vespasian in 67 CE.

The apocalyptic imagery in the Pesher seems more relevant to the chaos in Judaea at the time of Vespasian's invasion than it does of Pompey's conquest some 130 years previously:

> *when they hear all the b... ... of the final generation*
>
> [Pesher Habakkuk 2:7]

And reference to the *"priests of Jerusalem"* and the *"Last Days"* seems to indicate an almost welcoming acceptance that the temple will cease to be a place of Jewish worship:

> *...priests of Jerusalem*
> *The final (end time) ones who gather up wealth and take a*
> *cut from the spoils from the peoples and for the "Last Days"*
> *they give their wealth with spoil into the hands of the*
> *Roman army.*
>
> [Pesher Habakkuk 9:4-7]

Rebuilding David's fallen tent

The Acts of the Apostles described a council of the early church in Jerusalem that was held in about CE 50. Some present argued that all gentiles should be circumcised and obey the Law of Moses. Peter argued against imposing these requirements and Paul and Barnabas described their wonderful work amongst the gentiles. According to Acts it was James who had the last word:

> *When they finished, James spoke up. "Brothers," he said, "listen to me. Simon has described to us how God first intervened to choose a people for his name from the Gentiles. The words of the prophets are in agreement with this, as it is written:*
> *'After this I will return*
> *and rebuild David's fallen tent.*
> *Its ruins I will rebuild,*
> *and I will restore it,*
> *that the rest of mankind may seek the Lord,*
> *even all the Gentiles who bear my name,*
> *says the Lord, who does these things' —*
> *things known from long ago.*
> *It is my judgment, therefore, that we should not make it difficult for the Gentiles who are turning to God. Instead we should write to them, telling them to abstain from food polluted by idols, from sexual immorality, from the meat of strangled animals and from blood. For the law of Moses has been preached in every city from the earliest times and is read in the synagogues on every Sabbath."*
>
> [Acts 15:13-21]

One remarkable aspect of this passage is how it contrasts with the decision making process of the community described in the earlier part of Acts where decisions were made democratically.

It is also worth reflecting on our tendency to focus on the historical figures, such as James or Paul or *"Jesus"*, when we theorize about the founding of Christianity and ignore the underlying *zeitgeist*.

There was an enormous desire to see Jews and gentiles united. All convictions would have been questioned and among those

PART II

convictions surely would have been the exclusive nature of the Jewish faith and the taxing requirements for converts to it. The removal of the requirement for circumcision and prohibition on the eating of most foods made it much easier for converts.

A scroll of non-scriptural origin is the *"Damascus Document"*, a work that was known to scholars before the Qumran discovery, when fragments of a manuscript were found in the late 19th century in a room adjoining the Ben Ezra synagogue in Fustat near Cairo, Egypt. The document contains the following passage:

> *when the oracle of the prophet Isaiah son of Amoz came true, which says, "Days are coming upon you and upon your people and upon your father's house that have never come before, since the departure of Ephraim from Judah,"* *
> *that is, when the two houses of Israel separated, Ephraim departing from Judah.*

* Isaiah 7:17

[Damascus Document]

Ephraim was head of one of the twelve tribes of Israel. He was the younger son of Joseph. His mother was not a Jew but the daughter of a high priest and as Judaism is passed through the mother, then Ephraim was born a gentile, only becoming a Jew with the blessing of his grandfather Jacob.

In the passage above, the author is referring to a schism between the *"Jew"* and *"gentile"* houses of Israel, one that he sees reconciled under *"the books of the Torah"*:

> *The books of Torah are the tents of the king, as it says, "I will re-erect the fallen tent of David."* * *The king is <Leader of> the nation and the "foundation of your images" is the books of the prophets whose words Israel despised. The star is the Interpreter of the Torah who*

comes to Damascus, as it is written, "A star has left Jacob, a staff has risen from Israel." ** The latter is the Leader of the whole nation; when he appears, "he will shatter all the sons of Sheth."

* Amos 9:11 ** Num 24:1

[Damascus Document]

James' reference within Acts to rebuilding *"David's fallen tent"* is repeated here and if the star that has left Jacob is a reference to the Jesus Christ of James, it is not the only place where this reference is made:

"I, Jesus, have sent my angel to give you this testimony for the churches. I am the Root and the Offspring of David, and the bright Morning Star."

[Revelation 22:16]

There are numerous references to *"Damascus"* within the document and it is from these that the name of the document is derived. In language that will be familiar to Christian audiences, the document describes a new covenant in the land of Damascus:

They must keep the Sabbath day according to specification, and the sacred days and the fast day according to the commandments of the members of the new covenant in the land of Damascus, offering the sacred things according to their specifications. Each one must love his brother as himself, and support the poor, needy, and alien. They must seek each the welfare of his fellow, never betraying a family member according to the ordinance. Each must reprove his fellow according to the command, but must not bear a grudge day after day. They must separate from all kinds of

PART II

> *ritual impurity according to their ordinance, not befouling each his holy spirit, just as Elohim has told them so to do.*

The reference to the prophecy passage in Numbers betrays the author's Messianic expectations. What is clear is that the author saw Jews and gentiles united under a shared commitment to the law.

The Teacher of Righteousness

The *"Teacher of Righteousness"* or Moreh Tsedek referred to in many of the scrolls is the one through whom God would reveal to the community *"the hidden things in which Israel had gone astray"* [CD 3:12-15] and *"to whom God made known all the mysteries of the words of his servants the prophets"* [1QpHab 7:5]. Opponents of the *"Teacher of Righteousness"* are the *"Man of Lies"* and the *"Wicked Priest"*.

The identity of these three characters has been the subject of much debate. Some have theorized that the Teacher served as a High Priest in the second century BCE but was ousted by Judas Maccabeus. Some have theorized that he was the leader of the Essenes at Qumran. Robert Eisenman identifies the Teacher of Righteousness with James the Just, the head of the early church, whose sobriquet *"the Just"* can equally be translated as *"the Righteous"*. He identifies the *"Man of Lies"* as the apostle Paul himself and the *"Wicked Priest"* as Ananus, the High Priest who arranged for James' death.

There is the possibility, of course, that these are not sobriquets of historical characters at all, but archetypes. The scrolls are not historical documents but religious ones. Historical characters come and go but archetypes are timeless.

Philo had already interpreted Abraham, Isaac and Jacob, as a triumvirate of archetypal characters, representing those who had attained excellence in instruction, nature, and practice respectively.

Mark would interpret John, Peter and James as a triumvirate of archetypal characters, representing human reason, spirit and faith respectively.

The Teacher of Righteousness, the Man of Lies and the Wicked Priest represent another triumvirate of archetypes.

In the *Pesher Habakkuk* the Wicked Priest is described as follows:

> *Peshru about the wicked priest who is called by the name of "The Truth" He stands in prayer while watching over Israel. His heart is lifted up yet he abandons God and uses treachery by their laws for the sake of wealth. He rejoices and he gathers the wealth of the men of violence who rebel against God. And he receives the wealth of nations to add evil to himself by the guilt of his own way working in all the corrupt wanderings.*
>
> [Pesher Habakkuk 8:8-13]

> *Peshru about the "Wicked Priest" who (is given) into the hand of the Moreh*
> *Tsedek and the men of his council. God gives into His hand his enemies to answer him. (He visits them) with a plague in the bitterness of his soul because they had done wickedly against his "Chosen."*
>
> [Pesher Habakkuk 9:9-12]

> *Peshru about the "Wicked Priest" who pursues after the "Moreh Tsedek" to swallow him up in rage his hot (rage).*
>
> [Pesher Habakkuk 11:4-6]

In these short paragraphs, we have descriptions of pride, greed, anger and possibly lust. Surely, if the concern of a Holy Priest, a *"Messiah of Aaron"*, in the language of other Qumran scrolls, is for the spiritual, then the Wicked Priest is his antithesis. The concern of

PART II

the Wicked Priest is for his own feelings.

Similarly, the *"Man of Lies"*, also known as the *"Man of Mockery"* or *"Scoffer"* knows the rules but rejects them. In the *Pesher Habakkuk* again it states:

> *Pesher of the word about the flying [?] of the liar who leads many astray to the daughters of the city of vanity and by blood and to raise up a city by a lie. For the sake of (self) glory they lead many to serve vanity and for their own profit*
>
> [Pesher Habakkuk 10:9-11]

> *Pesher about the House of Absalom and the men of their council which fall silent in reproaching of the Moreh Tsedek. But they do not help him against the lying man who does violence to The Torah among all the nations and makes men as the fish of the sea*
>
> [Pesher Habakkuk 5:9-12]

Surely, if the concern of a Philosopher King or *"Messiah of Israel"*, in the language of other scrolls, is for law and justice then the Man of Lies is his antithesis. The Man of Lies rejects the laws. His concern is for his own interests.

Although we may regard the Qumran Jews as having an excessive attachment to the law, laws are necessary; as much in our own society as in Judaea two thousand years ago. Ultimately, laws are there to encourage harmonious social relations. A lawless society is a hostile one.

In the *Jewish War*, Josephus makes the following comment on the Essenes, the sect that is thought to have inhabited Qumran:

> *What they most of all honor, after God himself, is the name*

of their legislator whom if any one blaspheme he is punished capitally.

[Josephus: The Jewish War 2:8:9]

James himself states:

There is only one Lawgiver and Judge, the one who is able to save and destroy.

[James 4:12]

The lawgiver is thought to be a reference to Moses but rather than just being a reference to the one who brought the law to the chosen people, surely the lawgiver is also associated with Joshua who brought the law to the gentiles?

And surely, the *"Moreh Tsedek"* or *"Teacher of Righteousness"* is an archetype for someone who encourages compliance of the law because their concern is not for their own feelings nor for their own interests but for the feelings and interests of the community as a whole.

Notwithstanding, there were, no doubt, in the minds of the authors, those to whom the archetypes most aptly applied.

The Jerusalem Council

What we know of Christianity in the first 50 years of the first century is this:

The Acts of the Apostles states:

All the believers were together and had everything in common. They sold property and possessions to give to anyone who had need.

[Acts 2: 44-45]

PART II

The gospels and Josephus both attest that John the Baptist was a hugely popular figure who, through baptism in the river Jordan, symbolically cleansed the sins of those who repented. He was executed on the orders of Herod Antipas whose authority he threatened.

In his *"Roman History"* the Roman author Cassius Dio wrote of the period of Claudius' rule:

> *As for the Jews, who had again increased so greatly that by reason of their multitude it would have been hard without raising a tumult to bar them from the city, he did not drive them out, but ordered them, while continuing their traditional mode of life, not to hold meetings.*

There is a contradictory account in the *"Life of Claudius"* by Suetonius:

> *As the Jews were making constant disturbances at the instigation of Chrestus, he expelled them from Rome.*

There is some corroborating evidence for this latter course of action within Acts:

> *There he [Paul] met a Jew named Aquila, a native of Pontus, who had recently come from Italy with his wife Priscilla, because Claudius had ordered all Jews to leave Rome.*
>
> [Acts 18: 2]

Although admirably egalitarian, this was a movement that threatened authority.

Josephus wrote of a *"fourth philosophy"* that involved an inviolable attachment to liberty. This philosophy, popularized by Judas the Galilean, was particularly influential during this time.

By the removal of the requirement for circumcision and prohibition on the eating of most foods, Acts portrays the Jerusalem Council as an event that made it easier for gentiles to become Christians. It was also likely to be an event convened with some urgency, after the banishment of Jewish Christians from Rome the previous year, with an aim of moderating a movement that was seen as a threat to authority. And it was likely to be an event that gave tacit approval to Paul who:

> *meeting privately with those esteemed as leaders, I presented to them the gospel that I preach among the Gentiles.*
>
> [Galatians 2:1]

It seems likely that the Council was an event that established the rules permissible for the preaching of Christ and the conversion of gentiles and although Acts implies that James the Righteous made the final decision, in reality it was unlikely to have been such consensual acceptance of one person's authority. Acts itself indicates that there was division:

> *Then some of the believers who belonged to the party of the Pharisees stood up and said, "The Gentiles must be circumcised and required to keep the law of Moses."*
>
> [Acts 15:5]

No doubt there were some outside of the Council who disapproved of the compromises. In the *Pesher Habakkuk* it states:

> *"Look at the nations and watch—*
> *and be utterly amazed.*
> *For I am going to do something in your days*
> *that you would not believe,*
> *even if you were told.*
>
> [Habakkuk 1:5]

PART II

*it be told him ... the treacherous with a man all the liars ...
the Moreh Tsedek from the mouth of God and concerning
the trai(tors) ... the new (fragmented word) our belief in
the covenant of God ... those possessing ... and truth.
Pesher of the word ... ..gadiym to the last (aleph) days.
They are aro... ... ..oth which they will not believe when
they hear all the b... ... of the final generation from the
mouth of the priest which God gives in*

... to explain to all the words of His servants coming

[Pesher Habakkuk 2:1-9]

*Your eyes are too pure to look on evil;
you cannot tolerate wrongdoing.
Why then do you tolerate the treacherous?
Why are you silent while the wicked
swallow up those more righteous than themselves?*

[Habakkuk 1:13]

*Pesher about the House of Absalom[7] and the men of their
council which fall silent in reproaching of the Moreh
Tsedek. But they do not help him against the lying man
who does violence to The Torah among all the nations and*
makes men as the fish of the sea.

[Pesher Habakkuk 5:9-12]

---

[7] The House of Absalom is a reference to the story in 2 Samuel:13 where David's eldest son Amnon raped his half-sister Thamar. When Thamar's brother Absalom heard the news, he advised his sister to keep quiet. No punishment was meted out to Amnon and although Absalom never said a word about it to Amnon, he developed such a hatred for him that two years later he avenged his sister by arranging for Amnon to be killed.

Joseph of Arimathea

The characteristics of the Essenes described in the *Damascus document* is echoed in the writings of Josephus and if there were to be a gospel character that would be loathed by them, it would be Joseph of Arimathea. As the gospel states:

> *It was Preparation Day (that is, the day before the Sabbath). So as evening approached, Joseph of Arimathea, a prominent member of the Council, who was himself waiting for the kingdom of God, went boldly to Pilate and asked for Jesus' body. Pilate was surprised to hear that he was already dead. Summoning the centurion, he asked him if Jesus had already died. When he learned from the centurion that it was so, he gave the body to Joseph. So Joseph bought some linen cloth, took down the body, wrapped it in the linen, and placed it in a tomb cut out of rock. Then he rolled a stone against the entrance of the tomb.*
>
> [Mark 15:42–46]

Joseph is wealthy (he has his own tomb) and purchases a linen cloth. He is also a man of some prominence in the community. Josephus records the Essenes as being:

> *Contemptuous of wealth, they are communists to perfection, and none of them will be found to be better off than the rest*
>
> [Josephus: The Jewish War 2:8:3]

Joseph broke with Jewish law. On the evening before the Sabbath day which marks the start of the day of rest, devout Jews refrain from all activity. Joseph, however, not only purchases the linen cloth but takes Jesus down from the cross, wraps him in a shroud, lays him in a tomb hewn out of rock and then rolls a stone against the entrance to it. This is a considerable amount of effort for any one man. The *Damascus document* explains the rules regarding the day of rest:

> *They must keep the Sabbath day according to specification, and the sacred days and the fast day according to the commandments of the members of the new covenant in the land of Damascus, offering the sacred things according to their specifications.*
>
> [The Damascus Document]

Whilst Josephus gives more detail:

> *Moreover, they are stricter than any other of the Jews in resting from their labors on the seventh day; for they not only get their food ready the day before, that they may not be obliged to kindle a fire on that day, but they will not remove any vessel out of its place, nor go to stool thereon.*
>
> [Josephus: The Jewish War 2:8:9]

Despite being a prominent member of the council that condemned Jesus, it is doubtful Joseph would have had a position on the *"council of the people"* that is mentioned in the *Damascus document*:

> *So it is with all the men who entered the new covenant in the land of Damascus, but then turned back and traitorously turned away from the fountain of living water. They will not be reckoned among the council of the people.*
>
> [The Damascus Document]

That *"fountain of living water"* metaphor is equivalent to the *"Well"* metaphor used elsewhere in the Document. The following passage contains both an explanation of the *"Well"* and a reference to

Elohim or *"God"*:

> *the Well is the Torah, and its "diggers" are the captives of Israel who went out of the land of Judah and dwelt in the land of Damascus; because Elohim had called them all princes, for they sought Him and their honor was not denied by a single mouth.*
>
> [The Damascus Document]

The author of the *Damascus document* would have, no doubt, described Joseph of Arimathea as a *"boundary-shifter"*:

> *And such is the verdict on all members of the covenant who do not hold firm to these ordinances: they are condemned to destruction by Belial. That is the day on which Elohim will judge as He has said,*
> *"The princes of Judah were those like Boundary-Shifters on whom I will pour out wrath like water."*
>
> [The Damascus Document]

The significance of Joseph of Arimathea is explained by understanding his name.

"Arimathea" means *"Lion dead to the Lord"*. The Lion of Judah was the symbol of the tribe of Judah. Indeed it was from the tribe of Judah that David came and he replaced Saul as the King that met the challenge of the Philistine incursions with military might and re-united the twelve tribes into the kingdom of Israel.

In the Book of Genesis, Joseph is the son of Jacob and receives from his father a multi-colored coat. Philo sees in the reference to that coat an indication that Joseph is the consummate politician:

> *And it is not without a particular and correct meaning that*

PART II

Joseph is said to have had a coat of many colors. For a political constitution is a many-colored and multiform thing, admitting of an infinite variety of changes in its general appearance, in its affairs, in its moving causes, in the peculiar laws respecting strangers, in numberless differences respecting times and places.

[Philo: On Joseph]

Philo also sees significance in the fact that Joseph was a shepherd in his early years:

Now, this man began from the time he was seventeen years of age to be occupied with the consideration of the business of a shepherd, which corresponds to political business. On which account I think it is that the race of poets has been accustomed to call kings the shepherds of the people; for he who is skillful in the business of a shepherd will probably be also a most excellent king, having derived instruction in those matters which are deserving of inferior attention here to superintend a flock of those most excellent of all animals, namely, of men.

[Philo: On Joseph]

In this passage in Mark, there is a repetition of the phrase *"already dead"*[8]:

Pilate was surprised to hear that he was already dead.

---

[8] Pay attention to the doubling of a phrase

Summoning the centurion, he asked him if Jesus had already died. When he learned from the centurion that it was so, he gave the body to Joseph.

What was *"dead"*, surely, was the pre-incarnate Jesus Christ of James.

The divine reason, that was obsessed with the law and associated with the conquering hero of Israel, was rejected by the gentiles. This Jesus would not help bring forth God's kingdom.

The divine reason who was the Jesus Christ of James was too abstract a notion for most. This Jesus Christ would not help bring forth God's kingdom.

The Jesus Christ that did appeal was the divine logos made incarnate and shorn of Judaic nationalism and ideology, a Jesus Christ with whom people could identify. It is significant, of course, that it is Joseph of Arimathea who asks for the body.

PART II

Simon

Simon: Derived from Shimon (Hebrew) meaning "he has heard".

Paul

The earliest book of the New Testament is commonly regarded to be Saint Paul's first letter to the Thessalonians which is thought to have been composed at about 50-51 CE.

There is no contemporaneous record of Christianity before then. The half century timespan between 1 CE, formerly known as the first year of the Lord and the date of Paul's earliest New Testament letter comprise the *"dark ages"* of Christianity.

Paul, of course, was initially a passionate Jew, zealous for the law:

> *For you have heard of my previous way of life in Judaism, how intensely I persecuted the church of God and tried to destroy it. I was advancing in Judaism beyond many of my own age among my people and was extremely zealous for the traditions of my fathers.*
>
> [Galatians 1:13 – 15]

While revealing some sensitivity toward accusations of lying, Paul explains that it was three years after his conversion that he went to Jerusalem:

> *But when God, who set me apart from my mother's womb and called me by his grace, was pleased to reveal his Son in me so that I might preach him among the Gentiles, my immediate response was not to consult any human being. I*

> *did not go up to Jerusalem to see those who were apostles before I was, but I went into Arabia. Later I returned to Damascus.*
> *Then after three years, I went up to Jerusalem to get acquainted with Cephas and stayed with him fifteen days. I saw none of the other apostles—only James, the Lord's brother. I assure you before God that what I am writing you is no lie.*
>
> [Galatians 1:15 – 20]

The author of Acts also describes this event:

> *When he came to Jerusalem, he tried to join the disciples, but they were all afraid of him, not believing that he really was a disciple. But Barnabas took him and brought him to the apostles. He told them how Saul on his journey had seen the Lord and that the Lord had spoken to him, and how in Damascus he had preached fearlessly in the name of Jesus.*
>
> [Acts 9:26 – 27]

According to Acts, after a plot to kill him, Paul is sent to his home town of Tarsus:

> *He talked and debated with the Hellenistic Jews, but they tried to kill him.*
> *When the believers learned of this, they took him down to Caesarea and sent him off to Tarsus.*
>
> [Acts 9:29 – 30]

Barnabas later visited Paul and took him to Antioch where an early Church community had been established:

PART II

> *Then Barnabas went to Tarsus to look for Saul, and when he found him, he brought him to Antioch. So for a whole year Barnabas and Saul met with the church and taught great numbers of people. The disciples were called Christians first at Antioch.*
>
> [Acts 11:25 – 26]

His first Jerusalem visit is thought to have been at about 36-37 CE and his conversion experience to have been three years earlier in 33-34 CE. He undertook his first missionary journey in the company of Barnabas around 46-48 CE. Acts records how they travelled to Salamis and Paphos in Cyprus, Perga in Pamphylia, then four churches in the southern portion of the Roman province of Galatia, namely Pisidian Antioch, Iconium, Lystra and Derbe. After this, the apostles returned to Perga, and this time caught a ship at Attalia for their return to Antioch.

Fourteen years after his first visit, Paul returned once more to Jerusalem, presumably to attend the Council that was held in 50 CE:

> *Then after fourteen years, I went up again to Jerusalem, this time with Barnabas. I took Titus along also. I went in response to a revelation and, meeting privately with those esteemed as leaders; I presented to them the gospel that I preach among the Gentiles. I wanted to be sure I was not running and had not been running my race in vain.*
>
> [Galatians 2:1]

Paul's earliest canonical letter was written to the converts Paul had made in Thessalonica in the summer of 50 CE. It differs so obviously from James' much later letter. It is directed at a specific audience, one that is known to Paul and it is an affectionate and a much more pastoral letter than James' epistle.

Paul as he does in all his letters sets no store on adherence to laws but on the working of the Holy Spirit and his letter is full of encouragement:

> *We always thank God for all of you and continually mention you in our prayers. We remember before our God and Father your work produced by faith, your labor prompted by love, and your endurance inspired by hope in our Lord Jesus Christ.*
>
> *For we know, brothers and sisters loved by God, that he has chosen you, because our gospel came to you not simply with words but also with power, with the Holy Spirit and deep conviction. You know how we lived among you for your sake. You became imitators of us and of the Lord, for you welcomed the message in the midst of severe suffering with the joy given by the Holy Spirit.*
>
> *And so you became a model to all the believers in Macedonia and Achaia.*
>
> [1 Thess. 1: 2-7]

Also, whereas James' letter contains one reference to *"Lord Jesus Christ"*, one reference to *"Jesus Christ"* and one to *"Lord"*, Paul's earliest letter, despite being one of his shortest, contains thirteen references to *"Lord"*, seven to *"Lord Jesus"*, five to *"Lord Jesus Christ"*, three to *"Christ"* and two to both *"Christ Jesus"* and *"Jesus"*. In most places, these references can be replaced by the words *"divine reason"* and still make perfect sense.

However, the letter also introduces in its earliest existing written form, references to an incarnate Christ who was put to death by the Jews. There is no reference to the crucifixion at this stage:

> *For you, brothers and sisters, became imitators of God's churches in Judea, which are in Christ Jesus: You suffered*

PART II

> *from your own people the same things those churches suffered from the Jews who killed the Lord Jesus and the prophets and also drove us out. They displease God and are hostile to everyone*
>
> [1 Thess. 2: 14-15]

Although this sounds like a Christ of concrete reality, later in the letter Paul refers to Christ's death and resurrection as an article of faith rather than an historical event when in chapter 4 verse 14 he states:

> *For we believe that Jesus died and rose again*
>
> [1 Thess. 4:14]

Indeed Paul did not write of Christ's life but of his link to the one true God and the superiority of the one true God over the pagan alternatives:

> *...for they themselves report what kind of reception you gave us. They tell how you turned to God from idols to serve the living and true God, and to wait for his Son from heaven, whom he raised from the dead —Jesus, who rescues us from the coming wrath.*
>
> [1 Thess. 1: 9-10]

Despite Paul's preaching in Antioch, Salamis, Paphos, Perga, Pisilian Antioch, Iconium, Lystra and Derbe and despite his eighteen year ministry, the only correspondence of his that survives dates from after his attendance at the Jerusalem Council.

The reference in Acts to members of an early church community at Antioch being called *"Christians"* referred to a time before the Council. Likewise the comment by Suetonius that Jews *"who were making constant disturbances"* were expelled from Rome *"at the instigation of Chrestus"*.

Paul's first letter is the earliest reference we have to "Jesus".

It is highly speculative, of course, but it is possible, surely, that before the Council, Paul preached of a Christ that was subtly different from the Christ Jesus of whom he preached afterwards.

Paul and James

The letters of Paul have the capacity to both inspire and infuriate. Some of his writings are beautiful; others indicate a deep rooted belief in the inferiority of women:

> *Wives, submit yourselves to your own husbands as you do to the Lord. For the husband is the head of the wife as Christ is the head of the church, his body, of which he is the Savior.*
>
> [Ephesians 5:22 -23]

> *Every man who prays or prophesies with his head covered dishonors his head. But every woman who prays or prophesies with her head uncovered dishonors her head—it is the same as having her head shaved. For if a woman does not cover her head, she might as well have her hair cut off; but if it is a disgrace for a woman to have her hair cut off or her head shaved, then she should cover her head.*
> *A man ought not to cover his head, since he is the image and glory of God; but woman is the glory of man.*
>
> [I Corinthians 11: 4-7]

However, it would be a mistake to believe that Paul just infuriates our current day sensibilities. There is evidence that he was equally infuriating during his lifetime.

PART II

Paul was initially a passionate Jew, zealous for the law. After his conversion on the road to Damascus, you would maybe expect Paul to seek guidance from the disciples. Instead, it was three years before Paul met with Peter in Jerusalem and then only for fifteen days. Paul would not return to Jerusalem for another fourteen years.

In the second visit to Jerusalem, Paul hints at some agreement between him and Peter, James and John:

> *On the contrary, they recognized that I had been entrusted with the task of preaching the gospel to the uncircumcised, just as Peter had been to the circumcised. For God, who was at work in Peter as an apostle to the circumcised, was also at work in me as an apostle to the Gentiles. James, Cephas and John, those esteemed as pillars, gave me and Barnabas the right hand of fellowship when they recognized the grace given to me. They agreed that we should go to the Gentiles, and they to the circumcised. All they asked was that we should continue to remember the poor, the very thing I had been eager to do all along.*
>
> [Galatians 2:7-10]

It was a reconciliation that was to be short lived. Paul was very much his own man and he carried the single-minded determination that he exhibited before his conversion into his apostolic calling. In the process he ruffled a few feathers. In his letter to the Romans, dated at about 56 CE, he wrote:

> *What then shall we say? That the Gentiles, who did not pursue righteousness, have obtained it, a righteousness that is by faith; but the people of Israel, who pursued the law as the way of righteousness, have not attained their goal. Why not? Because they pursued it not by faith but as if it were by*

works. They stumbled over the stumbling stone.

[Romans 9:30-32]

The letter from James contains what seems like a rebuttal to this:

What good is it, my brothers and sisters, if someone claims to have faith but has no deeds? Can such faith save them? Suppose a brother or a sister is without clothes and daily food. If one of you says to them, "Go in peace; keep warm and well fed," but does nothing about their physical needs, what good is it?

In the same way, faith by itself, if it is not accompanied by action, is dead.

[James 2:14-17]

There certainly seems to have been some animosity between Paul and James. James had authority. He was, after all, the spiritual head of the church in Jerusalem. Yet in Galatians, there is something very revealing.

Paul uses both the name Peter and term Cephas to refer to Peter. The different appellations are used depending on the context. When Paul refers to Peter when James is referenced nearby, he refers to him as Cephas (meaning *"head"*). Otherwise he refers to Peter by his name. It is clear who Paul regarded as leader. James was not Cephas.

However, although Paul was a supporter of Peter, this didn't mean that he always agreed with him:

When Cephas came to Antioch, I opposed him to his face, because he stood condemned. For before certain men came from James, he used to eat with the Gentiles. But when they arrived, he began to draw back and separate himself

> *from the Gentiles because he was afraid of those who belonged to the circumcision group. The other Jews joined him in his hypocrisy, so that by their hypocrisy even Barnabas was led astray.*
>
> [Galatians 2:11-13]

Simon

The word *"tent"* as in *"rebuilding David's fallen tent"* is used as a metaphor by those who envisioned Jews and gentiles as united. The word *"tentmaker"* in Acts 18:2 is used in relation to Paul who had some success in working toward that goal:

> *There he met a Jew named Aquila, a native of Pontus, who had recently come from Italy with his wife Priscilla, because Claudius had ordered all Jews to leave Rome. Paul went to see them, and because he was a tentmaker as they were, he stayed and worked with them.*
>
> [Acts 18: 2]

Paul's success was based on his spreading of the story of the incarnate Christ who was crucified and resurrected. In this he wasn't alone. As Paul states:

> *On the contrary, they recognized that I had been entrusted with the task of preaching the gospel to the uncircumcised, just as Peter had been to the circumcised.*
>
> [Galatians 2:7]

Although Paul sometimes refers to Peter as Cephas, he does not in any of his letters refer to him as Simon. Neither is the name *"Simon"* used in the first letter of Peter. Indeed, the earliest writing in which the appellation *"Simon"* is likely to have been used for

INTERPRETING MARK

Peter is in gospel of Mark where Peter is named Simon Peter.

Why does the author use this name?

The name *"Simon"* derives from Hebrew and means *"he who hears"*. Gentiles were used to worshipping gods with whom they could identify and there was something in the death and resurrection myths, found in many cultures that spoke to the human heart. He realized – *"he who heard"* - that gentiles needed to identify with a bodily Christ.

Moreover, there is another disciple in the gospel of Mark that has the name Simon. This is *"Simon the Zealot"*. Isn't this the Simon who has been *"entrusted with the gospel to the uncircumcised"*? Isn't this the one who was *"extremely zealous ... for the traditions of my fathers"*? Isn't this Paul himself?

It was Paul and Peter who metaphorically brought Christ down to earth.

Later in the gospel, Jesus is at the house of Simon the Leper at Bethany (literally *"house of figs"*) when a woman enters with a flask of expensive ointment. The gospel states:

> *While he was in Bethany, reclining at the table in the home of Simon the Leper, a woman came with an alabaster jar of very expensive perfume, made of pure nard. She broke the jar and poured the perfume on his head. Some of those present were saying indignantly to one another, "Why this waste of perfume? It could have been sold for more than a year's wages and the money given to the poor." And they rebuked her harshly.*
> *"Leave her alone," said Jesus. "Why are you bothering her? She has done a beautiful thing to me. The poor you will always have with you, and you can help them any time you*

PART II

want. But you will not always have me

[Mark 14: 3-8]

Doesn't this passage echo the conflict between Paul and James? Isn't it reminiscent of the argument between faith and good works? Paul had the single minded determination to break down the barriers between Jews and Greeks by bringing the message of Christ to the gentiles, James had concern for the poor.

Isn't this Simon, the Leper, again Paul himself, ostracized by the early church community, anointing Christ by preaching reverentially of him?

All that we *"know"* about the *"human"* Christ from the letters of Paul is that he was crucified and was resurrected. These are flimsy grounds on which to establish a new religion. There is, however, another Simon referenced in the gospel:

> *A certain man from Cyrene, Simon, the father of Alexander and Rufus, was passing by on his way in from the country, and they forced him to carry the cross.*
>
> [Mark 15: 21]

This man named Simon, the passer-by who has heard.

This bit part player in the story of whom we know little except the remarkable biographical detail, unparalleled elsewhere in the gospel, that he was father of Alexander and Rufus[9].

This was the man who, following the deaths of Peter and Paul, took up the cross.

---

[9] Pay attention to an apparently superfluous expression in the text

Coptic tradition states that the author of Mark's gospel became the first bishop of Alexandria and that he was born in Cyrene.

Surely, this Simon is the author of the gospel himself.

Mary the mother of Jesus

Mary, the mother of Jesus, is mentioned in chapter 6, verses 1 – 6 of the gospel. Here Mark narrates how Jesus teaches at the synagogue in his home town. The inhabitants were astonished:

> *"Where did this man get these things?" they asked. "What's this wisdom that has been given him? What are these remarkable miracles he is performing? Isn't this the carpenter? Isn't this Mary's son and the brother of James, Joseph, Judas and Simon?*
>
> [Mark 6: 2-3]

As with Paul's stated profession in Acts, Jesus' stated profession is significant[10]. Whereas a carpenter creates by joining pieces of wood, Christianity was created by the joining of Judaism with Greek philosophy.

The name Mary is derived from Miriam that some scholars see as meaning *"sea of bitterness"*. First century Jews expressed bitterness and resentment that arose from the defilement of the temple by Antiochus, the later conquest of Judaea by the Romans, the imposition of the Herodian kings and the murder of the rightful heirs to Jewish political and spiritual rule – the Hasmonean descendants. Jesus was born from that *"sea of bitterness"* but so were

---

[10] Pay attention to the significance of a profession

his *"brothers"*:

- Judas (Judas the Galilean) who rejected the norms of the society he lived in, promoted a communal way of living where everyone was of equal standing and preached a philosophy that rejected external authority and encouraged people to look for the Messiah in their own hearts.

- James, a follower of Judas' teachings who, seeing how Judas' ideas were misinterpreted by those who, lacking any external authority, lost self-control, encouraged people to show restraint. He supplanted the Christ of Judas with Jesus Christ – a Christ (divine reason) who speaks as the internal authority and Jesus, the lawgiver who directs us to abide by the external authority of the law.

- Joseph (Joseph of Arimathea), the diplomats of influence who had a great desire to see the movement not come into conflict with authority. They recognized that gentiles saw tremendous value in the death and resurrection myths of pagan culture. At the Jerusalem Council, those of influence asked for a flesh and blood figure.

- Simon who created a bodily Messiah with whom people could identify – a Jesus Christ made incarnate who was crucified and resurrected.

Although gentiles responded to this new religion, Jews were less keen. As it states in the gospel:

> *Jesus said to them, "A prophet is not without honor except in his own town, among his relatives and in his own home." He could not do any miracles there, except lay his hands on a few sick people and heal them. He was amazed at their lack of faith.*
>
> [Mark 6: 4-6]

War

Mark: (Roman) derived from Mars, the God of War.

WHEREAS the war which the Jews made with the Romans hath been the greatest of all those, not only that have been in our times, but, in a manner, of those that ever were heard of; both of those wherein cities have fought against cities, or nations against nations; while some men who were not concerned in the affairs themselves have gotten together vain and contradictory stories by hearsay, and have written them down after a sophistical manner; and while those that were there present have given false accounts of things, and this either out of a humor of flattery to the Romans, or of hatred towards the Jews; and while their writings contain sometimes accusations, and sometimes encomiums, but nowhere the accurate truth of the facts; I have proposed to myself, for the sake of such as live under the government of the Romans, to translate those books into the Greek tongue, which I formerly composed in the language of our country, and sent to the Upper Barbarians;

[Josephus: The Jewish War - Preface]

The coming rebellion

The second earliest book of the New Testament is thought to be St Paul's second letter to the Thessalonians. It is very similar to the first and it is dated at about 51 CE. Presumably, Paul wrote this letter in order to clarify certain points. He certainly seemed anxious

PART II

to clarify the timing of the coming of the Lord:

> *Concerning the coming of our Lord Jesus Christ and our being gathered to him, we ask you, brothers and sisters, not to become easily unsettled or alarmed by the teaching allegedly from us—whether by a prophecy or by word of mouth or by letter —asserting that the day of the Lord has already come. Don't let anyone deceive you in any way, for that day will not come until the rebellion occurs and the man of lawlessness is revealed, the man doomed to destruction. He will oppose and will exalt himself over everything that is called God or is worshiped, so that he sets himself up in God's temple, proclaiming himself to be God. Don't you remember that when I was with you I used to tell you these things? And now you know what is holding him back, so that he may be revealed at the proper time. For the secret power of lawlessness is already at work; but the one who now holds it back will continue to do so till he is taken out of the way. And then the lawless one will be revealed, whom the Lord Jesus will overthrow with the breath of his mouth and destroy by the splendor of his coming.*
>
> [2 Thess. 2: 1-8]

The *"lawless one"* that Paul refers to is presumably any Messiah figure who aims to overthrow the yoke of Roman oppression but as for the *"one who now holds it back"*, there is surely only one plausible candidate.

Stephen

Traditionally, the importance of James the Just as an early church leader has been overlooked but historical documents are in agreement.

Commenting on a section of text in Josephus (that strangely is not present in any extant copies of his work), Eusebius writes:

> *So remarkable a person must James have been, so universally esteemed for Righteousness, that even the most intelligent of Jews felt this was why his martyrdom was immediately followed by the siege of Jerusalem.*
>
> [Eusebius Histories 2.23]

The death of James was such a significant event that it is mentioned in the non-scriptural writings of Josephus and Hegesippus. Strangely, it is not mentioned in the Acts of the Apostles. Instead there is a significant passage of 60 verses comprising the whole of chapter 7 of Acts given to the death of the mysterious character of Stephen. Commemorated as the first Christian martyr, Stephen is not independently referred to anywhere outside of Acts. Like James, Stephen is an eloquent speaker. Like James, he has authority. Like James, he is accused of blasphemy and is tried before the Sanhedrin. Like James, he is unjustly found guilty and sentenced to death by stoning. Like James, Stephen attracted the animosity of Paul (Acts states that Paul approved of the killing).

As he is dying, Stephen, like James, asks God to forgive his tormentors. As in the letter of James, through the whole of Stephen's speech there is no reference to the crucifixion or the resurrection, Indeed there is no reference to a bodily Christ at all. There is, however, a reference to the Son of Man:

> *But Stephen, full of the Holy Spirit, looked up to heaven and saw the glory of God, and Jesus standing at the right*

PART II

> *hand of God. "Look," he said, "I see heaven open and the Son of Man standing at the right hand of God."*
>
> *At this they covered their ears and, yelling at the top of their voices, they all rushed at him*
>
> [Acts 7: 55-57]

This is a passage that is similar to a passage that quotes James in Hegesippus:

> *Why ask ye me concerning Jesus the Son of man? He Himself sitteth in heaven, at the right hand of the Great Power, and shall come on the clouds of heaven.*

James is the Greek form of the name Jacob, the supplanter whose name was changed to Israel and about whom Philo wrote:

> *.... these things are not brought about without a struggle or without severe labor; but only when any one, having gone through all the labors of prudence, then proceeds to practice himself in the exercises of the soul and to wrestle against the reasonings which are hostile to it, and which seek to torment it; but it is the part of him who sees God not to depart from the sacred contest without the crown of victory, but rather to carry off the prize of triumph. And what more flourishing and more suitable crown could be woven for the victorious soul than one by which it will be able acutely and clearly to behold the living God? At least a beautiful prize is thus proposed for the soul which delights in the practice of virtue, namely, the being endowed with sight adequate to the clear comprehension of the only thing which is really worth beholding.*
>
> [Philo: On the Change of Names]

In his letter, James wrote:

> *Blessed is the one who perseveres under trial because, having stood the test, that person will receive the crown of life that the Lord has promised to those who love him.*
>
> [James 1: 12]

James was one who acutely and clearly beheld the living God. He was one of proven worth. He had won that promised *"crown"* - a word that has as a derivation the Greek name *"Stephen"*.

Prophecy

There are a number of references to historical events within the *Damascus Document*. One passage in the document states:

> *They considered their iniquity and they knew that they were guilty men, and had been like the blind and like those groping for the way for twenty years. But Elohim considered their deeds, that they had sought Him with a whole heart. So He raised up for them a teacher of righteousness to guide them in the way of His heart.*

The reference to twenty years may be significant if it is hypothesized that Judas the Galilean was crucified in the first year of Pilate's prefecture in 26 CE and James the Just came to prominence in 46 CE at the time of the famine. The document also includes the following passage:

> *Listen, all you who recognize righteousness, and consider the deeds of Elohim. When he has a dispute with any mortal, he passes judgment on those who spurn him. For when Israel abandoned him by being faithless, he turned away from them and from His sanctuary and gave them up*

> to the sword. But when He called to mind the covenant He made with their forefathers, He left a remnant for Israel and did not allow them to be exterminated. In the era of wrath – three hundred and ninety years at the time He handed them over to the power of Nebuchadnezzar king of Babylon – He took care of them and caused to grow from Israel and from Aaron a root of planting to inherit his land and to grow fat on the good produce of His soil.

The consensus is that the reference to the 390 figure is symbolic rather than historic, a reference to the prophet Ezekiel who foretells of the destruction of the first Jerusalem temple by the Babylonians under the command of Nebuchadnezzar in 597 BCE. Ezekiel wrote:

> "Now, son of man, take a block of clay, put it in front of you and draw the city of Jerusalem on it. Then lay siege to it: Erect siege works against it, build a ramp up to it, set up camps against it and put battering rams around it. Then take an iron pan, place it as an iron wall between you and the city and turn your face toward it. It will be under siege, and you shall besiege it. This will be a sign to the people of Israel.
>
> "Then lie on your left side and put the sin of the people of Israel upon yourself. You are to bear their sin for the number of days you lie on your side. I have assigned you the same number of days as the years of their sin. So for 390 days you will bear the sin of the people of Israel.
>
> [Ezekiel 4:1-5]

The author of the *Damascus document* was surely interpreting this ancient text in the light of his own time and in Ezekiel there are echoes of the same conflicts that bedeviled first century Judaea.

During the Jewish war, Jerusalem was under threat from the advancing Roman forces. But Judea was first Hellenized by the conquest of Alexander the Great in 332 BCE, three hundred and ninety three years before the death of James. Of the Essenes, Josephus wrote:

> *There are also those among them who undertake to foretell things to come, by reading the holy books, and using several sorts of purifications, and being perpetually conversant in the discourses of the prophets; and it is but seldom that they miss in their predictions.*
>
> [Josephus: The Jewish War 2:8:12]

Even in our own time we see the fascination that people have with fortune tellers and prophetic writings and surely it would have been the same back then. This text would have been read as a prophecy. Ezekiel continues:

> "After you have finished this, lie down again, this time on your right side, and bear the sin of the people of Judah. I have assigned you 40 days, a day for each year. Turn your face toward the siege of Jerusalem and with bared arm prophesy against her.
>
> [Ezekiel 4:6-7]

As Ezekiel alludes to a period of forty years for the sin of the house of Judah, the *Damascus document* predicts a period of forty years from the death of a Beloved Teacher until the destruction of all warriors:

> *Now from the day the Beloved Teacher passed away to the destruction of all the warriors who went back to the Man of the Lie will be about forty years.*

Surely, the end of all warriors is a prophecy for the end of all war and that Beloved Teacher a reference to James the Righteous.

PART II

Conflict

The sense that change was coming must have been almost palpable. Those educated in the works of Philo would have been aware of his words:

> *For all the things that are made by our arts when completed stand still and remain; but all those which are accomplished by the knowledge of God are moved at subsequent times. For their ends are the beginnings of other things; as, for instance, the end of day is the beginning of night. And in the same way we must look upon months and years when they come to an end as the beginning of those which are just about to follow them. And so the generation of other things which are destroyed, and the destruction of others which are generated is completed, so that that is true which is said that--*
> *And naught that is created wholly dies;*
> *But one thing parted and combined with others produces a fresh form.*
>
> [Philo: Legum Allegoriae I: III(7)]

For the devout, evidence from scripture contained a specific time-scale:

> *I have assigned you the same number of days as the years of their sin. So for 390 days you will bear the sin of the people of Israel.*
> *"After you have finished this, lie down again, this time on your right side, and bear the sin of the people of Judah. I have assigned you 40 days, a day for each year.*
>
> [Ezekiel 4:5-7]

From the conquest of Alexander the Great to the death of James there was a period of 393 years. The *Damascus document* was clear that Ezekiel was prophesying destruction of the Roman and allied forces in an additional forty years.

> *Now from the day the Beloved Teacher passed away to the destruction of all the warriors who went back to the Man of the Lie will be about forty years.*
>
> [The Damascus Document]

Expectation of conflict is evident throughout New Testament writings in the Book of Revelations, the letters of Paul and the gospels. Of the coming of the Lord Jesus Christ, Paul wrote:

> *It cannot happen until the Great Revolt has taken place*

In Mark's gospel too, it states:

> *But in those days, following that distress,*
> *the sun will be darkened,*
> *and the moon will not give its light;*
> *the stars will fall from the sky,*
> *and the heavenly bodies will be shaken.*
>
> *At that time people will see the Son of Man coming in clouds with great power and glory. And he will send his angels and gather his elect from the four winds, from the ends of the earth to the ends of the heavens.*
>
> *Now learn this lesson from the fig tree: As soon as its twigs get tender and its leaves come out, you know that summer is near. Even so, when you see these things happening, you know that it is near, right at the door. Truly I tell you, this generation will certainly not pass away until all these things*

PART II

have happened. Heaven and earth will pass away, but my words will never pass away.

[Mark 13:24-31]

That change was coming was universally accepted. What was disputed was the nature of that change. Some of the Qumran scrolls depict a bloody battle between the forces of good and evil that will end with the defeat of the Roman forces (the *"Kittim"*):

And he will destroy him and his army. [...] And you will swallow up all the uncircumcised and you will [...] And they will be righteous, and he will ascend to the height [...] one anointed with the oil of the kingdom of the [...]

[4Q458, fr.2, col.2]

As it is written in the book of Isaiah the prophet, And felled will be the thickets of the forest with an axe, and Lebanon by a mighty one will fall. A shoot will arise from the roots of Jesse, and a branch from his roots will bear fruit. Its interpretation is [...] the branch of David.
And they will judge the [...]. And the prince (nasi) of the Community, the branch of David, will put him to death [...] with tambourine and with dancing. And the priest will command [...] the slain of the Kittim.

[4Q285 5.1-6, commentary on Isaiah 10-11]

This apocalyptic imagery is most dramatically illustrated, however, in the extraordinary *War Scroll* which gives graphic details of the predicted bloody conflicts between the *"Sons of Light"* and *"Sons of Darkness"*:

Then at the time appointed by God, His great excellence shall shine for all the times of eternity; for peace and blessing, glory and joy, and long life for all Sons of Light. On the day when the Kittim fall there shall be a battle and horrible carnage before the God of Israel, for it is a day appointed by Him from ancient times as a battle of annihilation for the Sons of Darkness. On that day the congregation of the gods and the congregation of men shall engage one another, resulting in great carnage. The Sons of Light and the forces of Darkness shall fight together to show the strength of God with the roar of a great multitude and the shout of gods and men; a day of disaster. It is a time of distress for all the people who are redeemed by God. In all their afflictions none exists that is like it, hastening to its completion as an eternal redemption. On the day of their battle against the Kittim, they shall go forth for carnage in battle. In three lots the Sons of Light shall stand firm so as to strike a blow at wickedness, and in three the army of Belial shall strengthen themselves so as to force the retreat of the forces of Light. And when the banners of the infantry cause their hearts to melt, then the strength of God will strengthen the hearts of the Sons of Light. In the seventh lot: the great hand of God shall overcome Belial and all the angels of his dominion, and all the men of his forces shall be destroyed forever.

[War Scroll: The Description of the Eschatological War]

There was, of course, that reference in the Book of Numbers that seemed to prophesy a conquering Jewish Messiah:

A star *will come out of Jacob; a scepter will rise out of Israel. He will crush the foreheads of Moab, the skulls of all*

> *the people of Sheth. Edom will be conquered.*
>
> [Numbers 24.17-18]

The comet that appeared in 66 CE seemed an ominous portent:

> *Thus there was a star resembling a sword, which stood over the city [Jerusalem], and a comet, that continued a whole year.*
>
> [Josephus: The Jewish War 6:5:3]

There were some, however, who came to believe that the fulfillment of that prophecy was someone who was not a Jew at all.

Josephus

The resistance movement was divided into six regional commands. The most northerly region, Galilee, was put under the control of Josephus. By any standard Josephus' life was quite extraordinary. He was not an obvious choice for a military leader. In his youth he seemed destined for a religious life:

> *Moreover, when I was a child, and about fourteen years of age, I was commended by all for the love I had to learning; on which account the high priests and principal men of the city came then frequently to me together, in order to know my opinion about the accurate understanding of points of the law. And when I was about sixteen years old, I had a mind to make trim of the several sects that were among us. These sects are three: – The first is that of the Pharisees, the second that Sadducees, and the third that of the Essens, as we have frequently told you; for I thought that by this means I might choose the best, if I were once acquainted with them all*
>
> [Josephus: Life 2]

Nevertheless, at the start of the war and in a mass meeting at the Jerusalem Temple, Josephus was appointed as one of the army generals:

> *But John, the son of Matthias, was made governor of the toparchies of Gophnitica and Acrabattene; as was Josephus, the son of Matthias, of both the Galilees.*
>
> *Gamala also, which was the strongest city in those parts, was put under his command.*
>
> [Josephus: The Jewish War 2:20:4]

Josephus demonstrated great leadership qualities. He organized the fortifications of a number of towns in the region and trained an army. However, no body of men that Josephus could muster could match the Roman forces. The Emperor sent Vespasian with two legions of troops, X Fretensis and V Macedonica. He was joined by his son Titus who had set sail from Alexandria at the head of XV Apollinaris. It was in Galilee that they first landed and they moved swiftly through the region. Out of fear, Josephus' army deserted him and although he himself initially took refuge in the town of Tiberias, he eventually joined the rebel forces in the heavily fortified town of Jotapata. His account of the siege of that town bear testament to the indiscriminate, callous and brutal horror of war:

> *Then did Josephus take necessity for his counselor in this utmost distress, (which necessity is very sagacious in invention when it is irritated by despair,) and gave orders to pour scalding oil upon those whose shields protected them. Whereupon they soon got it ready, being many that brought it, and what they brought being a great quantity also, and poured it on all sides upon the Romans, and threw down upon them their vessels as they were still hissing from the heat of the fire: this so burnt the Romans, that it dispersed that united band, who now tumbled down*

> *from the wall with horrid pains, for the oil did easily run down the whole body from head to foot, under their entire armor, and fed upon their flesh like flame itself, its fat and unctuous nature rendering it soon heated and slowly cooled; and as the men were cooped up in their headpieces and breastplates, they could no way get free from this burning oil; they could only leap and roll about in their pains, as they fell down from the bridges they had laid. And as they thus were beaten back, and retired to their own party, who still pressed them forward, they were easily wounded by those that were behind them.*
>
> [Josephus: The Jewish War 3:7:28]

The Romans used siege weaponry, including an onager, a type of catapult used for hurling large rocks and a ballista, a type of high powered crossbow used for firing darts. Josephus describes the impact of these machines:

> *the force with which these engines threw stones and darts made them hurt several at a time, and the violent noise of the stones that were cast by the engines was so great, that they carried away the pinnacles of the wall, and broke off the corners of the towers; for no body of men could be so strong as not to be overthrown to the last rank by the largeness of the stones.*
> *And any one may learn the force of the engines by what happened this very night; for as one of those that stood round about Josephus was near the wall, his head was carried away by such a stone, and his skull was flung as far as three furlongs.*

In the day time also, a woman with child had her belly so violently struck, as she was just come out of her house, that the infant was carried to the distance of half a furlong, so great was the force of that engine.

[Josephus: The Jewish War 3:7:23]

Platforms to scale the wall were constructed by the Romans and little by little the height of the platforms increased. Finally, after forty seven days, the top of the wall was reached. The soldiers entered the city just before dawn when most of the rebels were still asleep. Some rebels managed to find hiding places but most were killed or captured. 1,200 prisoners were taken while the dead including those killed in the battles preceding the capture, were reckoned at 40,000. Josephus, meanwhile, with forty others, had taken refuge in a cave that was accessed from a deep pit and there for two days he remained hidden, until a woman of the party was captured and gave their position away. On hearing of the discovery of the rebel leader, Vespasian sent a request to Josephus to give himself up with a promise that his life would be spared:

Whereupon Vespasian sent immediately and zealously two tribunes, Paulinus and Gallicanus, and ordered them to give Josephus their right hands as a security for his life, and to exhort him to come up. So they came and invited the man to come up, and gave him assurances that his life should be preserved: but they did not prevail with him; for he gathered suspicions from the probability there was that one who had done so many things against the Romans must suffer for it, though not from the mild temper of those that invited him. However, he was afraid that he was invited to come up in order to be punished, until Vespasian sent besides these a third tribune, Nicanor, to him; he was one that was well known to Josephus, and had been his familiar

PART II

acquaintance in old time. When he was come, he enlarged upon the natural mildness of the Romans towards those they have once conquered; and told him that he had behaved himself so valiantly, that the commanders rather admired than hated him; that the general was very desirous to have him brought to him, not in order to punish him, for that he could do though he should not come voluntarily, but that he was determined to preserve a man of his courage. He moreover added this, that Vespasian, had he been resolved to impose upon him, would not have sent to him a friend of his own, nor put the fairest color upon the vilest action, by pretending friendship and meaning perfidiousness; nor would he have himself acquiesced, or come to him, had it been to deceive him.

Now as Josephus began to hesitate with himself about Nicanor's proposal, the soldiery were so angry, that they ran hastily to set fire to the den; but the tribune would not permit them so to do, as being very desirous to take the man alive. And now, as Nicanor lay hard at Josephus to comply, and he understood how the multitude of the enemies threatened him, he called to mind the dreams which he had dreamed in the night time, whereby God had signified to him beforehand both the future calamities of the Jews, and the events that concerned the Roman emperors. Now Josephus was able to give shrewd conjectures about the interpretation of such dreams as have been ambiguously delivered by God. Moreover, he was not unacquainted with the prophecies contained in the sacred books, as being a priest himself, and of the posterity of

> *priests: and just then was he in an ecstasy; and setting before him the tremendous images of the dreams he had lately had, he put up a secret prayer to God, and said, "Since it pleaseth thee, who hast created the Jewish nation, to depress the same, and since all their good fortune is gone over to the Romans, and since thou hast made choice of this soul of mine to foretell what is to come to pass hereafter, I willingly give them my hands, and am content to live. And I protest openly that I do not go over to the Romans as a deserter of the Jews, but as a minister from thee."*
>
> [Josephus: The Jewish War 3:8:1-3]

Although Josephus was on the point of surrendering, those with whom he shared his hiding place were less keen that he did so. His fellow Jews said to him:

> *We will lend thee our right hand and a sword; and if thou wilt die willingly, thou wilt die as general of the Jews; but if unwillingly, thou wilt die as a traitor to them."*
>
> [Josephus: The Jewish War 3:8:4]

Despite being fatigued and in a state of extreme stress with swords pointed at his throat, Josephus reports that following this threat, he delivered a speech that is impossibly eloquent. Nevertheless, at that moment in time, Josephus had a choice of whether to surrender to Vespasian's troops or to die. Josephus chose to surrender. Josephus was treated mercifully by Vespasian and indeed he became a great champion of the general:

> *For when the siege of Jotapata was over, and I was among the Romans, I was kept with much Care, by means of the great respect that Vespasian showed me. Moreover, at his command, I married a virgin, who was from among the*

captives of that country yet did she not live with me long, but was divorced, upon my being freed from my bonds, and my going to Alexandria.

However, I married another wife at Alexandria, and was thence sent, together with Titus, to the siege of Jerusalem, and was frequently in danger of being put to death; while both the Jews were very desirous to get me under their power, in order to have me punished

[Josephus: Life 75]

The Capernaum demoniac

Within the Old Testament there is only one reference to possession by an evil spirit and even that is uncertain. Samuel 16:14 reports: *"an evil spirit from the Lord troubled Saul"*.

Within the gospels, however, there are frequent references to Jesus casting out demons and fundamentalist Christians, Catholic orthodoxy and popular culture have fuelled a primitive belief that victims can be possessed by evil and supernatural forces.

You do not, however, need to subscribe to this belief to understand the references to demons in the gospel of Mark. There are very natural, very human explanations.

There are two major sections devoted to the healing of demoniacs. The healing of the Capernaum demoniac is one of the Galilean healing miracles in the early part of the gospel. The healing of the Gerasene demoniac occurs during a section of the gospel devoted to faith as commitment. In both passages at the same time as identifying Jesus as the Son of God, the *"victim"* expresses paranoia:

"What do you want with us, Jesus of Nazareth? Have you

come to destroy us? I know who you are—the Holy One of God!"

[Mark 1:24-25]

He shouted at the top of his voice, "What do you want with me, Jesus, Son of the Most High God? In God's name don't torture me!"

[Mark 5:7]

In the gospel, anxiety is an expression of spirit without faith. The demoniacs do have faith, of course, but it is an exclusive faith. The stories are likely to be allusions to historical events that took place during the Jewish War, the story of the Capernaum demoniac being a reference to the healing of an individual who identifies himself with a particular culture.

Josephus, the former head of the resistance movement in Galilee, became champion of Vespasian. This was an extraordinary turnaround and the Capernaum demoniac, surely, is an allusion to his *"conversion"*:

The people were all so amazed that they asked each other, "What is this? A new teaching—and with authority! He even gives orders to impure spirits and they obey him." News about him spread quickly over the whole region of Galilee.

[Mark 1:27-28]

Like many others, Josephus had been caught up in the excited and enthusiastic preparation for war. His was a spirit that lacked both faith in the divine and divine reason. In the subsequent gospel passage, at the house of Simon and Andrew, respectively the personifications of spirit and action, Simon's mother in law is lying in bed with a fever. The significance of the mother-in-law may seem strange but in Aramaic and Hebrew the term for mother-in-law (hamah) is very similar to the term for fever (hommah). It is a play on words[11]. After her healing, Simon's mother-in-law waits on Jesus and his disciples. Is this not an echo of the *"healing"* of Josephus?

Of course, if the Capernaum demoniac is an allegorical tale based on Josephus' *"healing"* then there must be significance in this small fishing village on the northern shore of the Sea of Galilee. And indeed there is, for it was in Capernaum, before his retreat to Jotapata, that Josephus himself developed a fever:

> *And I had performed great things that day, if a certain fate had not been my hindrance; for the horse on which I rode, and upon whose back I fought, fell into a quagmire, and threw me on the ground, and I was bruised on my wrist, and carried into a village named Cepharnome, or Capernaum.*
>
> *When my soldiers heard of this, they were afraid I had been worse hurt than I was; and so they did not go on with their pursuit any further, but returned in very great concern for me.*
>
> *I therefore sent for the physicians, and while I was under their hands, I continued **feverish** that day.*
>
> [Josephus: Life 72]

The Gerasene demoniac

Throughout Christian history, the account of the Gerasene Demoniac in Mark's gospel has perplexed Christian scholars. This is

---

[11] Pay attention to a play upon words

the story of the man possessed by a *"legion"* of unclean spirits that are cast into a herd of pigs that then run down a mountain side into a lake and drown.

Unlike most of the other gospel stories, it provides a wealth of incidental detail that poses awkward questions. For a start, Gerasa, the city of the Decapolis lies twenty miles from the nearest body of water. These pigs would have to run a very long way. Also, why at the end of the passage, is Jesus is asked to leave the neighborhood? What possible significance could this have?

There are a number of factors that may help to shed light on this tale.

Firstly, the story is position within the gospel in a section of scripture that deals with faith as commitment. That is *"doing"* as an expression of faith. This passage must relate to people's commitment in some way.

Secondly, the tale is related as a healing. Whatever that commitment is, it is not a good thing.

Thirdly, the author of the gospel was not interested in writing an historical record. He was concerned with creating myth. The incidental detail in the passage suggests an historical allegory where the overall cultural significance of the events that occurred holds far more importance than their historical detail.

By taking into account these factors and analysing the story itself, the tale seems best understood as a critique of the culture of the community that had a base at Qumran. Line by line we can see the parallels:

They came to the other side of the sea, to the country of

PART II

the Gerasene [12]

From the *Jewish War*, we know that shortly after Jericho was capture, Vespasian sent one of his generals to take Gerasa:

> *AND now Vespasian had fortified all the places round about Jerusalem, and erected citadels at Jericho and Adida, and placed garrisons in them both, partly out of his own Romans, and partly out of the body of his auxiliaries. He also sent Lucius Annius to Gerasa, and delivered to him a body of horsemen, and a considerable number of footmen. So when he had taken the city, which he did at the first onset, he slew a thousand of those young men who had not prevented him by flying away; but he took their families captive, and permitted his soldiers to plunder them of their effects; after which he set fire to their houses, and went away to the adjoining villages, while the men of power fled away, and the weaker part were destroyed, and what was remaining was all burnt down.*
>
> [Josephus: Jewish War 4:9:1]

The *"Gerasa"* mentioned in Josephus' account is unlikely to be a reference to the town on the Decapolis which is some miles north but a reference to a site somewhere nearer Jerusalem. If this is the case then surely the *"Gerasa"* mentioned in the gospel can also be a reference to this settlement somewhere near the Dead Sea.

And when Jesus had stepped out of the boat, immediately there met him out of the tombs a man

---

[12] Pay attention to a reference to an improbable geographical location

with an unclean spirit.

The *Community Rule*, the handbook for community members, states the proper attitude that the member of the community should have to others:

> They are to regard as felons all that transgress the law.
> He (the community member) is to bear unremitting hatred toward all men of ill repute, and to be minded to keep [ ] from them. He is to leave it to them to pursue wealth and mercenary gain, like servants at the mercy of their masters or wretches truckling to a despot.

An "unclean spirit" is one who rejects others out of hand such as those possessed by a spirit that bears "unremitting hatred toward all men of ill repute".

He lived among the tombs.

The numerous caves around the regions must have seemed like catacombs and were quite likely inhabited by some of the sects' members who fled the Roman advance.

And no one could bind him any more, not even with a chain, for he had often been bound with shackles and chains, but he wrenched the chains apart, and he broke the shackles in pieces. No one had the strength to subdue him.

This may well be a reference to the slavery that the Jewish people endured in Egypt and Babylon and under the oppressive regimes of the Seleucid Kings. Although Josephus wrote admiringly of the courage of the Essenes under torture:

> They condemn the miseries of life, and are above pain, by the generosity of their mind. And as for death, if it will be for their glory, they esteem it better than living always; and

PART II

> *indeed our war with the Romans gave abundant evidence what great souls they had in their trials, wherein, although they were tortured and distorted, burnt and torn to pieces, and went through all kinds of instruments of torment, that they might be forced either to blaspheme their legislator, or to eat what was forbidden them, yet could they not be made to do either of them, no, nor once to flatter their tormentors, or to shed a tear; but they smiled in their very pains, and laughed those to scorn who inflicted the torments upon them, and resigned up their souls with great alacrity, as expecting to receive them again.*
>
> [Josephus: Jewish War 2:8:10]

Night and day among the tombs and on the mountains

Literally, the tombs can refer to caves and the mountains to the mountainous region in which Qumran is located.

He was always crying out and cutting himself with stones.

Of the Essenes, Josephus wrote:

> *They also take great pains in studying the writings of the ancients, and choose out of them what is most for the advantage of their soul and body; and they inquire after such roots and medicinal stones as may cure their distempers.*
>
> [Josephus: Jewish War 2:8:6]

In addition the strict requirements for adherence to the Law suggest that these are emotionally repressed people. One consequence of emotional repression is self-harm, used to relieve feelings of anger or tension that get bottled up inside.

> *And when he saw Jesus from afar, he ran and fell down before him. And crying out with a loud voice, he said, "What have you to do with me, Jesus, Son of the Most High God? I adjure you by God, do not torment me."*

These zealots of the Essene community possess spirit without an all-encompassing faith and within the author's narrative model spirit lacking faith in the divine is vulnerable.

> *For he was saying to him, "Come out of the man, you unclean spirit!" And Jesus asked him, "What is your name?" He replied, "My name is Legion, for we are many."*

Here there is use of the Latin word "Legion" within the Greek text that is surely a reference to the Roman legion commanded by Vespasian.

> *And he begged him earnestly not to send them out of the country.*

This is a reference, surely, to the irrational attachment to the "promised land".

> *Now a great herd of pigs was feeding there on the hillside, and they begged him, saying, "Send us to the pigs; let us enter them."*

Here we have the irony of ironies. Those zealots with the obsessive attachment to the dietary restrictions of the Torah ask to be sent into the "unclean" animals.

> *So he gave them permission. And the unclean spirits came out, and entered the pigs, and the herd, numbering about two thousand, rushed down the steep bank into the sea and were drowned in the sea.*

We know that Vespasian commanded some captives to be thrown into the Dead Sea:

PART II

The nature of the lake Asphaltitis is also worth describing. It is, as I have said already, bitter and unfruitful. It is so light [or thick] that it bears up the heaviest things that are thrown into it; nor is it easy for anyone to make things sink therein to the bottom, if he had a mind so to do. Accordingly, when Vespasian went to see it, he commanded that some who could not swim should have their hands tied behind them, and be thrown into the deep, when it so happened that they all swam as if a wind had forced them upwards.

[Josephus: Jewish War 4:8:4]

The herdsmen fled and told it in the city and in the country. And people came to see what it was that had happened. And they came to Jesus and saw the demon-possessed man, the one who had had the legion, sitting there, clothed and in his right mind, and they were afraid. And those who had seen it described to them what had happened to the demon-possessed man and to the pigs.

Free from the group mentality, individuals can be sensible.

And they began to beg Jesus to depart from their region.

From Josephus, we know that Vespasian was urged to declare himself Emperor:

These were the discourses the soldiers had in their several companies; after which they got together in a great body, and, encouraging one another, they declared Vespasian emperor, and exhorted him to save the government, which was now in danger. Now Vespasian's concern had been for a considerable time about the public, yet did he not intend

> *to set up for governor himself, though his actions showed him to deserve it, while he preferred that safety which is in a private life before the dangers in a state of such dignity; but when he refused the empire, the commanders insisted the more earnestly upon his acceptance; and the soldiers came about him, with their drawn swords in their hands, and threatened to kill him, unless he would now live according to his dignity. And when he had shown his reluctance a great while, and had endeavored to thrust away this dominion from him, he at length, being not able to persuade them,*
>
> *yielded to their solicitations that would salute him emperor.*
>
> [Josephus: Jewish War 4:10:4]

Declaring himself Emperor meant moving the focus from Judaea and onto Rome and Vespasian did leave the region:

> *Vespasian then removed from Cesarea to Berytus, where many embassages came to him from Syria, and many from other provinces, bringing with them from every city crowns, and the congratulations of the people.*
>
> [Josephus: Jewish War 4:10:6]

As he was getting into the boat, the man who had been possessed with demons begged him that he might be with him. And he did not permit him but said to him, "Go home to your friends and tell them how much the Lord has done for you, and how he has had mercy on you." And he went away and began to proclaim in the Decapolis how much Jesus had done for him, and everyone marveled.

Qumran was a small fortified settlement that may have only held tens of permanent inhabitants and a few hundred fighters. It is surely likely that in CE 68 there were many in the community that slept in the nearby caves. During the Roman expedition against Qumran, these community members would have been completely helpless and many surely, would have surrendered to the Roman forces. Of course, for the die-hards, surrender would have been tantamount to betrayal and those who did surrender would surely have been fearful of the consequences should their *"betrayal"* become known.

Literary evidence from the scrolls indicates that many of the members of the community were fundamentalist in belief, extreme in behavior and divisive in their attitude. Evidence from the writing of Josephus indicates that they had a rigid hierarchical organization:

> *Now after the time of their preparatory trial is over, they are parted into four classes; and so far are the juniors inferior to the seniors, that if the seniors should be touched by the juniors, they must wash themselves, as if they had intermixed themselves with the company of a foreigner.*
>
> [Josephus: Jewish War 2:8:10]

Members of the community excluded themselves from others. Theirs was a faith that lacked divine spirit. Compare the story of the Gerasene demoniac with the story of the woman with the hemorrhage that follows immediately after. Within Jewish culture a menstruating woman was classed as unclean and to be touched by one regarded as defilement. Nevertheless, when she reaches out and touches his cloak, Jesus does not regard himself as being defiled. Indeed, he sends the woman away with a blessing. Is this not an echo of the *"healing"* of those at Qumran who chose not to fight?

The everlasting name

…. for the first, who is named Abraham, is a symbol of that virtue which is derived from instruction; the intermediate Isaac is an emblem of natural virtue; the third, Jacob, of that virtue which is devoted to and derived from practice.

[Philo: On Abraham]

Abraham, Isaac and Jacob

Philo was the greatest of the Jewish apologists who interpreted the Jewish scriptures in the light of Greek philosophy.

Aristotle wrote:

There are three things which make men good and virtuous; these are nature, habit, rational principle…… we learn some things by habit and some by instruction.

[Aristotle: Politics]

Philo echoed the teaching with reference to the fathers of the faith:

There are three different modes by which we proceed towards the most excellent end, namely, instruction, nature, and practice. There are also three persons, the oldest of the wise men who in the account given to us by Moses derive three names from these modes………………
for the sacred word appears thoroughly to investigate and to describe the different dispositions of the soul, being all of them good, the one aiming at what is good by means of

PART II

> *instruction, the second by nature, the last by practice..............;*
>
> *.... for the first, who is named Abraham, is a symbol of that virtue which is derived from instruction; the intermediate Isaac is an emblem of natural virtue; the third, Jacob, of that virtue which is devoted to and derived from practice.*
>
> [Philo: On Abraham]

And the three separate individuals are united together as one:

> *It happens then that they are all three of one household and of one family, for the last of the three is the son of the middle one, and the grandson of the first; and they are all lovers of God, and beloved by God, loving the only God, and being loved in return by him who has chosen, as the holy scriptures tell us, by reason of the excess of their virtues in which they lived, to give them also a share of the same appellation as himself; for having added his own peculiar name to their names he has united them together, appropriating to himself an appellation composed of the three names: "For," says God, "this is my everlasting name: I am the God of Abraham, and the God of Isaac, and the God of Jacob,"*
>
> [Philo: On Abraham]

A similar phrase is used in Mark's gospel. Some Saduccees test Jesus by asking whose wife a woman would be at the Resurrection after she married and was widowed by each of seven brothers in turn:

> *Jesus replied, "Are you not in error because you do not know the Scriptures or the power of God? When the dead*

> rise, they will neither marry nor be given in marriage; they will be like the angels in heaven. Now about the dead rising—have you not read in the Book of Moses, in the account of the burning bush, how God said to him, 'I am the God of Abraham, the God of Isaac, and the God of Jacob'? He is not the God of the dead, but of the living. You are badly mistaken!"
>
> [Mark 12:24-27]

The God of Abraham, the God of Isaac, and the God of Jacob is a God of the living and we should not be surprised if individuals who best epitomized excellence in instruction, nature and practice are themselves represented in Mark's gospel.

The God of Abraham

Mandaeism is a minority religion that until recently had its major population in Iraq where in 2003, there were 70,000 adherents. Due to the conflicts in that troubled country, the population in 2010 was estimated to be one tenth of that size.

The religion has pre-Christian roots but there are references to Christ within the text of one of their sacred books, the Book of John where Jesus implores God to baptize him:

> ....Therefore baptize me, O Yahya, with thy baptizing and utter o'er me the Name thy is wont to utter. If I show myself as thy pupil, I will remember thee in my writing: if I attest not myself as thy pupil then wipe out my name from thy page. Thou wilt for thy sins be hailed to account and I for my sins will be hailed to account." When Yeshu Messiah said this there came a letter out of the House of Abathur: "Yahya baptize the deceiver in the Jordan. Lead

PART II

him down into the Jordan and baptize him and lead him up again to the shore and there set him."

Then Ruha made herself like a dove and threw a cross over the Jordan and made its water change into various colors......

Within Mandean mythology, Abathur represents God and Ruha represents the emotional and passionate element representing spirit. Note how Ruha takes the form of a dove and when she throws a cross over the Jordan, the river that physically and metaphorically divided Jews and gentiles, the water, like Joseph's coat, became multi-colored. Toward the end of the chapter, Yeshu Messiah disappears to be replaced by Messiah Paulis:

....."O Jordan," she says "thou sanctifiest me and thou sanctifiest my seven sons." "The Jordan in which Messiah Paulis was baptized have I made into a trough. The bread which Messiah Paulis receives have I made into sacrament.' The drink which Messiah Paulis receives, have I made into a 'supper.' The head-band which Messiah Paulis receives, have I made into a 'priest-hood.'' The staff which Messiah Paulis receives, have I made into a 'dung' [-stick]." [? Gnosis of Life speaks] "Let me warn you, my brothers, let me warn you, my beloved! Let me warn you, my brothers, against the ....who are like unto the cross. They lay it on the walls; then stand there and bow down to the block.

The chapter ends with a warning:

Let me warn you, my brothers, of the god, which the carpenter has joined together. If the carpenter has joined together the god, who then has joined together the carpenter?"

Praised be Life and Life is Victorious

In contrast to Jesus, John the Baptist, although not regarded as the founder of the religion, is accorded special status. Indeed, the book of John portrays him as something of a Messiah figure. The book contains an extended pre-birth narrative where we are introduced to a *"Letter of Truth"* that in later chapters is passed to John himself. The text of the Book of John, unlike the books of the Bible, has a rhythmic quality with a repetition of phrases. Indeed the Book is more of a poetic than the prose narrative:

> *They took the Letter and put it in the hand of the Jews.*
> *They opened it, read in it and see that it does not contain what they would, that it does not contain what their soul wills.*
> *They took the letter and put it in the hand of Yôhânâ, saying: "Take, Rabbe Yôhânâ, Truth's Letter, which has come here to thee from thy Father."*
> *Yôhânâ opened it and read it and saw in it a wondrous writing. He opened it and read in it and became full of life.*
> *"This is, what I would, and this does my Soul will" He said.*

God spoke to Abram, telling him to leave his native land and his father's house for a land that he would show him.

God spoke to John and John asked people to respond to that internal authority and to cease from sinful works. For both Jews and gentiles, he symbolically washed away the sins of those who repented.

> **And a voice came from heaven: "You are my Son, whom I love; with you I am well pleased."**
>
> [Mark: 1:11]

PART II

The God of Jacob

The significance of Vespasian in bringing peace to a region that was riven with conflict should not be underestimated.

A prophecy in the Book of Numbers states:

> *A star will come out of Jacob; a scepter will rise out of Israel. He will crush the foreheads of Moab, the skulls of all the people of Sheth. Edom will be conquered.*
>
> [Numbers 24.17-18]

Far from this being a reference to a Jewish Messiah, Josephus suggests that Vespasian himself was the fulfillment of that prophecy:

> *But now, what did the most elevate them in undertaking this war, was an ambiguous oracle that was also found in their sacred writings, how, "about that time, one from their country should become governor of the habitable earth." The Jews took this prediction to belong to themselves in particular, and many of the wise men were thereby deceived in their determination. Now this oracle certainly denoted the government of Vespasian, who was appointed emperor in Judea.*
>
> [Josephus: The Jewish War 6:5:4]

There were others who were similarly minded:

> *There had spread over all the Orient an old and established belief, that it was fated for men coming from Judaea to rule the world. This prediction, referring to the Emperor of Rome –as afterwards appeared from the event– the people*

of Judaea took to themselves.

[Suetonius: Life of Vespasian 4.5]

The majority [of the Jews] were convinced that the ancient scriptures of their priests alluded to the present as the very time when the Orient would triumph and from Judaea would go forth men destined to rule the world. This mysterious prophecy really referred to Vespasian and Titus, but the common people, true to the selfish ambitions of mankind, thought that this exalted destiny was reserved for them, and not even their calamities opened their eyes to the truth.

[Tacitus, Histories 5.13]

There are allusions to the impact of Vespasian in the gospel of Mark within the story of the Capernaum and Gerasene demoniacs but there are other allusions.

In his *Histories*, Tacitus wrote:

In the months during which Vespasian was waiting at Alexandria for the periodical return of the summer gales and settled weather at sea, many wonders occurred which seemed to point him out as the object of the favor of heaven and of the partiality of the gods. One of the common people of Alexandria, well known for his blindness, threw himself at the Emperor's knees, and implored him with groans to heal his infirmity. This he did by the advice of the God Serapis, whom this nation, devoted as it is to many superstitions, worships more than any other divinity. He begged Vespasian that he would

PART II

deign to moisten his cheeks and eye-balls with his spittle. Another with a diseased hand, at the counsel of the same God, prayed that the limb might feel the print of a Caesar's foot. At first Vespasian ridiculed and repulsed them. They persisted; and he, though on the one hand he feared the scandal of a fruitless attempt, yet, on the other, was induced by the entreaties of the men and by the language of his flatterers to hope for success. At last he ordered that the opinion of physicians should be taken, as to whether such blindness and infirmity were within the reach of human skill. They discussed the matter from different points of view. 'In the one case,' they said, 'the faculty of sight was not wholly destroyed, and might return, if the obstacles were removed; in the other case, the limb, which had fallen into a diseased condition, might be restored, if a healing influence were applied; such, perhaps, might be the pleasure of the gods, and the Emperor might be chosen to be the minister of the divine will; at any rate, all the glory of a successful remedy would be Caesar's, while the ridicule of failure would fall on the sufferers.' And so Vespasian, supposing that all things were possible to his good fortune, and that nothing was any longer past belief, with a joyful countenance, amid the intense expectation of the multitude of bystanders, accomplished what was required. The hand was instantly restored to its use, and the light of day again shone upon the blind. Persons actually present attest both facts, even now when nothing is to be gained by falsehood.

[Tacitus: The Histories, 4:81]

Like Vespasian, the gospel reports Jesus curing a withered hand and in two passages restoring sight to the blind. In the first [8: 21-26], the sight of the blind man of Bethsaida is gradually restored, in the same way that Vespasian restores the sight of the blind man, by putting spittle on the man's eyes. There is also an historical allusion in the second passage [10: 46-51] where the sight of Bartimaeus is restored immediately. The author draws particular attention to the place name *"Jericho"* in this passage by repeating it. It was at Jericho that Vespasian first learnt of Nero's death and where he awaited instructions from the new Emperor:

> *Then they came to Jericho. As Jesus and his disciples, together with a large crowd, were leaving the city, a blind man, Bartimaeus (which means "son of Timaeus"), was sitting by the roadside begging. When he heard that it was Jesus of Nazareth, he began to shout, "Jesus, Son of David, have mercy on me!"*
>
> *Many rebuked him and told him to be quiet, but he shouted all the more, "Son of David, have mercy on me!" Jesus stopped and said, "Call him."*
>
> *So they called to the blind man, "Cheer up! On your feet! He's calling you." Throwing his cloak aside, he jumped to his feet and came to Jesus.*
>
> [Mark 10: 46-50]

As Vespasian awaited instructions from the new Emperor, his forces attacked the fortified stronghold of Qumran. The Essenes who inhabited Qumran awaited a Son of David, a conquering Messiah that was prophesied in the Book of Numbers, to free them from Roman rule. As is clear from the many of the scrolls, the Essenes considered themselves more worthy than others. In discarding his cloak, Bartimaeus is discarding his vanities.

In the writing of Philo, Jacob epitomized excellence in practice. He gained the authority that was due to his brother Esau. In 70 CE there was no one with greater authority in the Roman world than the new Emperor. His authority came from his reputation as a just and capable leader and on him laid the hopes of many who dreamed of a world free from conflict.

After Jesus spoke to Bartimaeus, the blind beggar no longer addressed him as *"Son of David"*. Although in the 2011 New International Version translation, he addresses Jesus as *"Rabbi"*, other translations differ. In the 1995 version of the New American Standard Bible, Bartimaeus addresses Jesus as *"Rabboni"*:

> *And answering him, Jesus said, "What do you want Me to do for you?" And the blind man said to Him, "Rabboni, I want to regain my sight!"*
>
> [Mark 10: 51]

This is the only place in the gospel where this title is used and it used to indicate the acceptance of authority. Rabboni in Hebrew means *"My master"*.

> ***"Go," said Jesus, "your faith has healed you." Immediately he received his sight and followed Jesus along the road.***
>
> [Mark 10: 51-52]

The God of Isaac

In all four gospels, Barabbas is the prisoner released in preference to Jesus. Matthew's gospel describes Barabbas as a *"notorious prisoner"*. In Luke's gospel, it states:

> *This man had been thrown into prison because of a riot in the city and murder.*

John's gospel describes Barabbas a *"bandit"*. In Mark's gospel, the nature of Barabbas is less clear cut. He is neither described as being notorious nor of being a bandit or insurrectionist. He is described as being in prison WITH the rebels who had committed murder during the uprising:

> *A man called Barabbas was in prison with the insurrectionists who had committed murder in the uprising.*
>
> [Mark 15:7]

In Mark's account, immediately after the release of Barabbas, Jesus is taken by the soldiers to the Praetorium where he is dressed as a king and mocked:

> *They put a purple robe on him, then twisted together a crown of thorns and set it on him. And they began to call out to him, "Hail, king of the Jews!" Again and again they struck him on the head with a staff and spit on him. Falling on their knees, they paid homage to him.*
>
> [Mark 15:17-19]

There are no details on the uprising mentioned in Mark's gospel but it surely alludes to the uprising in Alexandria in 38 CE and the central role in that played by Carabbas, described by Philo as that:

> *Certain madman ...... afflicted not with a wild, savage, and dangerous madness (for that comes on in fits without being expected either by the patient or by bystanders), but with an intermittent and more gentle kind*
>
> [Philo: Against Flaccus]

About the governor Flaccus, Philo relates:
> *he would have done right if he had apprehended the maniac and put him in prison*
>
> [Philo: Against Flaccus]

However, Flaccus did not imprison Carabbas. Instead, he was taken by the mob to the Gymnasium, where he was dressed as a king and

PART II

mocked. Philo relates that the mob:

> *setting him up there on high that he might be seen by everybody, flattened out a leaf of papyrus and put it on his head instead of a diadem, and clothed the rest of his body with a common door mat instead of a cloak, and instead of a scepter they put in his hand a small stick of the native papyrus which they found lying by the way side and gave to him; and when, like actors in theatrical spectacles, he had received all the insignia of royal authority, and had been dressed and adorned like a king, the young men bearing sticks on their shoulders stood on each side of him instead of spear-bearers, in imitation of the body-guards of the king, and then others came up, some as if to salute him, and others making as though they wished to plead their causes before him, and others pretending to wish to consult with him about the affairs of the state.*
> *Then from the multitude of those who were standing around there arose a wonderful shout of men calling out Maris; and this is the name by which it is said that they call the kings among the Syrians*
>
> [Philo: Against Flaccus]

And when the centurion, who stood there in front of Jesus, saw how he died, he said, "Surely this man was the Son of God!"

[Mark 15:39]

Sin

For sin is just this, what man cannot by its very nature do with his whole being; it is possible to silence the conflict in the soul, but it is not possible to uproot it.

[Martin Buber 1878 - 1965]

Harmony and discord

In the *Legum Allegoriae*, Philo wrote expansively on the significance of the number seven. He was not the first to first to see meaning in numbers. Some five hundred years previously, the Greek philosopher Pythagoras founded a movement that was akin to a religion. It was a movement that saw beauty in numbers and it attracted many followers.

Unfortunately for scholars, Pythagoras left no writings but his influence was enormous.

It was Pythagoras or one of his followers who demonstrated that in a right angled triangle, the square on the hypotenuse equals the sum of the squares on the other two sides.

It was Pythagoras or one of his followers who discovered the relationship between the length of a plucked string and the musical note it produces. The harmonies we hear when chords such as the octave, fifth and fourth are played were shown to have a purely mathematical basis. Lengths in the ratio of 2:1 always produced an octave, 3.2 a fifth, and 4:3 a fourth.

It was but a short jump to extrapolate from the discovery that the relationship between the first four numbers governed harmonies in music, the theory that the proper balance between four elements governed harmonies in other relationships.

PART II

It was a philosophy that influenced Plato and it underpinned his explanation of the cosmic soul in *Timaeus*. It also underpinned his explanation of the factors that governed our psychological health.

In *Phaedrus*, the character Simmias says:

> *"Our body being, as it were, strung and held together by the warm and the cold, the dry and the moist, and things of that sort, our soul is a sort of temperament and attunement of these, when they are mingled with one another well and in due proportion.*
> *If, then, our soul is an attunement, it is clear that, when the body has been relaxed or strung up out of measure by diseases and other ills, the soul must necessarily perish at once."*

[Plato, Phaedrus. 86 b7-c5]

This philosophy was not just used to explain the cosmos and our psychological health; it was also used to explain social well-being.

In his work, "On Mathematics Useful for the Understanding of Plato", written in approximately 100 CE, Theon of Smyrna wrote:

> *Unity is the principle of all things and the most dominant of all that is: all things emanate from it and it emanates from nothing. It is indivisible and it is everything in power. It is immutable and never departs from its own nature through multiplication ($1 \times 1 = 1$). Everything that is intelligible and not yet created exists in it; the nature of ideas, God himself, the soul, the beautiful and the good, and every intelligible essence, such as beauty itself, justice itself, equality itself, for we conceive each of these things as being one and as*

> *existing in itself.*
>
> *........One represents the principle of Unity from which all things arise. Two, the Dyad, represents Duality. This is the beginning of multiplicity and of strife, but is also the possibility of logos, denoting the relation of one thing to another:*
>
> [Theon of Smyrna, Mathematics Useful for Understanding Plato, 66]

The logos mentioned here is a product of Greek philosophy and ancient Greek thinkers had an all-encompassing world view that we simply do not share.

Plato inherited his idea of the hierarchical tripartite soul from Pythagoras. The tripartite soul of Philo is not hierarchical. It comprises equal value parts and is hugely useful in understanding conflict. Harmony occurs when elements of our own tripartite nature are in tune with the elements of the social or universal tripartite soul. Discord occurs when an element of our individual tripartite soul is out of tune with an element of the social or universal tripartite soul.

This prompts the question: *"What results if an element of our individual tripartite soul is out of tune with an element of the universal tripartite soul?"* It is a question that did not escape the attention of the author of the earliest canonical gospel.

Sins of the Passion

We know the Passion story so well. Catholic teaching is that the ancient story was passed on, either in a written form that is now lost or via oral tradition. The dramatic plot line, common to all three synoptic gospels, includes the betrayal, the preparation for the Paschal Supper, the Last Supper, the Agony in the Garden, the interrogation by the High Priest, Peter's denials, Pilate's interrogation and decision, the demands of the crowd and the scourging and crucifixion.

PART II

An alternative view to the orthodox Catholic teaching is that the story is a work that was created by the author of the earliest canonical gospel that was subsequently incorporated into the works of the later gospel writers.

Of the competing explanations there are compelling reasons why the latter is the more likely:

- The only information on the life of Jesus that is available from the letters that pre-dated the gospel of Mark is that Jesus was crucified under Pontius Pilate, was buried and resurrected. No other detail on his life is recorded.
- In James' letter there is no reference to an incarnate Jesus Christ.
- The gospel claims that in Jerusalem there was a custom that on the eve of Passover, Jewish leaders would request of the Roman governor the release of a prisoner, whom the governor was then obliged to set free. There is no independent evidence of this custom in all the religious and secular writings of this period.
- Much of the gospel of Mark appears to contain allusions to historical events at the time of the Jewish war not at the time of Pilate's governorship some 40 years earlier.
- Much of the gospel of Mark appears to identify Jesus with identifiable historical figures, most notably the general, later to be Emperor, Vespasian himself.
- In an allegorical interpretation of the gospel, there is an internal consistency within the narrative. As there are six psychological fractures represented by the Galilean healing miracles, so there are six social fractures exemplified by the major players within the Passion story.

The six significant players of the Passion story within the Gospel each demonstrate a different sin that reflects an element of the individual soul being out of tune with an element of the universal tripartite soul. The six players are:

Judas Iscariot

Judas Iscariot offered to betray Jesus and was promised money in return. During the arrest in the Garden of Gethsemane, in an act of feigned affection, he kissed Jesus and so indicated to those armed with swords and clubs, the man they should arrest. The sin of Judas is the expression of reason without divine spirit.

Peter

Peter made a spirited commitment to Jesus:

> *Peter declared, "Even if all fall away, I will not."*
>
> [Mark 14:29]

And

> *"Even if I have to die with you, I will never disown you."*
>
> [Mark 14:31]

However, at the high Priest's palace he denies Jesus three times. The sin of Peter is the expression of spirit without faith in the divine.

High Priest

Those in authority in the Jerusalem priesthood wanted rid of Jesus come what may. He was not arrested in response to an accusation. He was arrested and then evidence sought in order to convict him.

> *The chief priests and the whole Sanhedrin were looking for evidence against Jesus so that they could put him to death, but they did not find any*
>
> [Mark 14:55]

The sin of the Jerusalem priesthood is the expression of faith without divine spirit.

PART II

Pilate

Pilate had the responsibility for judging Jesus and evidently he could find nothing with which no convict him. In response to the crowd's demand that he crucify Jesus, he asked them:

> *"What crime has he committed?"*
>
> [Mark 15:14]

Nevertheless, he weakly accedes to the crowd's request:

> *Wanting to satisfy the crowd, Pilate released Barabbas to them. He had Jesus flogged, and handed him over to be crucified.*
>
> [Mark 15:15]

The sin of Pilate is the expression of reason without faith in the divine.

The crowd

There is no historical evidence for it but according to the Gospel narrative, at festival time Pilate used to release a prisoner - anyone the crowd asked for. Initially, the crowd approached Pilate to request their apparently customary favor. It is only after Pilate prompts them with a choice, that they become entrenched in their selection:

> *Now it was the custom at the festival to release a prisoner whom the people requested. A man called Barabbas was in prison with the insurrectionists who had committed murder in the uprising. The crowd came up and asked Pilate to do for them what he usually did.*
> *"Do you want me to release to you the king of the Jews?"* asked Pilate
>
> [Mark 15:6-9]

> *But the chief priests stirred up the crowd to have Pilate release Barabbas instead.*
>
> [Mark 15:11]

Pilate then asks the crowd whose passions are running high for advice on what to do with Jesus:

> *"What shall I do, then, with the one you call the king of the Jews?" Pilate asked them. "Crucify him!" they shouted.*
>
> [Mark 15:12-13]

The sin of the crowd is the expression of spirit without divine reason.

Jesus

Jesus was arrested and brought before the Sanhedrin where charges were brought against him:

> *"We heard him say, 'I will destroy this temple made with human hands and in three days will build another, not made with hands.'"*
>
> [Mark 14:57-58]

The high priest then rose in front of the assembly and asked Jesus:

> *"Are you not going to answer? What is this testimony that these men are bringing against you?" But Jesus remained silent and gave no answer.*
>
> [Mark 14:60]

Before Pilate, the chief priests brought many accusations against Jesus and Pilate asked him:

> *"Aren't you going to answer? See how many things they*

PART II

> *are accusing you of."*
> *But Jesus still made no reply, and Pilate was amazed.*
>
> [Mark 15:5]

In two passages in front of different audiences, Jesus refuses to speak. This may be indicative of a refusal to listen. If not, then it certainly indicates a refusal to explain.

In front of Pilate, when the procurator puts to him a question, "Are you the king of the Jews?" Jesus answers:

> *"You have said so"*
>
> [Mark 15:2]

This is an answer of someone who refuses to engage with the questioner. It is the first century equivalent of a twenty first century *"...Whatever"*.

Again, in front of the Sanhedrin, the high priest put a second question to him:

> *"Are you the Messiah, the Son of the Blessed One?"*
>
> [Mark 14:61]

The Christ or Messiah was regarded as the prophesied Son of David who would conquer Israel's foes and lead the nation into an age of peace and prosperity. Jesus' response sounds like a threat:

> *"I am," said Jesus. "And you will see the Son of Man sitting at the right hand of the Mighty One and coming on the clouds of heaven."*
>
> [Mark 14:62]

Certainly, it was a statement that in Mark's narrative elicited a strong reaction:

The high priest tore his clothes. "Why do we need any more witnesses?" he asked. "You have heard the blasphemy. What do you think?"

[Mark 14:63-64]

.. and from the assembled chief priests, scribes and elders:

They all condemned him as worthy of death.

[Mark 14:64]

With a literal interpretation of the Bible, Jesus' behavior seems baffling but with an allegorical interpretation it makes complete sense. In this passage Jesus doesn't listen, doesn't explain and is deliberately provocative in his language. Although it seems almost blasphemous to suggest it, his behavior represents a sin that is the expression of faith without divine reason.

The *"sins"*, exemplified by these six characters, have been woven together in one composite story designed to be used as a basis for moral teaching.

PART II

Divine reason

Truly, it is in darkness that one finds the light, so when we are in sorrow, then this light is nearest of all to us.

[Meister Eckhart (c. 1260 – c. 1327)]

Salome, Mary Magdalene and Mary the mother of James and Joseph

There are three Marys referenced in the gospel, two of whom, Mary of Magdala and Mary the mother of Joset and James are referenced on three occasions toward the end, at the crucifixion, at the burial and at the empty tomb.

"*Magdala*" is the Hebrew word for "*tower*" and surely Mary of Magdala is a reference to the bitterness engendered during the Jewish War that began in the settlement previously known as the "*Tower of Strato*".

Joseph and James are archetypes for where people look for authority. The one, "*Joseph*" by virtue of his name, "*God is increasing*", is the politician who obtains his sense of self-esteem from others. The other, "*James*", by contrast with a greatly developed inner world is the one, according to Philo, "*who delights in the practice of virtue*".

After the crucifixion, the gospel states:

> *Some women were watching from a distance. Among them were Mary Magdalene, Mary the mother of James the younger and of Joseph, and Salome.*

[Mark 15:40]

After the burial the gospel states:

> *So Joseph bought some linen cloth, took down the body,*

> *wrapped it in the linen, and placed it in a tomb cut out of rock. Then he rolled a stone against the entrance of the tomb.*
>
> *Mary Magdalene and Mary the mother of Joseph saw where he was laid.*
>
> [Mark 15: 46-47]

The tomb can be seen here as a metaphor for our hearts and that internal authority, the Word, is buried within us. The author is encouraging us to look to the Word within our own hearts. Mary's son James is not mentioned here[13]. James, delighting in the practice of virtue, is aware of where to look for the logos.

At the empty tomb, the gospel states:

> *When the Sabbath was over, Mary Magdalene, Mary the mother of James, and Salome bought spices so that they might go to anoint Jesus' body. Very early on the first day of the week, just after sunrise, they were on their way to the tomb and they asked each other, "Who will roll the stone away from the entrance of the tomb?"*
>
> *But when they looked up, they saw that the stone, which was very large, had been rolled away. As they entered the tomb, they saw a young man dressed in a white robe sitting on the right side, and they were alarmed.*
>
> *"Don't be alarmed," he said. "You are looking for Jesus the Nazarene, who was crucified. He has risen! He is not*

---

[13] Pay attention to noteworthy omissions

here. See the place where they laid him. But go, tell his disciples and Peter, 'He is going ahead of you into Galilee. There you will see him, just as he told you.'"

[Mark: 16:1-7]

Here the author is encouraging us to roll away the stone from our hearts and engage with other people. Mary's son Joseph, the politician, is not mentioned. Joseph does not need to be reminded to engage with others.

On all three occasions, Salome is also present. Here the author is telling us that, in times of distress, it is through divine reason that we find peace.

Worship

For millennia, humankind has worshipped in communal and shared celebration. Our gods personify that which we value. They help forge both a sense of common values and a sense of common identity. To worship, (literally *"to acknowledge the worth of"*) is to physically attest to that which we value.

Before Christianity, non-Jews worshipped one or more gods, each representing that which they valued. With the introduction of Christianity that belief system changed. The gods that were worshipped were replaced by one God with three natures that parallel the three natures of the tripartite soul. This was a God that spoke to a common humanity, a God of the divine incorporating a God of divine reason and a God of divine spirit and this religion had the potential of being a greatly cohesive force underpinned by an enlightened theology.

Part III

The strongest proof that we are made in the image and likeness of the Trinity is this: only love can make us happy, because we live in relation to others, we live to love and to be loved. Using an analogy taken from biology we could say that the human beings carry in their 'genomes' the profound traces of the Trinity, of God-Love

[Pope Benedict XVI]

The Catholic Church

In his letter to the Smyrnaeans in about 110 CE, St Ignatius wrote:

> *See that ye all follow the bishop, even as Jesus Christ does the Father, and the presbytery as ye would the apostles; and reverence the deacons, as being the institution of God. Let no man do anything connected with the Church without the bishop. Let that be deemed a proper Eucharist, which is [administered] either by the bishop, or by one to whom he has entrusted it.*
>
> *Wherever the bishop shall appear, there let the multitude [of the people] also be; even as, wherever Jesus Christ is, there is the Catholic Church.*
>
> [St Ignatius: Letter to the Smyrnaeans 8]

This is the first recorded use of the term "*Catholic (or universal) Church*".

PART III

In 325 CE, at the Council of Nicaea, a creed was formulated and that was used to exclude those who failed to profess it. The church became more institutionalized and from that day since, the "*universal*" church has become ever more exclusive.

Many of the actions of the leaders within the historical Church are indefensible. Despite it all, the Church has miraculously survived. However, it is not the historical sins that have inflicted most harm on its accessibility, it is the teachings.

The doctrine of infallibility was defined dogmatically in the First Vatican Council of 1869-1870, fifteen hundred and forty five years after the Council of Nicaea and states that a teaching of the Pope on faith or morals when declared as infallible MUST be held by every Catholic.

Strangely, there is some confusion over what Papal statements are infallibly defined and the estimate of the number of such statements varies considerably. The one statement on which there is general agreement that it meets the defined criteria for infallibility was the declaration of Pope Pius XII in 1950, sixteen hundred and twenty five years after the Council of Nicaea:

> *By the authority of our Lord Jesus Christ, of the Blessed Apostles Peter and Paul, and by our own authority, we pronounce, declare, and define it to be a divinely revealed dogma: that the Immaculate Mother of God, the ever Virgin Mary, having completed the course of her earthly life, was assumed body and soul into heavenly glory.*

Even without the backing of papal infallibility, there are plenty of other church teachings that tax our credulity. Change, if it comes, comes at a glacial pace. Many still remember the fear of God instilled by priests who taught that failure to attend Sunday Mass was a mortal sin for which, without confession, Catholics would receive everlasting punishment in Hell.

From the earliest years of the church, people have found great meaning in the story of the death and resurrection of Jesus Christ but it is wrong when meaningful myth lapses into meaningless fiction and that failing is compounded when that meaningless fiction is venerated.

From the earliest years of the church, there have been different interpretations of the Christian story but it is wrong when what should be a matter of opinion is dogmatically declared and that failing is compounded when the rational voice is anathematized.

From the earliest years of the church, attendance at a regular liturgical service and the coming together of community has been a crucial aspect of the Christian faith but it is wrong when grown adults are coerced into attending and that failing is compounded when the coercion involves threats of punishment.

From the earliest years of the church, the doctrine of the Trinity has had great prominence in the Christian liturgy but it is wrong to dismiss it as a divine mystery beyond our understanding and that failing is compounded by an unwillingness or inability to understand and explain the philosophy that formed it.

From the earliest years of the church, the regular liturgy contained elements that survive in the present-day Mass. The Catholic Church describes the Mass as *"the source and summit of the Christian life"*. It is certainly the common experience that Catholics share and despite the rules and rituals and dogmas and doctrines introduced by the institutionalized church, the Mass still contains the seeds of a Christianity that is not just worth preserving. It contains the seeds of a Christianity that is worth evangelizing.

PART III

Introductory rites

Greeting

The Mass is introduced by the priest with the Trinitarian greeting:

> *"The grace of the Lord Jesus Christ and the love of God and the communion of the Holy Spirit be with you all."*

To which the congregation reply:

> *"And with your spirit".*

+++

Names are testimonies of how we used to define ourselves. The names of Skinner, Smith and Fisher and many more are evidence of how we used to define ourselves by profession.

These are outnumbered only by the frequency with which we used to define ourselves by our relationships. The names Andrews, James, Jones and Peters are clan names with the *"Son of"* equivalents of Anderson, Jameson, Johnson and Peterson.

We don't just define ourselves by our family and profession, of course, but also by our community, our nationality and our beliefs, whatever they may be.

We have need for identity. Identity is good.

And yet, it has a negative side. In defining what we are, we are also defining what we are not.

There's no way we are English. We're not pompous and arrogant.

Heaven forbid we're not atheist, those godless heathens.

And God spare us from the Muslims with their fatwas and their jihads.

Of course, the overwhelming majority of English are not pompous and arrogant.

The overwhelming majority of those that call themselves atheists are good people.

The overwhelming majority of Muslims are peaceful, law abiding citizens.

As well as giving us a sense of belonging and purpose, identity gives evidence of where our allegiance lies and fuels stereotyping, prejudice and division.

It is a useful exercise to imagine stripping away the aspects of your life that give you your identity.

Imagine leaving your home and cutting all contact with your friends, family and community.

Imagine discarding your religion.

Imagine denying your nationality.

Imagine leaving your job and ignoring the skills you have learned.

Imagine… There's just you and the world and it seems a very scary place.

And yet, this is exactly what Jesus called his disciples to do.

In the process, the disciples discarded the cultural preconceptions and prejudices that they held of other peoples. They discarded the archaic and meaningless rules and rituals that cluttered their faith and set them apart from others. And in its place they forged a new identity - one that Jesus, in Mark's gospel, used to describe himself.

PART III

Not the *"Son of Joseph"* – the identification with a family; not the *"Son of David"* – the identification with a tribe; not the *"Son of Israel"* – the identification with a religion; but the *"Son of Man"* - the identification with all humanity.

Penitential Rite and Kyrie

I confess to almighty God,
and to you, my brothers and sisters,
that I have greatly sinned
in my thoughts and in my words,
in what I have done,
and in what I have failed to do;
through my fault
through my fault
through my most grievous fault

…..................... extract from Penitential rite.

It is not known when the Penitential rite was added to the liturgy but a reference to confession of one's faults is made in a second century documentary source. The penitential rite is followed by the Kyrie where we ask God for mercy. The earliest documentary evidence for the inclusion of the Kyrie into Latin mass was in the fourth century.

+++

Christmas can be a time of great joy. It can also be a time of great unhappiness. It has that effect. It amplifies emotions. Up and down the land, feelings are expressed in a similar vein to these:

"Your mother's not coming on Christmas Day is she? She'll only criticize."

Wouldn't it be good if someone with authority would exorcise these negative feelings?

"It's all left to me. I have to do everything and I can't think of everything. Make your own dinner!"

PART III

Wouldn't it be good if someone with authority would calmly explain that everything will be OK?

> *"Well, it's my wife that does all the organizing and preparation. I just turn up on the day."*

Wouldn't it be good if someone with authority would firmly insist that you made a contribution?

> *"I know we agreed to go out on Boxing Day but I forgot and I've asked the neighbors around. I don't want to disappoint them."*

Wouldn't it be good if someone with authority would forgive you?

> *"I don't agree with your uncle. I've never agreed with your uncle. I'm not having your uncle around and that's that"*

Wouldn't it be good if someone with authority would firmly insist that it is not acceptable to exclude someone simply because you don't see eye to eye?

> *"I'm not going to bother with others. I want to spend Christmas on my own"*

Wouldn't it be good if someone with authority would gently implore you to reach out and let other people into your life?

The beauty of scripture is that it speaks to different people in different ways but for some the ailments, described in the Galilean healing miracles, in the gospel of Mark are metaphors for states of mind and Jesus is exactly that voice of authority.

Isn't the Capernaum demoniac fearful because he is not open hearted?

Isn't Simon's mother in law, in an effort to do right by her daughter, stressed in making preparations for Simon's guests?

Isn't the leper parasitically living off someone else's good will?

Isn't the paralytic, torn as he is between different commitments, paralyzed by guilt?

Isn't the man with the withered hand inhibited in reaching out because of his small-minded intolerance of others?

Isn't the woman with the hemorrhage isolated because she doesn't wish to bother with others?

The emotions we feel and attitudes we hold are as old as humanity itself but we shouldn't always respond to them. Instead we should listen to that Voice of Authority.

There's one way to have a joyful and peaceful experience at the festive time of year. That is to put Christ into Christmas.

PART III

Gloria

The Gloria begins with the words sung by the angels at Christ's birth (Luke 2:14):

> *"Glory to God in the highest,*
> *and peace to his people on earth."*

To this verse others were added very early, forming a doxology, or short hymn of praise to God. In some form the Gloria dates back to at least the third century, maybe earlier.

+++

Why do we do anything?

It is a question that we rarely consider.

Our body is an interconnected mass of bone, tissue, nerves, vessels and organs. What gives it life?

What makes a new born baby gasp for its first breath?

What is lost when a dying man breathes his last?

The ancients used the word *"spirit"* to describe the animating force present in all living things – an invisible, elusive power, portrayed as a breath or wind. However, the word refers to not just that which gives life, but also that which shapes it.

In their energy, enthusiasm and readiness to explore new possibilities, spirited children shape their life but, as parents know, they can make themselves vulnerable, they can be frustratingly unreliable and they can push boundaries too far.

As we get older, experience blunts our sense of invulnerability and sharpens our sense of what is important and new possibilities become fewer as the choices we make limit the opportunities available.

And spirit is gradually, though not completely, superseded by faith – not necessarily religious or spiritual faith but the everyday common or garden faith; the faith that is fashioned by our experiences. The faith that, among a myriad of other chores, gets clothes washed, rooms tidied and dinners cooked. This is a faith that gets things done because they have to be done. It is faith as commitment – to work, family and community.

Unlike spirit, faith is reliable. It does not push boundaries but informs and guides our relationships with others.

Spirit and faith are antagonistic. While spirit is radical, faith is conservative. While spirit is the engine of change, faith is the force of continuity.

Both faith and spirit find expression. Action is the physical expression of spirit. Reason is the interpretation of faith.

Faith, spirit, reason and action can be considered as aspects of being, and while faith, spirit and reason are aspects of the psyche, or mind, action is an aspect of the body.

This is what we all share in common. This is what it is to be human.

In the gospel of Mark, during the passage on the Transfiguration [9:5], Peter is portrayed as energetic:

> *Peter said to Jesus, "Rabbi, it is good for us to be here. Let us put up three shelters—one for you, one for Moses and one for Elijah."*

He is portrayed as enthusiastic [11:21]:

> *"Rabbi, look! The fig tree you cursed has withered!"*

He is portrayed as ready to explore new possibilities [8:29]:

PART III

> *Peter answered, "You are the Messiah."*

He is portrayed as vulnerable [10:28]:

> *"We have left everything to follow you!"*

He is also portrayed as unreliable when following his declaration [14:29]:

> *"Even if all fall away, I will not."*

he denies Jesus three times [14:66–72].

Finally, he is portrayed as pushing boundaries too far when he remonstrates with Jesus [8:32–33], leading to Jesus' declaration:

> *"Get behind me, Satan!" he said. "You do not have in mind the concerns of God, but merely human concerns."*

The name Peter means "*rock*" but this portrayal is anything but "*rock-like*". Indeed, Peter, in Mark's gospel represents the personification of spirit.

What of the other disciples?

Throughout, the entire gospel, the disciple John makes just one remark by himself [9: 38]:

> *"Teacher," said John, "we saw someone driving out demons in your name and we told him to stop, because he was not one of us."*

John provides a description of the disciples' behavior and a justification for them. John represents the personification of reason.

John and Simon Peter are two of the four disciples called at the beginning of the gospel [1:16-20].

If Peter represents the personification of spirit, then his "*brother*"

Andrew represents the personification of action. If John represents the personification of reason, then his *"brother"* James represents the personification of *"faith"*.

In the gospel, Jesus is alone with the first four disciples on just one occasion. During the eschatological discourse that comprises chapter 13, in a discussion about the temple [13:2], Jesus states:

> *"Do you see all these great buildings?" replied Jesus. "Not one stone here will be left on another; every one will be thrown down.*

The four disciples question him privately [13:3-4]:

> *"Tell us, when will these things happen? And what will be the sign that they are all about to be fulfilled?"*

What follows is a discourse from Jesus incorporating a number of instructions aimed at faith (*"Watch out that no one deceives you"* - [13:5]), reason (*"Whenever you are arrested and brought to trial, do not worry beforehand about what to say"* - [13:11]), spirit (*"Be on guard! Be alert"* - [13:33]) and action (*"When you see 'the abomination that causes desolation' standing where it does not belong—let the reader understand—then let those who are in Judea flee to the mountains."* - [13:14]).

Furthermore, Jesus is alone with James, Peter and John on three occasions.

Jesus takes these disciples to the house of Jairus and there he brings Jairus' daughter back to life.

In the living death that is depression, Christ speaks to faith, spirit and reason to give purpose to life.

During the transfiguration, Jesus takes these disciples to the top of a high mountain where Jesus' clothes become dazzlingly white and Moses and Elijah appear.

PART III

After a spiritual experience, Christ speaks to faith, spirit and reason to give meaning to that experience.

In the garden of Gethsemane, Jesus takes these three disciples so far and instructs them to keep awake while he walks on further; when he returns he finds them sleeping.

In times of distress, Christ seems far away and nothing prepares us for grief.

Of course, these metaphors work only if the respective aspects of the psyche were apparent in the disciples' actual life or teachings.

So, read the 1st Letter of Peter and see the significance of the word "*spirit*".

Read the 1st Letter of James and see the significance of the word "*faith*".

Read the 1st Letter of John and see the significance of the word "*logos*" or "*reason*".

This idea of human nature underpins the narrative structure of Mark's gospel. With this idea established in the mind, the gospel of Mark can be read with a perspective of our very human, often unthinking, often unfeeling, often vulnerable natures being addressed by the divine.

Liturgy of the word

First Reading

The normal Sunday Mass in the Catholic Church includes three bible readings. Except during the Easter season, the first reading is from the Old Testament, in recognition of Christianity's Jewish heritage. Often the Old Testament reading is from one of the prophets, through whom, in the words of the Nicene Creed, the Holy Spirit had spoken.

+++

Trust is where faith meets spirit

+++

At the birth of Christianity, people were deeply divided.

On one side of the divide lay the Greeks with their scientists and their philosophers – emphasizing the rational. On the other side lay the Jews and their religion – emphasizing commitment. On either side of the divide lay a whole host of preconceptions.
Through the eyes of the Jews, it seemed that the Greeks had no boundaries to their private life; they were free to do what they chose. Their worship of the human form seemed a sacrilegious adoration of the physically desirable and they seemed to have little respect for the sanctity of life; abortion and euthanasia were freely practiced, divorce was common and the elderly were frequently treated with contempt. The Greeks were seen as immoral and Greek culture with its god for every interest as individualistic and corrupting.

Through the eyes of the Greeks, the Jews were a tribal people that excluded themselves from others; the Jewish practice of circumcision was barbaric and most of the rules and regulations, including the prohibition on the eating of certain foods, detailed in the book of law, the Torah, were simply incomprehensible. The Jews were seen as irrational with no interest in philosophy or the natural sciences and the Jewish worship of a one supreme God was seen as a naïve superstition.

Two hundred years previously, the Syrian ruler, Antiochus IV banned circumcision, banned Jews from possessing the Book of law (the Torah) and commanded the temple be used for sacrifice to pagan gods.

Any infringement of these prohibitions was punishable by death.

A Jewish rebellion overthrew the rule of the Seleucid King and the subsequent re-consecration of the Temple is still marked today as the Jewish holiday Hanukkah.

By the time Israel came under Roman rule with the conquest by Pompey in 63 BCE, Israel was a nation segregated geographically (Hellenized Jews and gentiles populated the Decapolis, a collection of towns that, with the exception of Damascus, were all located in Galilee, with most of the towns lying on the eastern side of the Jordan river) and culturally (the scribes and Pharisees were determined to adhere to the strict prohibitions and regulations laid out in the Torah).

The two cultures were united only in their mutual distrust.

Sections of scripture overlap slightly in the gospel but the section of scripture on *trust* is closely linked to passages that make reference to Bethsaida, firstly in 6:45 where Jesus walks on water and secondly in 8:22 and the curing of the blind man of Bethsaida. Bethsaida means merciful.

The section of scripture itself is bounded by the two stories of the feeding miracles where bread is used as a metaphor for trust. It is a good metaphor. We instinctively trust those that feed us.

In the feeding of both the five thousand [6:30-44] and the four thousand [8:1-10], Jesus blesses the loaves and fishes before breaking the bread and giving it to his disciples to distribute among the gathered crowd – of Jews, in the first case and Hellenized Jews and gentiles in the second. In both cases those gathered followed Jesus' example and shared the food they had so all were satisfied.

Trust requires acceptance of others. Trust is where faith meets spirit.

These two passages encompass a section of scripture where Jesus confronts that which divides the two communities – the archaic and meaningless rules and regulations that cluttered the Jewish faith and set it apart from others.

In chapter 7, verse 6-8, he quotes from the prophet Isaiah:

> *This people honors me only with lip-service,*
> *while their hearts are far from me.*
> *The worship they offer me is worthless,*
> *the doctrines they teach are only human regulations.*

After the second feeding miracle, there are further passages that describe that which we should not trust.

We should not put our trust in those, like the Pharisees, who discriminate against others on the basis of their religion nor the Herodians, who value power and wealth above all other things. [8:14-15].

We should not, like those demanding a sign from Heaven [8:11-13], see in natural phenomena such as comets, a message from God.

Instead, we should listen to the words of Jesus [8:17-21] who, in exasperation, reiterates a message that is clearly not being understood:

> *"Do you not yet understand? Have you no perception? Are your minds closed? Have you eyes that do not see? ears that*

PART III

do not hear? Or do you not remember? When I broke the five loaves among the five thousand, how many baskets full of scraps did you collect?" They answered, 'Twelve'. "And when I broke the seven loaves for the four thousand, how many baskets full of scraps did you collect?" And they answered, 'Seven'. Then he said to them, "Are you still without perception?"

It is only in building trust in others that we can truly build God's kingdom.

Second Reading

The second reading in the Sunday Mass comes from the New Testament. Usually the second reading is from one of Paul's letters. The letters contain very many references to Jesus Christ, to some God made man, to others the divine logos. Paul's letters themselves allow for both interpretations.

+++

Interpretation is where faith meets reason

+++

Two patients listen to the same explanation of a new treatment.

One is hopeful, the other resigned.

Two parents read the same school report.

One is encouraged, the other frustrated.

Two politicians listen to the same speech.

One is enthusiastic, the other skeptical.

Yet when prompted, there is unanimity. Both patients wish to act in the best interests of their own health, both parents in the best interests of their own children, both politicians in the best interests of their own country.

We interpret the same words in different ways and our interpretation is colored by a myriad of influences; our hopes and expectations, our beliefs and values, our identity, understanding and temperament.

Interpretation is where faith meets reason.

PART III

Regrettably, considerable conflict is caused not by differences between two faiths but by different interpretations of the same faith.

In the gospel of Mark, two passages on the use of parables act as bookends for a section of scripture that deals with interpretation.

In the first passage, [4:10-12], Jesus is asked, by his disciples, what the parables mean. He replies:

> *"The secret of the kingdom of God has been given to you. But to those on the outside everything is said in parables so that they may be ever seeing but never perceiving, and ever hearing but never understanding; otherwise they might turn and be forgiven!"*

The second passage [4:33-34], reiterates the message of the first:

> *With many similar parables Jesus spoke the word to them, as much as they could understand. He did not say anything to them without using a parable. But when he was alone with his own disciples, he explained everything.*

People interpret Mark's gospel in different ways. Some read it literally. Others, for whom the miracle stories offend their sense of natural reason, point to the passages above as evidence of an underlying allegorical meaning.

People should not be inhibited in talking about their understanding. Although, it is usually the believers in the literal interpretation who speak loudest, we should follow the example of the deaf and mute man in the Gospel [7:31-36] who after his healing by Jesus, began to speak plainly.

However, we should avoid imposing our understanding on others. What matters to the author of the gospel is not our interpretation but how we respond to it.

As illustrated in the parable of the sower [4:1-10 and 13 -20], we respond to the Word in different ways.

Some, where the seed falls on rocky ground, are enthusiastic until there are difficulties when they fall by the wayside.

Some, where the seed falls among thorns, have so many commitments that the Word is smothered.

Some, where the seed falls alongside the path, stand to the side and observe until something else attracts their attention.

But for some, where the seed falls in rich soil, their spirit is encouraged and they respond with hope and enthusiasm tempered with realism. When trials come, their faith keeps them steadfast and their reason doesn't stand idly by but is involved in overcoming hurdles and reconciling conflicts.

In the parable of the lamp, Christ invites us to proclaim the Word.

In the parable of the measure, Christ invites us to live by the Word.

If we live by the Word then, as in the parable of the seed growing by itself, the Word will flourish.

If the Word flourishes then, as in the parable of the mustard seed, the Word will spread.

Christ calls us to respond to the Word of God with one mind and act in the best interests of us all. It is this that creates the harvest. It is this that brings forth the kingdom.

PART III

Gospel

The word gospel derives from the Old English gōd-spell meaning *"good news"* and within conventional Christianity refers to one of the four Gospels included in the New Testament which relate the stories of Jesus Christ's actions. In Mass, during the reading of the Gospel, the congregation stands.

+++

Commitment is where faith meets behavior

+++

Definition: Jairus – from Hebrew meaning "God enlightens".

+++

The transition from childhood to adulthood is a process of great significance in the life of every one of us.

In some traditional societies, the process was marked by a rite of passage when, for a short period, the adolescent was cast out into the wilderness.

In Native American culture, this was called a *"Vision Quest"*, in Australian Aboriginal culture, a *"Walkabout"*. Physically, the young person was required to fend for themselves. Psychologically, it gave them an opportunity to evaluate what was and what was not important.

Perhaps the closest thing to a *"Vision Quest"* that young people in our society experience is when they leave home.

If you are old enough, it is a useful exercise to cast your mind back and try to recollect the feelings you experienced when you moved away from home.

At times, life seems exciting and full of possibilities. You have moved away from the sphere of direct parental influence and are free to do whatever you like.

At other times that very same freedom makes you feel uncertain and vulnerable; buffeted by external influences and internal conflicts as Jesus in the gospel of Mark [1:12 -13]:

> *At once the Spirit sent him out into the wilderness, and he was in the wilderness forty days, being tempted by Satan. He was with the wild animals, and angels attended him.*

By the very nature of their age, what young people often lack, that older people possess, is commitment. Young people often lack a commitment to a vocation, a career, a partner, a family, a community, a social group; commitment to anything without which one feels very lost and alone. Commitment is where faith meets behavior.

Two passages in the gospel of Mark act as bookends for a section of scripture that deals with commitment. In the first, Jesus is asleep in a boat when the wind picks up and waves crash into the vessel. On awakening, Jesus rebukes the sea and instructs the wind to be calm again.

The second passage is the famous story of Jesus walking on water.

In between these two passages lie the interconnected stories of the daughter of Jairus and the woman with the hemorrhage.

Jairus, a synagogue official urgently approached Jesus and fell at his feet:

> *"My little daughter is dying. Please come and put your hands on her so that she will be healed and live."*

[Mark 5:23]

On the way to the official's house Jesus is approached by a woman

PART III

who had a hemorrhage for twelve years:

> *She had suffered a great deal under the care of many doctors and had spent all she had, yet instead of getting better she grew worse.*
>
> [Mark 5:26]

An allegorical interpretation of this passage is that this woman, who spent all she had, had been living the good life, apart from the community. In Jewish culture of the time, a menstruating woman was regarded as unclean and to be touched by one was considered defilement. Yet this woman reached out, touched the cloak of Jesus and was immediately healed:

> *"Daughter, your faith has healed you. Go in peace and be freed from your suffering."*
>
> [Mark 5:34]

While Jesus was still speaking, people arrived to break the news to the official that his daughter was dead."

Jesus overheard them speaking and said to the official:

> *"Don't be afraid; just believe."*
>
> [Mark 5:36]

Being an official at the synagogue, Jairus would have been an important, busy and relatively affluent member of the community.

It's easy to imagine that his daughter would have had every wish granted and every whim indulged. She would have lacked for nothing except for her parents' attention. Emotionally neglected, she would have felt that her parents didn't care and her behavior would have become ever more extreme.

When they arrived at the official's house, Jesus turned out the loud and superficial acquaintances that were causing a commotion and went to see the child with her mother, her father, James, Peter and John.

In addressing her as "*Little girl*", Jesus established the proper relationship with the daughter. Then taking her by the hand, he didn't ask, he didn't implore, but told her to get up. She did and began to walk about and Jesus told the parents to give her something to eat.

Both the woman and young girl lacked spirit and when spirit dies it is faith alone that gives purpose to life. The woman with the hemorrhage, isolated by her riches for so long, had the faith as commitment that allowed her to reach out to others. The girl, too young to have developed a steadfast faith of her own, relied on the faith as commitment of her parents to save her.

We should not, of course, quash the natural spirit within our children. Children should not be oppressed. But neither should we allow that spirit free rein.

We should have respect for our children but we should also expect them to show respect for others and have respect for themselves.

We should provide security for and be tolerant of our children. But we should also set boundaries on their behavior and not accede to their every request. Children need to be able to learn to cope with rejection.

We should engage with our children (and praise them for the good that they do) and in that interaction demonstrate right values in the way we live our lives.

Then when the time eventually comes for our children to leave home, they will, at least, be equipped to make the right choices.

PART III

Credo

*We believe in the Holy Spirit, the Lord, the giver of life, who **proceeds** from the Father and the Son... He has spoken through the Prophets.*

[Excerpt from the Nicene Creed]

And they asked him, "Why do the teachers of the law say that Elijah must come first?"

Jesus replied, "To be sure, Elijah does come first, and restores all things"

[Mark 9:11-12]

+++

The creed is a statement of belief first introduced into the Catholic Church at the First Ecumenical Council of Nicaea. The council, held in 325, was initiated by Constantine the Great. Constantine's aim was to have a united Church free from divisive arguments. The purpose of the creed is to refute heresies, predominantly Arianism. In contrast to the two simple commandments given by Jesus in Mark's Gospel, which were to love God and your neighbor, the very nature of the creed is divisive. The words are designed to exclude everyone who does not believe in an historical God made man.

But if the historical evidence suggests otherwise, if scriptural exegesis suggests otherwise and if our God-given skepticism tells us otherwise, how can we honestly proclaim it?

+++

If there be nothing, good or bad,
But chaos for a soul to trust,

> *God counts it for a soul gone mad,*
> *And if God be God, He is just.*
>
> *And if God be God, He is Love;*
> *And though the Dawn be still so dim,*
> *It shows us we have played enough*
> *With creeds that make a fiend of Him.*

[Edwin Arlington Robinson: excerpt from The Children of the Night (1897)]

+++

"Do you believe in God?"

It's a simple question, isn't it? Are you a theist or an atheist? It's a simple question but a divisive one; to be avoided at dinner parties. It's a question that, depending on the depth of conviction of the questioner, can either sort the rational from the superstitious or the saved from the damned.

On one side of the divide lies pure reason represented by science – emphasizing the rational. On the other side lies faith represented by religion – emphasizing commitment. On either side of the divide lie a whole host of preconceptions.

Ever since the age of enlightenment, there has been an uneasy relationship between science and Christianity as scientific discoveries challenged religious certainties. The work of Galileo challenged the orthodox view of a geocentric universe. The work of Darwin challenged the creationist view of life. Discoveries in geology challenged the accepted understanding of the age of the earth. In modern times, and at least partly as a result of the Church's consistently conservative stance whenever there are scientific and social developments, church attendance in Western Europe has been in a state of perpetual decline. There are many educated people who express, sometimes with ridicule, sometimes with regret, their disbelief in God.

PART III

"Do you believe in God?"

Firstly, it depends what is meant by *"believe"*? Does it mean whether you give your rational assent to a proposition as in – *"Do you believe the earth is round?"* Or does it mean whether you ascribe to a particular set of values as in *"Do you believe that people should have consideration for others?"*

Secondly, it depends on the nature of the God that is understood by the questioner. I am not just splitting hairs. The questioner may have a conception of God that you don't share. Indeed if either you or the questioner is a theological skeptic, the God that you or they do not believe in may simply not exist.

Maybe the question is not so simple after all.

God is commonly perceived as an otherworldly deity looking down from on high, while rewarding the good, punishing the bad and performing the occasional miracle. But the good are not always rewarded and the bad are not always punished while science baulks at giving any credence to a supernatural explanation for *"miracles"*.

Faith is sometimes seen as an unquestioning belief in the historical veracity of the scriptural narrative, in the case of Christianity, this being the gospel narrative. Indeed the gospels are often preached as being a literal truth.

It is easy to portray Christianity like this as a primitive superstition that has been superseded by modern science; its followers deluded. A good proportion of people in Western Europe, if asked if they believed in the Christian God, would respond with a resounding *"No"*.

And yet, what is often overlooked is that during the late middle ages in Western Europe there was a rediscovery of the classical works of the ancient Greeks and it was towards the end of a period of extraordinary scientific achievements, particularly in the fields of geometry and astronomy, from the teachings of Pythagoras (c. 500 BCE) to the production of Ptolemy's Almagest (approx. 170 CE), that the gospels themselves were written.

A common misunderstanding of religious scripture is that it in some way purports to be history. It is not. Although the gospels in the New Testament may contain allusions to historical events they are designed to be interpreted and we should not be surprised if they reflect the ideas, the philosophies and the social and political realities of the time in which they were written. Christianity was born in an age of tremendous conflict. It was also an age where intellectual endeavor was highly valued and encouraged. The writer of the gospel according to Mark, the earliest gospel in the New Testament canon, was highly educated. It is inconceivable that he was unaware of the philosophical and scientific achievements of the society of which he was part. If we imagine his experiences and read his gospel as an allegorical tale rather than as a literal truth, we may be able to discern a different narrative and perceive a God that is not an other-worldly deity but one who is described in the first letter of John [John 4: 8]:

> *"Whoever does not love does not know God, because God is love."*

In John's words love is not a characteristic of God. It is a definition.

"Do you believe in Love?"

Surely that is something that all of us can believe in.

PART III

Intercessions

The General Intercessions have been part of the Christian liturgy since the early church. The following format is common:

- The presider invites all the faithful to pray on a particular topic.
- The assembly prays in silence.
- The presider then recites a *"collect"* prayer that collects the silent prayer of the assembly into a concluding spoken prayer to God.
- The assembly assents to this prayer.
- The process is repeated with the next topic.

+++

Definitions: Jesus – New Testament form of Joshua means "God is Salvation"

Nazareth – Separated, generally supposed to be the Greek form of the Hebrew "netser", a "shoot" or "sprout." (esp. offshoot of Judaism)

+++

In any list of the most inspirational figures of the 20th Century, the names of Mahatma Gandhi, Martin Luther King and Nelson Mandela would have great prominence. These were figures who are widely held in high regard and who commanded great loyalty from their followers.

However, despite their admirable personal qualities, if they had lived at a different time or in a different place, they would be unknown.

What made them inspirational was their courage in speaking out and articulating that which people knew, in their heart of hearts, was right.

And that message inspired revolutionary movements that threatened the status quo and challenged authority.

Each of these individuals paid the price for speaking out. While Gandhi and King were assassinated, Mandela was arrested and imprisoned.

However, despite the assassinations and imprisonment, the challenge to authority persisted as the strength of feeling of the people was fuelled by a deep sense of injustice.

+++

If there was any list of the most inspirational figures of the 1st Century, the name of John the Baptist would loom large.

This was a figure who was widely held in high regard and who commanded great loyalty, even devotion, from his followers:

> "... for everyone held that John was a real prophet"
>
> [Mark 11:33]

However, despite his admirable personal qualities, if he had lived at a different time or in a different place he would be unknown.

What made him inspirational was his courage in speaking out when no-one else would:

> "It is written in the book of the prophet Isaiah:
> Look, I am going to send my messenger before you:
> he will prepare your way.
> A voice cries in the wilderness:
> Prepare a way for the Lord,

PART III

> *make his paths straight.*
> *And so it was that John the Baptist appeared in the wilderness,*
> *proclaiming a baptism of repentance for the forgiveness of sins."*
>
> [Mark 1:2-4]

The message from John was an inspiration to others:

> *"All Judaea and all the people of Jerusalem made their way to him and as they were baptized by him in the river Jordan they confessed their sins."*
>
> [Mark 1:5]

.. because it articulated that which people knew, in their heart of hearts, was right:

> *"It was at this time that Jesus came from Nazareth in Galilee and was baptized in the Jordan by John. No sooner had he come up out of the water than he saw the heavens torn apart and the Spirit, like a dove, descending on him. And a voice came from heaven, 'You are my Son, the Beloved, my favor rests on you".*
>
> [Mark 1:9-11]

The message threatened the status quo and was a challenge to the authority of the time:

> *"Now it was .... Herod who had sent to have John arrested, and had him chained up in prison because of Herodias, his brother Philip's wife whom he had married. For John had told Herod, 'It is against the law for you to*

have your brother's wife'."

[Mark 6:17-18]

... and John paid the price for speaking out:

"So the king at once sent one of the bodyguards with orders to bring John's head. The man went off and beheaded him in prison"

[Mark 6:27-28]

However, despite the arrest and execution, a movement was born as the strength of feeling of the people was fuelled by a deep sense of injustice:

"After John had been arrested, Jesus went into Galilee. There he proclaimed the Good News from God. 'The time has come' he said 'and the kingdom of God is close at hand. Repent, and believe the Good News'."

[Mark 1:14-15]

... and the challenge to authority persisted:

*"...... King Herod had heard about him, since by now his name was well known.
Some were saying, 'John the Baptist has risen from the dead, and that is why miraculous powers are at work in him'. Others said, 'He is Elijah'; others again, 'He is a prophet, like the prophets we used to have'. But when Herod heard this he said, 'It is John whose head I have cut off; he has risen from the dead'."*

[Mark 6:14-16]

Throughout human history, there has been conflict often fuelled by a deep sense of injustice. Brother against brother, black against white, nation against nation, religion against religion, Jew against Greek.

Jewish scripture speaks of a future Messiah who will end conflict and bring forth a time of peace and harmony between people and nations.

But peace and harmony cannot be imposed. They must start in the heart of every one of us. So whenever, we see injustice, we shouldn't wait for the inspirational figure but we should have the courage to speak out and act according to that which we know, in our heart of hearts, is right. For that is the voice of divine reason. That is the voice of the Messiah. That is the voice of Christ:

> *"Jesus and his disciples left for the villages round Caesarea Philippi. On the way he put this question to his disciples, 'Who do people say I am?" And they told him. 'John the Baptist,' they said 'others Elijah; others again, one of the prophets. 'But you,' he asked 'who do you say I am?' Peter spoke up and said to him, 'You are the Christ'. And he gave them strict orders not to tell anyone about him."*
>
> [Mark 8:27-30]

Liturgy of the Eucharist

Sanctus

The Sanctus is a short hymn of holiness said or sung as the final words of the Preface of the Eucharistic prayer, the prayer of consecration of the bread and wine:

> *Holy, Holy, Holy Lord God of hosts.*
> *Heaven and earth are full of your glory.*
> *Hosanna in the highest.*
> *Blessed is he who comes in the name of the Lord.*
> *Hosanna in the highest*

It dates as far as the first century. St. Clement of Rome makes reference to it in his first letter to the Corinthians:

> *For the Scripture says: Ten thousand times ten thousand stood ready before Him, and thousand times one thousand ministered to Him, and cried out: "Holy, Holy, Holy is the Lord of hosts; the whole creation is replete with His splendor." And so we, too, being dutifully assembled with one accord, should, as with one voice, cry out to Him earnestly, so that we may participate in His great and glorious promises.*

+++

Despite the high regard in which the philosophy of Plato has historically been held, there is something disconcerting about his readiness to make judgments of others.

Nowhere is this illustrated more clearly than in the Timaeus where Plato describes his vision of the ideal state. For one class of citizens,

Plato proposes that procreation be arranged by lottery – a lottery that is fixed so that the *"good"* of either sex be coupled and the *"bad"* of either sex be coupled. The offspring would be separated so that the progeny of the *"bad"* would be dispersed among the *"inferior"* citizens whilst those of the *"good"* would be educated in the finest arts.

+++

Spiritual faith is something to be developed and something to be nurtured. Regrettably, the term *"faith"* is almost universally used for something static – either as a belief in the unproven or as a synonym for one's religious identity.

Two passages in the gospel of Mark relate the story of a cure of a blind man. These two passages act as bookends for a section of scripture that deals with a gradual revelation of faith. In the first [8:21-26], the sight of the blind man of Bethsaida is gradually restored. In the second [10:46-51], the sight of the blind man of Jericho is restored immediately.

These sections are separated by three prophecies of the Passion. In the first section, Peter, as the personification of spirit, in response to Jesus' question *"Who do you say I am?"* declares: *"You are the Christ!"*

For the Jewish people, the Christ-figure, the Messiah, was the *"hoped-for"* leader that would lead them in their struggle for freedom from Roman rule. Peter's declaration is followed by the first prophecy of the Passion, where Jesus completely undermines this concept of Messiah-ship. Peter's reaction in remonstrating with Jesus leads to Jesus' rebuke in front of all the disciples:

> *"Get behind me, Satan!" he said. "You do not have in mind the concerns of God, but merely human concerns."*
>
> [Mark 8:33]

Christ rejects a faith that is based on a desire to impose

our will on others.

Closely following the second prophecy of the Passion is a statement from John, as the personification of reason: "Master, we saw a man who is not one of us, casting out devils in your name, and because he was not one of us, we tried to stop him". Jesus responds:

> "Do not stop him," Jesus said.
> "For no one who does a miracle in my name can in the next moment say anything bad about me, for whoever is not against us is for us.

[Mark 8:39-40]

Christ rejects a faith that is based on a belief that we are more virtuous than others.

The third prophecy of the Passion is followed by the request of James, as the personification of faith, and John as the personification of reason, to be allowed to sit at the right and left of Christ in glory. Faith and reason without divine spirit is the voice of conviction, and it is the voice of conviction that speaks loudest. For this reason, [3: 17], Jesus gives James and John the name "*Boanerges*" or "*Sons of Thunder*". But the response of Jesus to their request is:

> "You will drink the cup I drink and be baptized with the baptism I am baptized with, but to sit at my right or left is not for me to grant. These places belong to those for whom they have been prepared."

[Mark 8:39-40]

Christ rejects a faith that is based on the final vanity; the conviction that the sacrifice of oneself for that faith makes us more worthy than others.

The name of the blind man of Jericho is Bartimaeus – a name that is a fusion of Aramaic ("*Bar*" - meaning "*Son of*") and Greek

(*"Timaeus"*). After being called by Jesus, Bartimaeus discards his cloak. Before he does so, he addresses Jesus as *"Son of David"* – a title of the conquering Messiah. After he discards his cloak, he addresses Jesus as Rabboni (master).

Like Bartimaeus discarding his cloak, it is only AFTER we discard our vanities that we can hear the voice of TRUE authority. Like Bartimaeus with his sight restored, it is only then that we can recognize Christ.

Agnus Dei

The Agnus Dei (Lamb of God) is an invocation comprising three short lines that is either sung or said during the breaking of bread during Mass:

> *Lamb of God, you take away the sins of the world, have mercy on us.*
>
> *Lamb of God, you take away the sins of the world, have mercy on us.*
>
> *Lamb of God, you take away the sins of the world, grant us peace.*

The invocation was introduced in the Mass, relatively late, by Pope Sergius in the seventh century in a defiant response to the Byzantine ruling that Christ was not to be depicted as an animal.

+++

It is not that Judas arranged to have Jesus arrested that hurt. It is that he exploited the trust and friendship of others for his own ends.

It is not that the Chief Priests put Jesus on trial that hurt. It is that they pressed for the ultimate sanction because they felt threatened.

It is not that Peter denied knowing Jesus that hurt. It is that he made a commitment that he failed to honor.

It is not that both the High Priest and Pilate questioned Jesus that hurt. It is that Jesus didn't listen, he didn't explain and he was dogmatic and deliberately provocative in his language.

It is not that Pilate was put in the position of passing judgment on Jesus that hurt. It is that he avoided the responsibility that was rightfully his.

PART III

It is not that the crowd asked for Barabbas that hurt. It is that they rejected Pilate's suggestion out of spite.

These are the sins that cause relationships to fracture:

- When we exploit others' trust and friendship for our own benefit
- When we are intolerant of others or intolerant of different ideas or perspectives and react harshly when we feel threatened
- When we fail to honor a commitment
- When we don't listen or explain or are dogmatic or deliberately provocative in our language
- When we avoid the responsibility that is rightfully ours
- When we act impetuously with no thought of the consequences

But something overcomes all sins.

Respect for and commitment to others. That selfless but often painful and difficult love, exemplified by Christ in the crucifixion, bears its fruit in the resurrection. The kingdom of God is there to be created.

Interlude

A queue of people snakes its way to a series of checkout tills within the High street store. Each person in the queue is holding one or more items or a basket of items. There is constant noise; a chatter of children and checkouts.

"Next please!"

The person at the head of the queue presents themselves to the available checkout girl. The items are scanned and bagged, the total cost tallied. The card is inserted into the plastic box and numbers are pressed. After a few seconds a receipt is generated.

This act is almost sacramental. I have chosen these items. They are an expression of my individuality. Through this transaction, my existence is affirmed.

Our advertising industry demonstrates the sin of Judas by creating needs where none are recognized and stoking desires where none are felt.

We respond, of course, seduced by these promptings, with the sin of the crowd and purchase that which is unnecessary with no consideration of the consequences of our actions.

The sin of Peter is commonplace. Relationships and marriages break down with a frequency that must amaze our parents brought up in the belief that whatever fate held, you made the best of what you had. The only commitment that matters nowadays is commitment to one's own interests.

By avoiding their responsibility toward the common good, bankers demonstrate the sin of Pilate as they pocket ever bigger bonuses on the back of short term profits and long term losses for banks that are *"too big to fail"*.

And the ever-increasing individualism fuels an ever more virulent capitalism with its powerful dynamic toward making the poor ever poorer, as businesses seek ways to cut costs, and the rich ever richer, as businesses seek the *"very best"* people for the top jobs. And it is these *"very best"* people who, like the rich people in the temple, feign philanthropy in public while in private they strive to avoid paying their due.

So we look to the Church to offer the powerful counterbalance to this increasing individualization of society. But the Church, stuck with the legacy of almost seventeen hundred years espousing the theology of power, struggles to find the language that is meaningful to contemporary society. It is being marginalized because it cannot reach out. Many clergy, displaying the sin of the Jesus, fail to listen and fail to explain because they do not have ready recourse to language that will enable them to explain. Instead they fall back on outmoded and useless dogma.

And woe betides those who challenge religious teachings. The church is no democracy. The dissenting voice is the voice of the trouble maker. Exhibiting the sin of the High Priest, with claims of heresy and threats of excommunication, the dissenting voices are marginalized. The media, meanwhile, feign outrage for like sex, gossip and scandal, outrage sells.

And the fruits of our sins will be made manifest. We are a people of superficial faith and young people without faith will create a faith of their own, however destructive that may be.

And we will look on in helpless bewilderment.

Communion

The Holy Communion or Eucharist (literally "*Thanksgiving*") is the earliest Christian ritual incorporated into the Mass. Paul's first letter to the Corinthians (c. 57 CE) makes reference to it:

> "*The Lord Jesus on the night when he was given up took bread, and when he had given thanks, he broke it, and said, 'This is my body which is for you. Do this in remembrance of me.' In the same way also the cup, after supper, saying, 'This cup is the new covenant in my blood. Do this, as often as you drink it, in remembrance of me'.*"
>
> [1 Corinthians 11:23-26].

The term communion itself is derived from Latin "*communion*" which means "*sharing in common*".

+++

A queue of people starts forming in the center aisle at the front of the church. People sit in rows of seats on either side of the aisle. As one row of seats empties, people in the row behind stand up and follow. Each row of people joins the main queue by merging in the center aisle with the row opposite. Some people stay seated. Those in the queue present themselves to the priest.

For those who have their arms crossed across their chest, the priest performs a blessing. For the others he proffers a thin wafer. The recipient may have their hands prepared ready to receive the wafer, left hand cupped on top of right. Alternatively, they may stand with mouth open and tongue slightly extruded. The priest places the wafer in the hands or on the tongue while intoning the words:

> "*The Body of Christ*"

The recipient replies "*Amen*", and those receiving the wafer in their hand, then place it on their tongue.

The mood is appropriately solemn as, in turn, each individual presents themselves to the priest:

The boy with the mischievous grin, the gawky and self-conscious teenager, the harassed parent with the unruly child, the wealthy man of some importance in the community, the woman gently leading her aged and confused mother, the young man trying to find meaning in a seemingly selfish world, the woman suffering from anxiety and prone to depression, the family with little money but lots of love, the courageous woman confronting the community for the first time after losing her husband, the lonely and isolated elderly man, the middle aged man recently made redundant and desperate for the opportunity of another job, the feisty woman who wishes to shake things up and the serious man who wishes things to stay the same. There are many who receive the blessing; those who have not yet been baptized or been given instruction in the sacrament, those who have divorced and remarried, those who consider themselves not to be in a state of grace. They, nevertheless, partake in the same ritual; at this moment they are part of the same community. There are black, white, Asian, young and old, people from all nations and of all temperaments.

This is a sacrament. It has something that is felt. It is a feeling of communality. It is a realization that we are all one people in God.

Concluding rite

Dismissal

Surprisingly perhaps, the concluding part of the Mass is one of the most important.

The term "*Mass*" itself is derived from the Latin word missa (dismissal). In Christian usage, the word "*dismissal*" has come to imply a "*mission*".

+++

For millennia, humankind has worshipped in communal and shared celebration. Our gods have personified that which we have valued. They have helped forge a sense of common identity. To worship, (literally "*to acknowledge the worth of*") is to physically attest to that which we value. But for a Christian, what does it mean to worship God?

Christianity is centered on the person of Jesus Christ and the message of Jesus was one of inclusion. He gave two commandments – to love God and to love your neighbor.

It is deeply ironic therefore, that in the history of the Church there has been such conflict between different interpretations of Christ's true nature.

So was he simply a man or was he the incarnation of a supernatural being?

It is perfectly possible to read the gospel of Mark, the earliest gospel in the New Testament canon, and conclude that he was neither. That is the nature of myth. It is a story that illuminates truths about the human condition. It is not meant to be understood literally.

Nevertheless, during the Last Supper at the breaking of bread, the

PART III

gospel does reveal something of Jesus' nature

Bread has been used previously in the gospel as a metaphor for faith as trust – (in the feeding of the multitudes and in 8:14-21 where Jesus warns his disciples to be on their guard against the yeast of the Pharisees and the Herodians). It is a good metaphor. From the time we are infants, we instinctively trust those that feed us.

Jesus invites us to have trust in him – the voice of true authority. However, Jesus doesn't just show the bread, he shares it with his disciples. It is only after this that Jesus makes his declaration: *"This is my body"*.

We know the phrase so well but we scarcely pause to think of its significance. It is in the physical actions that follow from trust in Christ that Christ himself is made manifest.

Shortly after the Last Supper [14:28], Jesus says to his disciples:

> *"But after I have risen, I will go ahead of you into Galilee."*

The author draws special attention to this phrase by repeating it[14], just before the original ending of the gospel [16:7]. At the tomb, the young man in the white robe tells the women:

> *But go, tell his disciples and Peter, 'He is going ahead of you into Galilee. There you will see him, just as he told you.'*

This repeated phrase links the Eucharist with the Resurrection and the reference to Galilee points the reader back to the inspirational actions and healing miracles at the beginning of the gospel.

---

[14] Pay attention to the repetition of statements previously made

It is these that we are invited to emulate. It is in the emulation that Christ is made manifest. It is in the emulation that the risen Christ is seen.

For good or for ill, the world we live in is created by our words and actions. The calling for any follower of the divine reason, personified by Jesus Christ, is that in our day to day lives, we embody that voice of true authority and play a part in shaping it.

Epilogue

All human knowledge takes the form of interpretation.

[Walter Benjamin]

Imagination is more important than knowledge

[Albert Einstein]

Wicked men obey from fear; good men, from love

[Aristotle]

One of the most difficult things is not to change society, but to change yourself

[Nelson Mandela]

Be the change in the world you want to see

[Ghandi]

When the winds of change blow, some people build walls and others build windmills

[Chinese proverb]

We must learn to live together as brothers or perish together as fools

[Martin Luther King]

He who wishes to secure the good of others has already secured his own

[Confucius]

"I saw a stranger yester' een. I put food in the eating place, drink in the drinking place, music in the listening place, And in the sacred name of the Triune, he blessed myself and my house, my cattle and my dear ones, And the lark sang in her song, Often, often, often goes the Christ in the stranger's guise"

[from Celtic rune of hospitality c. 6th century CE]

EPILOGUE

Spirit

I enjoy going down to the harbor in the evening, especially in the summer, on those days like this, when the wind blows the moist warm air in from the sea. I frequently sit here, unobtrusively looking, listening and dreaming. From where I sit now I can just hear the waves gently lap against the harbor wall. To my left a boat is unloading its cargo and there is lots of shouting of instructions and frequent cursing and exchanges of abuse.

I can taste the salt in the sea air. Further down the coast sea water is captured in shallow lagoons and evaporated by the sun. The white mineral that remains is a valuable commodity that has been used for millennia as a preservative, to improve the taste of food and as a season for offerings to deities. I remember the instruction in Leviticus:

> *Season all your grain offerings with salt. Do not leave the salt of the covenant of your God out of your grain offerings; add salt to all your offerings.*

Judaism itself had developed over hundreds of years. The best spiritual experiences of the people had been captured and preserved in the scriptures. However, I have lost the taste for Judaism. For most Jews, it appears, all that has been preserved is a dry bone carcass. That which was once a highly cohesive force is now a highly divisive one. Perhaps, in time, all religious faiths develop in the same way. Religious authority is fallible. Ultimately, we need to have faith in our own judgments.

When the sun sets and the moon and stars of the cosmos start to become visible, the fire on top of the lighthouse is lit. It is an extraordinary sight. Set on the small island of Pharos that is connected to the mainland by the man-made causeway of the Heptastadion, the lighthouse is 140 meters high and comprises three levels. The first and second levels are closed to the elements but the top level is exposed. This contains the small platform that is covered by an ornate roof supported by four columns. On the platform stands the brazier that holds the fire. Behind the platform is the mirror that reflects the light from the fire out to sea.

The lighthouse serves as a beacon to guide sailors to the city. It is said that the light is visible from 47 km away.

It is a marvelous metaphor. For the mariners, the lighthouse is the guiding light in the darkness. For us all, Christ is the guiding light in our lives.

In my dream there were four sea-faring vessels. The first was a big roughly hewn boat like a warship supporting a tall proud mast. At first this vessel headed toward the light but a storm rose up and blew her off course. The deckhands shouted to each other to lower the sail. Some argued that the sail shouldn't be lowered as they were making such good speed. Some thought that it wasn't their job to lower the sail and shouted back that if anyone wanted the sail lowered they should do it themselves. Others couldn't hear the instructions the storm was so strong. As the deckhands argued the boat was wrecked on the rocks.

The second was such a sleek and narrow boat that there was really only room for one person on board. She had a sharply pointed bow and glided beautifully through the water leaving no trace in her wake; but she headed away from the light and was lost in the darkness.

The third was a tall and very old vessel that moved very slowly because her hull was encrusted with barnacles. She had three decks. The top deck housed the captain and his officers, the middle deck housed the stewards and the bottom deck housed the passengers. The captain, officers and stewards were all unmarried men. Once a week the stewards would descend to the bottom deck and share a meal with the passengers.

"Look at what happened to the first boat", they would say, *"She sailed straight until the storm blew up and then the crew argued so much that the vessel was blown off course and crashed into the rocks"*.

EPILOGUE

"Look at what happened to the second boat", they would say, *"She sailed off course and was lost in the darkness"*.

"Stay with us", they would say, *"for we are the one true ship and we are heading toward the light. Do as your captain tells you for he is never wrong."*

But many of the passengers did not want to do as the captain told them for they knew that he was often wrong. Some left the ship altogether but many stayed for they knew of nowhere else to go.

But there was a fourth boat. She was small with only one deck but she was broad. To look at her one would think that she was quite unstable. This vessel headed toward the light. Sometimes she was blown off course but when this happened, a hand on the tiller would redirect her. Sometimes she was tossed about by a storm but when this happened, the crew would lower the sail until the storm had passed. And this vessel made great progress for everyone aboard had trust in her.

Reason

Unlike in much of continental Europe, there was no revolution in Britain in the 18th, 19th or early 20th centuries. There was no wave of rebellion that swept the country in 1848. Yet there was still change and there were some who shared a similar vision to intellectual revolutionaries such as Proudhon and Marx but were more practical and less stridently ideological.

Robert Owen was a visionary. He was born in 1771, the son of a saddler from Newtown in Mid Wales. He was convinced that people are products of both their heredity and their environment. Owen thought that if there were improvements in an individual's environment then the character of that individual would be improved along with it. This was a conviction that drove Owen to invest heavily in the establishment of an experiment in social community in New Lanark in Scotland.

The town of New Lanark was centered on four textile factories. Before Owen took over, children from as young as five were working for thirteen hours a day in the textile mills. He stopped employing children under ten who instead were required to attend the schools that Owen had built. New Lanark had the first infant school in the world, a crèche for working mothers, a comprehensive education system for children and evening classes for adults. He also provided free medical care and discounted retail shops where profits were passed on to his employees.

The ideas of Robert Owen still seem remarkably relevant for today. He was a strong believer in social inclusion and early intervention. His schools were not just available to those of New Lanark but for any child of the surrounding neighborhood where:

> *They would receive the same care and attention as those who belong to the establishment. Nor will there be any distinction made between the children of those parents who*

EPILOGUE

are deemed the worst, and of those who may be esteemed the best members of society: indeed I would prefer to receive the offspring of the worst, if they shall be sent at an early age; because they really require more of our care and pity and by well-training these, society will be more essentially benefited than if the like attention were paid to those whose parents are educating them in comparatively good habits.

[Address to the Inhabitants of New Lanark, 1st Jan 1816]

He was concerned with people's rights:

In advanced age, and in cases of disability from accident, natural infirmity or any other cause, the individual shall be supported by the colony, and receive every comfort which kindness can administer.

[Constitution, laws, and Regulations of a Community 1826]

Women will be no longer made the slaves of, or dependent upon men.... They will be equal in education, rights, privileges and personal liberty.

[Book of the New Moral World: Sixth Part, 1841]

However, he also made plain the responsibilities of the community members:

Parents shall be answerable for the conduct of their children, and householders for their lodgers. None of the inhabitants of the same village shall injure any of the fences about it, or upon the farm, whether stone, dyke, railings, or hedges; nor any of the houses, ground, or plantings, nor any of the company's property, of whatever nature it may be; but, on the contrary, when they see children or others committing such damage, they shall immediately cause them to desist from it, or if that shall not be in their power, give notice at the principal counting-house of the offences, and who are the offenders.

As there are a very great variety of religious sects in the world (and which are probably adapted to different constitutions under different circumstances, seeing there are many good and conscientious characters in each), it is particularly recommended, as a means of uniting the inhabitants of the village into one family, that while each faithfully adheres to the principles which he most approves, at the same time all shall think charitably of their neighbors respecting their religious opinions, and not presumptuously suppose that theirs alone are right.

[Rules and Regulations for the Inhabitants of New Lanark, 1800]

Owen was inspired by a vision of a new world of universal harmony:

What ideas individuals may attach to the term Millennium" I know not; but I know that society may be formed so as to exist without crime, without poverty, with health greatly improved, with little, if any misery, and with intelligence and happiness increased a hundredfold; and no obstacle whatsoever intervenes at this moment except ignorance to prevent such a state of society from becoming universal..............

[Address to the Inhabitants of New Lanark, 1st Jan 1816]

EPILOGUE

Is it not the interest of the human race, that everyone should be so taught and placed, that he would find his highest enjoyment to arise from the continued practice of doing all in his power to promote the well-being, and happiness, of every man, woman, and child, without regard to their class, sect, party, country or color.

[From a Paper Dedicated to the Governments of Great Britain, Austria, Russia, France, Prussia and the United States of America, published by Robert Owen, 1841.]

It was important to Owen that he influenced others. He published many books, made many speeches and distributed many pamphlets.

In one two month period he spent £4,000, in those days an enormous sum of money, publicizing his activities. In his speeches, Owen argued that he was creating a *"new moral world, a world from which the bitterness of divisive sectarian religion would be banished"*.

In 1815 he lobbied parliament, distributing to MPs a pamphlet he wrote, Observations on the Effects of the Manufacturing System that contained the draft of a factory reform bill. This called for a limit on working hours to twelve a day, including one and a half hours for meals; preventing the employment of children under the age of ten; limiting the hours of those aged under twelve to six hours per day; and providing basic education for employed children.

A modified version of this bill became law in 1819. It was not as far reaching as Owen would have liked but the issue was on the agenda. More comprehensive legislation on working conditions was introduced in 1825, 1833 and 1842.

Both the French anarchist Proudhon and Owen were concerned with the interests of the workers but whereas Proudhon advocated the somewhat ideological mutualism, Owen is regarded as the father of the much more practical cooperative movement. However, unlike other great social reformers of Victorian Britain and despite his fervent convictions, which must have seem religious, even *"Christian"*, to some, he was not a Christian himself. Indeed he held religion in low regard:

> *all religions are based on the same ridiculous imagination, that make man a weak, imbecile animal; a furious bigot and fanatic; or a miserable hypocrite.*
>
> [Gerald O'Hara: Dead men's embers]

Nevertheless, in 1854, at the grand old age of 83 and after a series of *"sittings"* with the American medium Maria B. Hayden, Robert Owen became a fervent spiritualist. This must have seemed a surprising volte face from someone supposed to have been an avowed atheist.

Owen claimed to hear the voice of many deceased but well respected men, including Thomas Jefferson. The purpose of these communications was:

> *to change the present, false, disunited and miserable state of human existence, for a true, united and happy state…to prepare the world for universal peace, and to infuse into all the spirit of charity, forbearance and love.*
>
> [Frank Podmore: Robert Owen, a biography - Vol. 2]

Some may say that at that stage Owen's mental faculties were in decline. Yet he was perfectly capable of writing the most articulate letters. Some may say that he was fooled by his medium into believing such nonsense. Yet the most convincing mediums are the ones who truly believe that they are channels to the dead. Some may say that both he and the medium suffered from the same delusions created from a combination of wishful thinking and active imaginations. Some may say that the spirit of Thomas Jefferson really did speak from beyond the grave….

But maybe, just maybe, the voice that spoke was the same as the voice of Osiris that spoke to Horus, the voice of Elijah that spoke to Elisha, the voice of John the Baptist that inspired many, the voice that is described throughout the gospel of Mark. Maybe, just maybe, the voice that spoke was the living and eternal voice of divine reason that speaks to us all, if we are just willing to listen.

Faith

One of the teachers of the law came and heard them debating. Noticing that Jesus had given them a good answer, he asked him, "Of all the commandments, which is the most important?"

"The most important one," answered Jesus, "is this: 'Hear, O Israel: The Lord our God, the Lord is one. Love the Lord your God with all your heart and with all your soul and with all your mind and with all your strength.' The second is this: 'Love your neighbor as yourself.' There is no commandment greater than these."

"Well said, teacher," the man replied. "You are right in saying that God is one and there is no other but him. To love him with all your heart, with all your understanding and with all your strength, and to love your neighbor as yourself is more important than all burnt offerings and sacrifices."

When Jesus saw that he had answered wisely, he said to him, "You are not far from the kingdom of God." And from then on no one dared ask him any more questions.

[Mark 12:28-34]

+++

They were preparing to leave Jerusalem for the port of Caesarea when a woman, who had been a religious for twelve years, approached them. She knelt at the feet of Jesus, bowed her head

EPILOGUE

and said:

> "Holy One, give us a sign so that others may believe"

Jesus answered:

> "Sister, why do you call me holy? No one is holy but God alone. Have faith. Look up and be at peace, for in your search for signs you fail to see that which is there before you".

The woman looked up and at the same time reached out her hand. As she did so, the clouds parted and Jesus was bathed in a bright light:

> "Master", said the woman, "I see you clearly".

Then Jesus said:

> "Come, sister, let me help you to your feet"

And he took her hand and helped her to her feet.

Jesus then left the city with the disciples. As they passed through the city gates, James and John addressed him:

> "Master", they said, "See how thick and high are these walls. Surely, nothing can breach these defenses."

Jesus replied:

> "It is because you are so untrustworthy that these walls were built. This is a city of men. The city of God has no walls".

On the journey, John questioned him privately:

> "Master", he said, "I know you are to leave us. What needs

to happen before your return?"

Jesus answered:

> "Listen and understand. A tower of Babel will be created in my name as men strive to reach the heavens. People will speak but not explain. Others will listen but not understand. I tell you solemnly, until that tower is leveled by my Father in heaven, the Son of man will not return".

Then Peter said to him:

> "Master, we will glorify your mother and hold her as exulted and she will appear to us".

Jesus replied:

> "My son, may the Holy Spirit inspire you. May she guide you and comfort you. Let there be music and singing and dancing. Let there be praise for our heavenly Mother. But in all this, do not be deceived. It is not my earthly mother who will appear before you for my earthly mother was not of flesh and blood".

They reached the port of Caesarea and boarded a boat for Alexandria. When they reached the city they left the boat and, as they hadn't yet eaten, they found a quiet place to sit down.

No sooner had they sat down than some men of science, seven in number, approached Jesus in order to confront him:

> "You charlatan!" exclaimed the leader, "We hear what you say but we cannot believe and without proof we will not believe".

Jesus replied:

EPILOGUE

"Quiet brothers and be at peace, for in your search for truth you fail to see the Truth that is here before you. Stay awhile and eat with us".

They had with them a few small loaves and fishes and Jesus took the loaves, gave thanks, broke the loaves and gave them and the fishes to his disciples to distribute. As the men took the offering, the clouds parted and Jesus was bathed in a bright light. One of the men said:

"Teacher, I see you clearly".

Jesus said to the man:

"My brother, remember this and you will not be far from the kingdom".

And Jesus travelled with his disciples through Alexandria and beyond. He met with Men and Women, Black and White, Gay and Straight, Catholic and Protestant, Christian and Jew, Muslim and Hindu, people of all religions and none. Many saw him clearly and many followed him but those who sought him were very afraid…

Ω

Appendix – Psychological and social fractures

Fracture	INTERNAL (Psychological) Expression	Example	EXTERNAL (Social) Expression	Example
Spirit without Divine Reason	stress	Simon's mother in law	acting impetuously with no regard for the consequences	The crowd
Spirit without Faith in the Divine	anxiety	Capernaum demoniac	being unreliable	Peter
Faith without Divine Reason	guilt	paralytic	using provocative language / failing to listen or explain	Jesus
Faith without Divine Spirit	prejudice	man with withered hand	acting harshly when feeling threatened	High Priest
Reason without Divine Spirit	avoidance of others / ignorance of others	woman with hemorrhage	betraying / exploiting others	Judas
Reason without Faith in the Divine	taking others for granted	leper	avoiding responsibility	Pilate
Reason without both Spirit and Faith	depression	daughter of Jairus	despair	The crucified Christ

References

Bible extracts (except for extracts from Books of the Apocrypha) are from the 2011 New International Version. Extracts from the Books of the Apocrypha (Wisdom, Maccabees I and Maccabees II) are taken from The New Jerusalem Bible.

Online references obtained via:

http://www.biblegateway.com.

Many of the other references were obtained from online sources, most of which amazingly are free of charge. The URL from which the source material was obtained will be listed but there is, of course, no guarantee that links will remain current.

An English translation of the complete works of Josephus including the *Jewish War*, *Antiquities*, *Life* and *Against Apion* are all available in a downloadable pdf document:

http://www.sounddoctrine.net/history/WorksofFlaviusJosephus.pdf

It is this translation that has been used throughout the document except the reference to Jewish War 2:8:3 where the superior 1959 translation by G.A. Williamson has been used.

http://www.radio-yahweh.com/dam-doc/Damascus-Document-01.pdf

Prologue

Spirit:

Dei Verbum from 2nd Vatican council:

http://www.vatican.va/archive/hist_councils/ii_vatican_council/documents/vat-ii_const_19651118_dei-verbum_en.html

Reason:

Alexandria described in Cosmos by Carl Sagan:

http://physics.weber.edu/carroll/honors-time/cosmos.htm

Faith:

Extracts from St. Patrick's Breastplate taken from *"St. Patrick's Breastplate"* within *"An Introduction to Celtic Christianity"*, edited by James P. Mackey, pub. T&T Clark Ltd., 1989. The translation is by Fr. Noel Dermot O'Donoghue. This is also available at:

http://www.spms.org/stpatricksmissionarysociety/main/St_Patrick_Breastplate.htm

The Hinton St Mary floor mosaic:

http://www.britishmuseum.org/explore/highlights/highlight_objects/pe_prb/t/the_hinton_st_mary_mosaic.aspx

Emperor Magnentius coins:

http://wildwinds.com/coins/ric/magnentius/i.html

Emperor Magnentius: attitude toward pagans and Christians:

http://en.wikipedia.org/wiki/Magnentius

Alexandria and Judaea

15th Year of Tiberius' reign (28 CE)

The description of ancient Alexandria was obtained from *Geography book XVII* by Strabo (ca. 64/63 BCE – ca. 24 CE):

REFERENCES

http://rbedrosian.com/Classic/strabo17.htm

16th Year of Tiberius' reign (29 CE)

As evidenced from Claudius' letter, Jews had attempted to take part in the gymnastic games:

> *I explicitly order the Jews not to agitate for more privileges than they formerly possessed, ... and not to force their way into gymnasiarchic or cosmetic games....*

http://www.csun.edu/~hcfll004/claualex.html

Alexandria

Letter from Aristeas:

http://www.ccel.org/c/charles/otpseudepig/aristeas.htm/

Inscription recording a Jewish dedication of a synagogue to Ptolemy and his wife Berenice

[Sir John Pentland Mahaffy, The History of Egypt under the Ptolemaic Dynasty, New York 1899 p. 192]

Extracts from Plutarch's *Life of Antony* has been taken from the following:

http://penelope.uchicago.edu/Thayer/E/Roman/Texts/Plutarch/Lives/Antony*.html

Background to Book of Wisdom from Introduction to the Book of Wisdom within *The Jerusalem Bible, Study Edition*.

[p. 1042, The Jerusalem Bible, Study Edition, pub. Darton, Longman and Todd]

The tripartite soul

21st Year of Tiberius' reign (34 CE)

Description of the library at Alexandria:

http://en.wikipedia.org/wiki/Library_of_Alexandria

Description of Ctesibius (of Alexandria) and his invention of the clepsydra:

http://en.wikipedia.org/wiki/Ctesibius

Eratosthenes (Chief librarian of Alexandria library) condemned those who divided the world into Greeks and barbarians:

http://en.wikipedia.org/wiki/Eratosthenes

Heron (of Alexandria) credited with the invention of the aelopile:

http://en.wikipedia.org/wiki/Hero_of_Alexandria

Euclid (of Alexandria), often known as the father of geometry:

http://en.wikipedia.org/wiki/Euclid

22nd Year of Tiberius' reign (35 CE) - 1

Aristotle's explanation of the use of rhetoric for different means of persuasion is Book 1 Chapter 2 of Rhetoric:

http://rhetoric.eserver.org/aristotle/rhet1-2.html

22nd Year of Tiberius' reign (35 CE) - 2

Philo describes the therapeutae, a contemplative community living on the far side of Lake Mareotis near Alexandria in his book "*On the Contemplative Life*":

http://www.earlychristianwritings.com/yonge/book34.html

REFERENCES

Plato and the tripartite psyche

American Declaration of Independence:

http://en.wikipedia.org/wiki/United_States_Declaration_of_Independence

Letter from Thomas Jefferson to John Adams April 11, 1823:

http://www.stephenjaygould.org/ctrl/jefferson_adams.html

Letter from Thomas Jefferson to John Adams October 12, 1813:

http://www.encyclopediavirginia.org/Letter_from_Thomas_Jefferson_to_John_Adams_October_12_1813

Letter from Thomas Jefferson to John Adams July 5, 1814:

http://www.yamaguchy.com/library/jefferson/1814b.html

Portrait statues in Library of Congress:

http://myloc.gov/ExhibitSpaces/MainReadingRoom/PortraitStatues/Pages/default.aspx

Plato's discussion of the tripartite nature of the soul is to be found in Book 4 of the Republic:

http://classics.mit.edu/Plato/republic.5.iv.html

Plato's allegory of the charioteer and the chariot is to be found in the Phaedrus:

http://classics.mit.edu/Plato/phaedrus.html

The universal psyche

Plato's description of the cosmic soul is to be found in his *Timaeus*:

http://classics.mit.edu/Plato/timaeus.html

Some information on Moderatus of Gades and Apollonius of Tyana with speculation that they both may have been representative of the neo-Pythagorean school of philosophy is given here:

http://www.sacred-texts.com/eso/sta/sta03.htm

Philo's interpretation of the Genesis story is to be found in Legum Allegoriae Book I:

http://www.earlychristianwritings.com/yonge/book2.html

An appraisal of Bruno Bauer's work (*Bruno Bauer and Early Christianity*) was written in 1882 by Frederick Engels. This records Bauer's theory that Philo was the father of Christianity:

http://www.marxists.org/archive/marx/works/1882/05/bauer.htm

Women

Meaning of the word "*widow*" in the scriptures:

http://www.earlyjewishwritings.com/text/philo/book10.html

[Philo: On the Unchangeableness of God XXIX (137)]

Motherhood of Mary by Cyril:

http://www.crossroadsinitiative.com/library_article/1197/Divine_Motherhood_of_Mary___St._Cyril_of_Alexandria.html

[Cyril of Alexandria: Divine Motherhood of Mary]

Report on the death of Hypatia:

http://cosmopolis.com/alexandria/hypatia-bio-socrates.html

[Socrates Scholasticus: Ecclesiastical History]

REFERENCES

Numbers

It is in *Legum Allegoriae Book I* (IV-VII) that Philo's enthusiasm for the number seven is expressed:

http://www.earlychristianwritings.com/yonge/book2.html

Healing

3rd Year of Tiberius' reign (36 CE) - 1

Philo describes the therapeutae as healers in his work *"On the Contemplative Life"* I:2:

> *the deliberate intention of the philosopher is at once displayed from the appellation given to them; for with strict regard to etymology, they are called therapeutae and therapeutrides, {from therapeuoμ, "to heal."} .... because they process an art of medicine more excellent than that in general use in cities (for that only heals bodies, but the other heals souls which are under the mastery of terrible and almost incurable diseases, which pleasures and appetites, fears and griefs, and covetousness, and follies, and injustice, and all the rest of the innumerable multitude of other passions and vices, have inflicted upon them)*

http://www.earlychristianwritings.com/yonge/book34.html

23rd Year of Tiberius' reign (36 CE) – 2

Again Philo describes the practice of the therapeutae in interpreting scripture as allegory and in great detail, their weekly and seven-weekly celebrations. The book includes this extraordinary quote regarding the celebration of the therapeutae:

And the young men who are standing around attend to this explanation no less than the guests themselves who are sitting at meat. And these explanations of the sacred scriptures are delivered by mystic expressions in allegories, for the whole of the law appears to these men to resemble a living animal, and its express commandments seem to be the body, and the invisible meaning concealed under and lying beneath the plain words resembles the soul, in which the rational soul begins most excellently to contemplate what belongs to itself, as in a mirror, beholding in these very words the exceeding beauty of the sentiments, and unfolding and explaining the symbols, and bringing the secret meaning naked to the light to all who are able by the light of a slight intimation to perceive what is unseen by what is visible.

http://www.earlychristianwritings.com/yonge/book34.html

Conflict

4th Year of Caligula's reign (40 CE)

Josephus' attack on the slanders of Apion is contained in his book known as "*Against Apion*":

http://www.earlyjewishwritings.com/text/josephus/apion2.html

Josephus gives details of the embassy to Caligula in *Antiquities* 18:8:1:

> *There was now a tumult arisen at Alexandria, between the Jewish inhabitants and the Greeks; and three ambassadors*

REFERENCES

were chosen out of each party that were at variance, who came to Caius. Now one of these ambassadors from the people of Alexandria was Apion, who uttered many blasphemies against the Jews; and, among other things that he said, he charged them with neglecting the honors that belonged to Caesar; for that while all who were subject to the Roman empire built altars and temples to Caius, and in other regards universally received him as they received the gods, these Jews alone thought it a dishonorable thing for them to erect statues in honor of him, as well as to swear by his name. Many of these severe things were said by Apion, by which he hoped to provoke Caius to anger at the Jews, as he was likely to be. But Philo, the principal of the Jewish embassage, a man eminent on all accounts, brother to Alexander the alabarch, and one not unskillful in philosophy, was ready to betake himself to make his defense against those accusations; but Caius prohibited him, and bid him begone; he was also in such a rage, that it openly appeared he was about to do them some very great mischief. So Philo being thus affronted, went out, and said to those Jews who were about him, that they should be of good courage, since Caius's words indeed showed anger at them, but in reality had already set God against himself. In "On the Embassy to Gaius", Philo gives some extraordinary detail about Caligula and the hatred the Jewish people developed for him:

http://www.earlychristianwritings.com/yonge/book40.html

1st Year of Caligula's reign (37 CE)

Plato's argument in the Republic for society to be ruled by a philosopher king:

http://classics.mit.edu/Plato/republic.7.vi.html

Explanation of the reason for why there are 31 days in August is taken from *The Calendar* p.47 [David Ewing Duncan: The Calendar, Fourth Estate, 1999]:

Suetonius gives a detailed account of the life of Caligula, including a remark about his *"falling sickness"* (epilepsy) in his work on the 12 Caesars (50:2):

http://penelope.uchicago.edu/Thayer/E/Roman/Texts/Suetonius/12Caesars/Caligula*.html

2nd Year of Caligula's reign (38 CE) - 1

In *"Against Flaccus"*, Philo gives a detailed critique of the governor of Alexandria, Flaccus, during the uprising in CE 38:

http://www.earlychristianwritings.com/yonge/book36.html

Judas

2nd Year of Caligula's reign (38 CE) - 2

A description of Pilate withdrawing his plan to erect standards to Caesar within Jerusalem, after being confronted with the crowd willing to die to prevent it, is given by Josephus (*Jewish War* 2:9:2-3).

4th Year of Vespasian's reign (73 CE) - 1

In the *Jewish War* (2:13:3), Josephus gives a description of the Sicarii:

> *When the country was purged of these, there sprang up*

> *another sort of robbers in Jerusalem, which were called Sicarii, who slew men in the day time, and in the midst of the city; this they did chiefly at the festivals, when they mingled themselves among the multitude, and concealed daggers under their garments, with which they stabbed those that were their enemies; and when any fell down dead, the murderers became a part of those that had indignation against them; by which means they appeared persons of such reputation, that they could by no means be discovered. The first man who was slain by them was Jonathan the high priest, after whose death many were slain every day, while the fear men were in of being so served was more afflicting than the calamity itself; and while everybody expected death every hour, as men do in war, so men were obliged to look before them, and to take notice of their enemies at a great distance; nor, if their friends were coming to them, durst they trust them any longer; but, in the midst of their suspicions and guarding of themselves, they were slain. Such was the celerity of the plotters against them, and so cunning was their contrivance.*

In the *Jewish War* (7:10:1), Josephus gives a description of the exiled Sicarii in Alexandria:

> *WHEN Masada was thus taken, the general left a garrison in the fortress to keep it, and he himself went away to Caesarea; for there were now no enemies left in the country, but it was all overthrown by so long a war. Yet did this war afford disturbances and dangerous disorders even in places very far remote from Judea; for still it came to pass that many Jews were slain at Alexandria in Egypt; for as*

many of the Sicarii as were able to fly thither, out of the seditious wars in Judea, were not content to have saved themselves, but must needs be undertaking to make new disturbances, and persuaded many of those that entertained them to assert their liberty, to esteem the Romans to be no better than themselves, and to look upon God as their only Lord and Master. But when part of the Jews of reputation opposed them, they slew some of them, and with the others they were very pressing in their exhortations to revolt from the Romans; but when the principal men of the senate saw what madness they were come to, they thought it no longer safe for themselves to overlook them. So they got all the Jews together to an assembly, and accused the madness of the Sicarii, and demonstrated that they had been the authors of all the evils that had come upon them. They said also that "these men, now they were run away from Judea, having no sure hope of escaping, because as soon as ever they shall be known, they will be soon destroyed by the Romans, they come hither and fill us full of those calamities which belong to them, while we have not been partakers with them in any of their sins." Accordingly, they exhorted the multitude to have a care, lest they should be brought to destruction by their means, and to make their apology to the Romans for what had been done, by delivering these men up to them; who being thus appraised of the greatness of the danger they were in, complied with what was proposed, and ran with great violence upon the Sicarii, and seized upon them; and indeed six hundred of them were caught immediately: but as to all those that fled into Egypt and to the Egyptian Thebes, it was not long ere they were caught also, and brought back, whose courage, or whether we ought to call it madness, or hardiness in their opinions, everybody was amazed at. For when all sorts of torments and vexations of their bodies that could be devised were made use of to them, they could not get any one of them to comply so far as to confess, or seem to confess, that Caesar was their lord; but they preserved their own opinion, in spite of all the distress they were brought to, as if they received these torments and the fire itself with bodies insensible of pain, and with a soul that in a manner rejoiced under them. But what was most of all astonishing to the beholders was the courage of the children; for not one of these children was so far overcome by these torments, as to name Caesar for their lord. So far does the strength of the courage [of the soul] prevail over the weakness of the body.

Society and spirit without faith in the divine

A description of the 3rd Marquess of Bute:

http://www.caerphilly.gov.uk/chronicle/english/diggingdeeper/famousfaces/johnpatrickcrichtonstuart.htm

Communist Manifesto of Mark and Engels:

http://www.marxistsfr.org/archive/marx/works/download/manifest.pdf

Proudhon's call to revolution is obtainable from below:

http://fair-use.org/p-j-proudhon/general-idea-of-the-revolution/

James

6th Year of Claudius' reign (46 CE)

An account of the famine in Judea in 46 CE is given by Josephus in Antiquities (20:5:2)

1st Year of Nero's reign (55 CE)

The Golden Rule described in wikipedia:

http://en.wikipedia.org/wiki/Golden_Rule

6th Year of Nero's reign (60 CE)

Wikipedia entry on Eisenman including his summarized opinion of James:

http://en.wikipedia.org/wiki/Robert_Eisenman

Jesus

The 39th holy letter of Athanasius can be viewed here:

http://www.ccel.org/ccel/schaff/npnf204.xxv.iii.iii.xxv.html

The reference to James in the Gospel of Thomas is available at the link below:

http://www.gnosis.org/naghamm/gthlamb.html

Joseph

The following link is a letter of Hadrian to his brother in law Servianus in about 132 CE that contains a description of the Christians of Alexandria:

REFERENCES

http://penelope.uchicago.edu/Thayer/E/Roman/Texts/Historia_Augusta/Firmus_et_al*.html

15th Year of Nero's reign (69 CE) – 2

The Dead Sea scrolls have long been a source of academic controversy. A long standing question has been the identity of three central characters found in many of the scrolls. These are the *"Teacher of Righteousness"*, the *"Wicked Priest"* and the *"Man of Lies"*. Controversially, Robert Eisenman, an American academic and biblical scholar, identifies Paul as the *"Man of Lies"* and James as the *"Teacher of Righteousness"* in his 1986 publication *James the Just in the Habakkuk Pesher*.

Information on the history of the Dead Sea scroll research can be found here:

http://virtualreligion.net/iho/dss.html

Information on Qumran is to be found in Wikipedia:

http://en.wikipedia.org/wiki/Qumran

8th Year of Claudius' reign (48 CE)

Quote from Strabo in his work *Geography* (I:2:3):

> *As I was saying, Eratosthenes contends that the aim of every poet is to entertain, not to instruct.*

http://penelope.uchicago.edu/Thayer/E/Roman/Texts/Strabo/1B1*.html

Reference in Plato's *Timaeus* to the three kinds of soul.

http://classics.mit.edu/Plato/timaeus.html

9th Year of Claudius' reign (49 CE)

In 41 CE, three years after the uprising, Claudius wrote his letter to the Alexandrians:

http://www.csun.edu/~hcfll004/claualex.html

Qumran

Although the author of this site disagrees with the dating of the *Pesher Habakkuk* suggested by Robert Eisenman (see below), the site does provide translations of the Pesher. It is useful if the commentary is read side by side with the related verse:

http://www.moellerhaus.com/habdir.htm

The Teacher of Righteousness

Somewhat of a controversial figure, Robert Eisenman argues within his book, James the Brother of Jesus, that the Teacher of Righteousness and the Man of Lies mentioned within many of the Dead Sea Scrolls are references to James the Just and Paul respectively:

James the Brother of Jesus: The Key to Unlocking the Secrets of Early Christianity and the Dead Sea Scrolls   (Penguin, 1998).

http://www.roberteisenman.com/

Joseph

Philo writing on the meaning of the name Joseph (On Joseph: VII: 32):

http://www.earlychristianwritings.com/yonge/book23.html

REFERENCES

Simon

Simon

There is a well-established association of the apostle Mark with Alexandria and he is regarded as the founder of the Coptic Church.

http://en.wikipedia.org/wiki/Coptic_Orthodox_Church_of_Alexandria

War

8th Year of Nero's reign (62 CE)

A report of the death of James is reported in Josephus (Antiquities 20:9:1).

10th Year of Nero's reign (64 CE)

Cornelius Tacitus in *Annals* (15:44) reports on the actions of Nero in burning Christians after the great fire of Rome:

> *But all human efforts, all the lavish gifts of the emperor, and the propitiations of the gods, did not banish the sinister belief that the conflagration was the result of an order. Consequently, to get rid of the report, Nero fastened the guilt and inflicted the most exquisite tortures on a class hated for their abominations, called Christians by the populace. Christus, from whom the name had its origin, suffered the extreme penalty during the reign of Tiberius at the hands of one of our procurators, Pontius Pilatus, and a most mischievous superstition, thus checked for the moment, again broke out not only in Judaea, the first source of the evil, but even in Rome, where all things*

hideous and shameful from every part of the world find their center and become popular. Accordingly, an arrest was first made of all who pleaded guilty; then, upon their information, an immense multitude was convicted, not so much of the crime of firing the city, as of hatred against mankind. Mockery of every sort was added to their deaths. Covered with the skins of beasts, they were torn by dogs and perished, or were nailed to crosses, or were doomed to the flames and burnt, to serve as a nightly illumination, when daylight had expired.

Nero offered his gardens for the spectacle, and was exhibiting a show in the circus, while he mingled with the people in the dress of a charioteer or stood aloft on a car. Hence, even for criminals who deserved extreme and exemplary punishment, there arose a feeling of compassion; for it was not, as it seemed, for the public good, but to glut one man's cruelty, that they were being destroyed.

http://classics.mit.edu/Tacitus/annals.11.xv.html

12th Year of Nero's reign (66 CE) – 1

A description of the incident in Caesarea Maritima that sparked the war is reported by Josephus in *War* 2:14:4.

A description of the events in Jerusalem when Florus was insulted is reported in *War* 2:14:6-9.

Halley's Comet appeared in 66 CE:

http://en.wikipedia.org/wiki/Halley%27s_Comet

12th Year of Nero's reign (66 CE) – 2

REFERENCES

Details on the taking of Masada are reported in *Jewish War* 2:17:2.

Details on the treachery in Scythopolis are reported in *Jewish War* 2:18:3.

15th Year of Nero's reign (69 CE) – 3

A report of Josephus in Alexandria is in Life (Josephus) 75.

An image said to be of Josephus is available in Wikipedia

http://en.wikipedia.org/wiki/Josephus

15th Year of Nero's reign (69 CE) – 1

Assent of Tiberias Alexander to Vespasian's bid for Emperor reported in *Jewish War* 4:10:6.

Stephen

Actions of James are described in Eusebius *Histories Book II* where the author quotes from the writer Hegesippus:

> *The aforesaid Scribes and Pharisees therefore placed James upon the pinnacle of the temple, and cried out to him and said: 'You just one, in whom we ought all to have confidence, forasmuch as the people are led astray after Jesus, the crucified one, declare to us, what is the gate of Jesus.'*
> *And he answered with a loud voice, 'Why do you ask me concerning Jesus, the Son of Man? He himself sits in heaven at the right hand of the great Power, and is about to come upon the clouds of heaven.'*

http://www.newadvent.org/fathers/250102.htm

Philo explains the significance of the name Jacob (James in Greek) in *"On the Change of Names"* (XII: 82):

> *And what more flourishing and more suitable crown could be woven for the victorious soul than one by which it will be able acutely and clearly to behold the living God? At least a beautiful prize is thus proposed for the soul which delights in the practice of virtue, namely, the being endowed with sight adequate to the clear comprehension of the only thing which is really worth beholding.*

http://www.earlychristianwritings.com/yonge/book20.html

Conflict

Extracts from the Dead Sea Scrolls 4Q458 and 4Q285 were taken from here:

http://www.livius.org/men-mh/messiah/messiah_07.html

The translation of the War Scroll from Qumran is available here:

http://www.meta-religion.com/World_Religions/Christianity/Other_Books/Dead_Sea_Scrolls/the_war_scroll.htm

The Capernaum Demoniac

A reference to the claim that in Hebrew the words for *"fever"* and *"mother-in-law"* are similar:

http://vridar.wordpress.com/2010/12/12/more-puns-in-the-gospel-of-mark-people-and-places/

The book referenced in this blog is:

Paul Nadim Tarazi: The New Testament: an introduction. Volume

REFERENCES

1, Paul and Mark

The everlasting name

1st Year of Vespasian's reign (70 CE) – 1

Josephus on Alexandria (*Jewish War* 4:11:5):

> *And now, as Vespasian was come to Alexandria, this good news came from Rome, and at the same time came embassies from all his own habitable earth, to congratulate him upon his advancement; and though this Alexandria was the greatest of all cities next to Rome, it proved too narrow to contain the multitude that then came to it.*

Abraham, Isaac and Jacob

Aristotle's account of the three things that make men virtuous is in Politics (Book 7):

http://www.constitution.org/ari/polit_07.htm

Philo's *"everlasting name"* is explained in "*On Abraham*" X:51:

> *"For,"* says God, *"this is my everlasting name: I am the God of Abraham, and the God of Isaac, and the God of Jacob"*

http://www.earlychristianwritings.com/yonge/book22.html

God of Abraham

The Mandaen Book of John includes a text on the baptism of Jesus (§ 30):

> *"Let me warn you, my brothers, let me warn you, my*

beloved! Let me warn you, my brothers, against the . . . who are like unto the cross. They lay it on the walls; then stand there and bow down to the block. Let me warn you, my brothers, of the god which the carpenter has joined together. If the carpenter has joined together the god, who then has joined together the carpenter?"

http://www.sacred-texts.com/chr/gno/gjb/gjb-2-1.htm

God of Isaac

An account of the treatment of Carabbas during the uprising of 38 CE is given by Philo in Against Flaccus (VI: 36):

http://www.earlychristianwritings.com/yonge/book36.html

God of Jacob

The claim that Vespasian fulfilled the prophecy within Jewish scripture was made among others by Suetonius in 12 Caesars – Vespasian 4:5:

http://penelope.uchicago.edu/Thayer/E/Roman/Texts/Suetonius/12Caesars/Vespasian*.html

The description of Vespasian's *"healings"* in Alexandria is reported by Tacitus in *History Book 4*:

http://www.sacred-texts.com/cla/tac/h04080.htm

Sin

Harmony and discord

The idea of an *"attuned"* soul is explained in Plato's *Phaedrus*:

http://classics.mit.edu/Plato/phaedrus.html

REFERENCES

Divine Reason

Salome, Mary Magdalene and Mary the mother of James and Joseph

Josephus reports on the name change of Strato's Tower in *Antiquities* 14:4:4:

> *Besides those that had been demolished, and also of the maritime cities, Gaza, and Joppa, and Dora, and Strato's Tower; which last Herod rebuilt after a glorious manner, and adorned with havens and temples, and changed its name to Caesarea. All these Pompey left in a state of freedom, and joined them to the province of Syria.*

The Catholic Church

The letter of St Ignatius to the Smyrnaeans is available here:

http://www.earlychristianwritings.com/text/ignatius-smyrnaeans-longer.html

The doctrine of the assumption is available on the Vatican website:

http://www.vatican.va/holy_father/pius_xii/apost_constitutions/documents/hf_p-xii_apc_19501101_munificentissimus-deus_en.html

Order of the Mass:

http://catholic-resources.org/ChurchDocs/Mass.htm

Epilogue

Reason

Quotations from Robert Owen are taken from the Robert Owen web site: http://www.robert-owen.com/

Made in the USA
Charleston, SC
07 September 2012